The Evolving American Presidency Series

Series Foreword:

The American Presidency touches virtually every aspect of American and world politics. And the presidency has become, for better or worse, the vital center of the American and global political systems. The Framers of the American government would be dismayed at such a result. As invented at the Philadelphia Constitutional Convention in 1787, the Presidency was to have been a part of a government with shared and overlapping powers, embedded within a separation-of-powers system. If there was a vital center, it was the Congress; the Presidency was to be a part, but by no means, the centerpiece of that system.

Over time, the presidency has evolved and grown in power, expectations, responsibilities, and authority. Wars, crises, depressions, industrialization, all served to add to the power of the presidency. And as the United States grew into a world power, presidential power also grew. As the United States became the world's leading superpower, the presidency rose in prominence and power, not only in the U.S., but on the world stage.

It is the clash between the presidency as invented and the presidency as it has developed that inspired this series. And it is the importance and power of the modern American presidency that makes understanding the office so vital. Like it or not, the American Presidency stands at the vortex of power both within the United States and across the globe.

This Palgrave series recognizes that the Presidency is and has been an evolving institution, going from the original constitutional design as a Chief Clerk, to today where the president is the center of the American political constellation. This has caused several key dilemmas in our political system, not the least of which is that presidents face high expectations with limited constitutional resources. This causes presidents to find extra-constitutional means of governing. Thus, presidents must find ways to bridge the expectations/power gap while operating within the confines of a separation-of-powers system designed to limit presidential authority. How presidents resolve these challenges and paradoxes is the central issue in modern governance. It is also the central theme of this book series.

Michael A. Genovese
Loyola Chair of Leadership
Loyola Marymount University
Palgrave's *The Evolving American Presidency,* Series Editor

The Second Term of George W. Bush
    edited by Robert Maranto, Douglas M. Brattebo, and Tom Lansford

The Presidency and the Challenge of Democracy
    edited by Michael A. Genovese and Lori Cox Han

Religion and the American Presidency
    edited by Mark J. Rozell and Gleaves Whitney

Religion and the Bush Presidency
    edited by Mark J. Rozell and Gleaves Whitney

Test by Fire: The War Presidency of George W. Bush
    by Robert Swansbrough

American Royalty: The Bush and Clinton Families and the Danger to the American Presidency
    by Matthew T. Corrigan

Accidental Presidents: Death, Assassination, Resignation, and Democratic Succession
    by Philip Abbott

Presidential Power in Action: Implementing Supreme Court Detainee Decisions
    by Darren A. Wheeler

President George W. Bush's Influence over Bureaucracy and Policy: Extraordinary Times, Extraordinary Powers
    edited by Colin Provost and Paul Teske

Assessing George W. Bush's Legacy: The Right Man?
    edited by Iwan Morgan and Philip John Davies

Acting Presidents: 100 Years of Plays about the Presidency
    by Bruce E. Altschuler

America Responds to Terrorism: Conflict Resolution Strategies of Clinton, Bush, and Obama
    by Karen A. Feste

Presidents in the Movies: American History and Politics on Screen
    edited by Iwan W. Morgan

Presidents in the Movies

American History and Politics on Screen

Edited by
Iwan W. Morgan

First published in 2011 by
PALGRAVE MACMILLAN®
in the United States—a division of St. Martin's Press LLC,
175 Fifth Avenue, New York, NY 10010.

Where this book is distributed in the UK, Europe and the rest of the world,
this is by Palgrave Macmillan, a division of Macmillan Publishers Limited,
registered in England, company number 785998, of Houndmills,
Basingstoke, Hampshire RG21 6XS.

Palgrave Macmillan is the global academic imprint of the above companies
and has companies and representatives throughout the world.

Palgrave® and Macmillan® are registered trademarks in the United States,
the United Kingdom, Europe and other countries.

ISBN: 978–0–230–11328–2

Library of Congress Cataloging-in-Publication Data

Presidents in the movies : American history and politics on screen /
edited by Iwan W. Morgan.
p. cm.—(The evolving American presidency series)
ISBN 978–0–230–11328–2 (alk. paper)
1. Presidents in motion pictures. 2. Motion pictures—Political aspects—
United States. 3. Historical films—United States—History and criticism.
4. Motion pictures and history. I. Morgan, Iwan W.

PN1995.9.P678P65 2011
791.43'635873—dc22   2010044900

A catalogue record of the book is available from the British Library.

Design by Newgen Imaging Systems (P) Ltd., Chennai, India.

First edition: May 2011

10 9 8 7 6 5 4 3 2 1

Printed in the United States of America.

To four people with whom I have watched many movies—
albeit in different eras.
My brother, Hywel,
and my present-day fellow film fans,
Theresa, Humphrey, and Eleanor.

Contents

Contributors

Harry Keyishian is professor of English at Fairleigh Dickinson University and director of Fairley Dickinson University Press. His publications include *Screening Politics: The Politician in American Movies* (2006) and *The Shapes of Revenge: Victimization, Vengeance and Vindictiveness in Shakespeare* (1995).

Kingsley Marshall is a film critic and a lecturer in film studies at University College, Falmouth. He is currently working on a study of movie representations of U.S. politicians.

Iwan W. Morgan is professor of U.S. studies and director of the United States Presidency Centre at the Institute for the Study of the Americas, School of Advanced Study, University of London. He has written extensively on U.S. presidents, including *Nixon* (2002), a short biography of the thirty-seventh president. His most recent book *The Age of Deficits: Presidents and Unbalanced Budgets from Jimmy Carter to George W. Bush* (2009) was awarded the American Politics Group's Richard E. Neustadt Prize. He also coedited *Assessing George W. Bush's Legacy: The Right Man?* (2010).

Brian Neve is senior lecturer in politics at the University of Bath. He has authored numerous books and articles on film, including *Film and Politics in America: A Social Tradition* (1992) and *Elia Kazin: The Cinema of an American Outsider* (2009), and has coedited *"Un-American Hollywood": Politics and Film in the Blacklist Era* (2007).

Ian Scott is senior lecturer in American studies at Manchester University. He has written extensively on the connection between film and politics, including *American Politics in Hollywood Film* (to be issued in a new edition in 2010). His latest book is *From Pinewood to Hollywood: British Filmmakers in American Cinema, 1910–1969* (2010).

Melvyn Stokes is senior lecturer in history at University College, London. He is coeditor of *Identifying Hollywood Audiences: Cultural Identity at the Movies* (1999) and the author of *The Birth of a Nation:*

The History of the Most Controversial Motion Picture of All Time (2008). His most recent book is *Gilda* (2010).

Mark Wheeler is reader in politics at London Metropolitan University. He is the author of *Politics and the Mass Media* (1997) and *Hollywood: Politics and Society* (2006). His next book, *Celebrity Politics: Image and Identity in Modern Political Communications*, appears in 2012.

Mark White is professor of history at Queen Mary, University of London. His books include *Missiles in Cuba: Kennedy, Khrushchev, Castro and the 1962 Crisis* (1997), *The Kennedys and Cuba: The Declassified Documentary History* (1999), and *Against the President: Dissent and Decision-making in the White House—A Historical Perspective* (2007). He has also written *Kenneth Branagh: A Life* (2005), a biography of the British actor-director.

Introduction

Iwan W. Morgan

American history and politics have been staple elements of movies since the emergence of the U.S. film industry in the early twentieth century. Cinematic interpretation of presidents, real and imagined, has been central to celluloid exploration of the nation's past and present. At one level, the focus on the president conforms to the conventions of movie drama that one good man (and in some recent instances, woman) can make a difference. More significantly, moviemakers have depicted presidents as symbols of the nation's spirit, values, and historical destiny.

A number of scholarly works have examined portrayals of presidents, both actual and fictional, in cinematic films and made-for-television movies and miniseries.[1] This study has a more specialized focus on the depiction of real presidents in Hollywood films that have had a theatrical release. Such an approach does not imply any assumption about the superiority of cinematic over television representations. Indeed it is widely recognized that the HBO miniseries *John Adams* (2008) set a new standard for filmic portrayal of an American president. There have also been high-quality made-for-television presidential movies, notably about George Washington, Abraham Lincoln, Harry Truman, John F. Kennedy, and Lyndon B. Johnson.[2] By and large, however, cinematic movies featuring American presidents offer a more interesting blend of symbol and substance than their television counterparts. A Hollywood film has to get its message across within the constraints of the conventional three-act format and the need for commercial success in a mass market. Television movies can pack in more detail because they tend to be longer, less expensive to make, and more focused on niche markets. They are also relatively more faithful to the factual record because many are adaptations of historical studies rather than based on original screenplays.

The essays in this volume are primarily concerned with analyzing the cinematic representations of eight occupants of the White House: Abraham Lincoln (1861–1865), Andrew Johnson (1865–1869), Theodore Roosevelt (1901–1909), Woodrow Wilson (1913–1921), Franklin D. Roosevelt (1933–1945), John F. Kennedy (1961–1963),

Richard Nixon (1969–1974), and George W. Bush (2001–2009). In exploring movies featuring these presidents, the contributors strike a number of common themes.

- Image, message, and myth are prioritized over historical accuracy and complexity.
- The presidents of the nineteenth and early twentieth centuries are interpreted more in terms of the moviemakers' present rather than of their own times.
- The focus tends to be on the president rather than the presidency as an institution, thereby putting the emphasis on individual character instead of organizational structures and the broader aspects of the American polity
- For the most part, presidents are celebrated as idealistic, wise, and dependable guardians of the national interest, rather than ambitious, self-interested, and materialistic, thereby promoting the view that there is nothing wrong with American democracy so long as power is in the hands of intelligent and far-sighted visionaries.
- From Hollywood's founding through to the 1960s, presidents have been glorified as the embodiments of America's mission to be the "Redeemer Nation" with a God-given destiny to act as the beacon of liberty and democracy for all mankind, but the corrosive effects of the Vietnam and Iraq Wars and Watergate have produced a darker image in films dealing with post-Kennedy presidents.

To contextualize the presidents and movies under consideration, it is necessary to briefly review the presidents and the presidency in history, presidents in film, and the comparative perspective of national leaders in British movies. This chapter then closes with a brief synopsis of the contributions to the volume.

Presidents and the Presidency: A Brief History

The founders invented the presidency at the Constitutional Convention of 1787 in recognition that the single-branch national legislature format of the Articles of Confederation, the American republic's first experiment in self-government, had not proved effective. To assuage concerns that the new office would become excessively powerful, they designed it to be a constrained institution that operated in a system of government in which it shared powers with the legislative and judicial branches. More than two hundred years later, the forty-fourth president, Barack Obama (2009–), exercises leadership under largely the same Article II constitutional provisions as had the first president, George Washington (1789–1797).[3]

Of course, the early twenty-first-century presidency is a vastly different office in terms of its responsibilities, the expectations placed on it, and its organizational structure. The contemporary president is leader of the only global superpower, manager of the world's largest economy, and head of a government with huge domestic program commitments. Writing in the 1950s, political scientist Clinton Rossiter identified ten different roles for the modern office: chief of state; chief executive; commander-in-chief; chief diplomat; chief legislator; chief of party; voice of the people; protector of the peace; manager of prosperity; and world leader.[4] Some of these duties were recent developments; others had a longer history but their performance necessitated far greater endeavor than required of early presidents. To assist in their discharge, modern presidents have a White House staff (the number of aides has fluctuated between four hundred and five hundred since the 1960s) and an umbrella organization, the Executive Office of the President, created in 1939 and composed of various agencies (some permanent, notably the Office of Management and Budget and the National Security Council, others temporary) that provide advisory, policy coordination, and administrative support. Their skill in organizing this army of aides to get the most out of them is an important foundation for the success of their leadership.[5]

Nevertheless, continuity coexists with change for modern presidents because they still operate under long-standing constitutional restraints. In the words of scholar Edward Corwin, the Constitution is "an invitation to struggle" between the different branches of government that share power within its institutional framework of checks and balances. An important and ongoing part of the presidency's history, therefore, has been its involvement in a perpetual tug-of-war for ascendancy with the Congress in particular.[6]

In recognition of the constraints upon the modern presidency, many scholars regard the formal powers of the office, which allow for command, as less important than its informal powers, which facilitate leadership and influence. The former are limited, often shared, and derived from the Constitution; the latter are rooted in personal skill, historical situation, and the process of politics. In arguably the most famous study of the modern presidency, political scientist Richard

Neustadt conceptualized its real power as that of persuasion, which depended on winning support through bargaining, manipulation, the agency of reputation, and public opinion mobilization. Crucial to this was the president's unique capacity to speak for all Americans as their only nationally elected leader and to them via the modern mass media.[7]

Despite its growing responsibilities in modern times, the evolution of the presidency from chief clerk to chief executive of government over more than two centuries has hardly been linear and consistent over the entire history of the institution. As Edward Corwin noted in 1957, only one-third of the first thirty-three presidents had contributed to the expansion of their office, while "things have either stood still or gone backward" under the others.[8] The power of the presidency ebbed and flowed in the first one hundred and fifty years of its existence. In the nineteenth century, the strong presidencies of Thomas Jefferson (1801–1809), Andrew Jackson (1829–1837), and Abraham Lincoln all gave way to the normalcy of the office's constrained authority in their aftermath. Theodore Roosevelt and Woodrow Wilson seemingly pioneered the modern presidency in the first two decades of the twentieth century, but there followed an era of presidential retrenchment in the 1920s. It was Franklin D. Roosevelt's presidency that truly marked the permanent transformation of the office to meet the need for strong leadership at home and abroad from the 1930s onward.[9]

The presidency has remained the key actor in U.S. politics since FDR's day, but its level of authority has still not been constant. Presidential power was at its peak from the 1930s to the 1970s, receded in reaction to Vietnam and Watergate, revived under Ronald Reagan (1981–1989), slipped again in the 1990s, and reached new peaks under George W. Bush. As scholar Michael Genovese has indicated, the three words that best sum up the presidency are "ELASTIC, ADAPTABLE, and VARIABLE." In his view it is a chameleon-like institution that "has been able to transform itself to what the times needed, what ambitious officeholders grabbed, what the people wanted, and what world events and American power dictated."[10]

Unsurprisingly, rating the performance of the holders of this protean office has become a significant scholarly enterprise since the first survey was conducted by Harvard historian Arthur Schlesinger Sr. in 1948. While there is no universal standard for assessing them, presidents are broadly judged on the basis of: the scale of problems they faced and their success in dealing with them; their vision for the nation; their moral authority and character; and the long-term effects of their actions. Conservatives have long complained that this approach tends to discriminate in favor of liberal-oriented presidents who have expanded the role of government. Nevertheless, the now regular presidential polls have shown remarkable similarity in their top and bottom rankings, regardless of the ideological leanings of those conducting them.[11]

Lincoln tends to be rated the greatest president, with FDR and Washington in either second or third place. The remainder of the top ten usually includes Thomas Jefferson, Theodore Roosevelt, Harry Truman (1945–1953), and Woodrow Wilson, and, on occasions, Lyndon Johnson (1963–1969). More recent polls have also ranked one or more of the following in this pantheon as appreciation of their achievements grows with time: Dwight Eisenhower (1953–1961), John F. Kennedy, and Ronald Reagan. Their rise has tended to push Andrew Jackson and James Polk (1845–1849) out of their "near great" status in early polls. Bringing up the rear, the "failures" generally include Warren Harding (1921–1923), Franklin Pierce (1853–1857), Andrew Johnson, and, the lowest rated in many polls, James Buchanan (1857–1861). Richard Nixon was initially among them until growing awareness that his presidency entailed more than Watergate propelled him into the lower reaches of the top thirty in twenty-first-century surveys. Ulysses S. Grant (1869–1877) has made a similar rise in acknowledgment of his sincere but unsuccessful efforts to make post–Civil War Reconstruction work.[12] Polls conducted shortly after George W. Bush's departure from office, however, tended to add his name to the "failed presidents" roster.[13]

Only Lincoln, FDR, and Washington are widely considered to have been "great," but Jefferson, Theodore Roosevelt, and Truman also have their champions. All these presidents encountered great challenges, adopted an activist approach to leadership, demonstrated a high degree of political skill in advancing their aims, and showed a strong sense of moral purpose. Their greatness emanated from the confluence of opportunity, ability, and vision. Each governed in times of great change and some did so in the face of crisis; each had the skills to make the presidency the institution of leadership that the times warranted; and each set a new course for the nation that was rooted in its eternal values.

All three of these elements have been essential to presidential success. Bill Clinton (1993–2001) used to bemoan the absence of crisis in his presidency on grounds that this denied him the opportunity for greatness.[14] However, crisis and great challenges alone are not enough. America's greatest president, Abraham Lincoln, was preceded and succeeded by men who are generally considered to be among its worst presidents (Pierce, Buchanan, and Andrew Johnson) because they lacked the skill and vision to deal with the momentous sectional divisions of their day. Although George W. Bush had opportunity and ability (despite what some critics claim), his war-on-terror leadership lacked a moral compass to keep it true to America's values. The vision to chart a new course for the nation in times of change is the ultimate mark of presidential greatness, but this is most effectively done through reinterpretation of the past.

In political scientist Stephen Skowronek's conception, the presidency exerts greatest influence when it is both an *order-shattering* institution that rejects current orthodoxy and an *order-creating* one that shapes the nation's future. In doing so, however, it must also be an *order-affirming* institution "in that the disruptive effects of the exercise of presidential power must be justified in constitutional terms broadly construed as the protection, preservation, and defense of values emblematic of the body politic."[15] The perfect illustration of this was Abraham Lincoln's Gettysburg address in 1863, which rejected the pre–Civil War order and envisioned a future free from slavery through America's rededication to founding principles. And no one better explained presidential agency to link America's past and future than Franklin D. Roosevelt. The presidency, he declared in 1932, "is pre-eminently a place of moral leadership. All our great Presidents were leaders of thought at times when certain historic ideas in the life of the nation had to be clarified."[16]

As "leaders of thought," presidents who make their mark on American history do not by themselves create the conditions for change but draw authority and influence from their capacity to give expression to broader political forces that challenge old orthodoxies. Washington understood that he was a symbol of national unity after the divisiveness of the Confederation period; Jefferson articulated the political and economic aspirations of agrarian democracy; Lincoln ultimately identified with the abolitionist movement in transforming the Civil War into a conflict to end slavery; Theodore Roosevelt's domestic agenda drew inspiration from the Progressive reform movement; Franklin D. Roosevelt responded to the needs of urban, blue-collar labor for activist government to create jobs, support trade union rights, and develop a basic welfare state; and Harry Truman upheld the interests of the Roosevelt voter coalition at home and met the communist challenge abroad. In like vein, the most effective post-Truman presidents identified their office with new forces in society. John F. Kennedy and Lyndon B. Johnson promoted the interests of the civil rights movement, while Ronald Reagan did the same for the newly emergent conservative movement.

The president may not operate in a political vacuum, but presidential reputation is closely tied to individual character. As Ronald Reagan's scriptwriter, Peggy Noonan, put it, "In a president, character is everything...He doesn't have to be clever; you can hire clever...But you can't buy courage and decency; you can't rent a strong moral sense. A president must bring those with him."[17] In literal terms, the first part of this statement is hyperbolic, but overall its sense is accurate. This is not to suggest that America's "great" and "near great" presidents were perfect human beings. Idealists they may have been, but they would not have risen so high without being hugely ambitious, manipulative, and sometimes untrustworthy—and their ideas on gender and race rarely rose above their times. Nevertheless, they were, for the most part, wise, bold, and far-sighted in their dedication to America's interests and values. Other than Thomas Jefferson, they were not particularly learned, but all were intelligent in both the analytic (capacity to weigh up options) and emotional (free from defective impulse) senses. Typifying this, FDR was famously characterized as possessing "a second rate intellect, but a first rate temperament" (Richard Nixon was thought to have the opposite attributes).[18] Finally, America's best presidents have had a sense of restraint in their desire to expand their power without undermining the Constitution.

In moments of crisis, particularly in wartime, presidents have acted beyond the letter and spirit of the Constitution in the belief that strong leadership was essential to address the dangers facing the nation. However, such instances were exceptional and temporary until the advent of the Cold War in the late 1940s involved the United States in a nearly fifty-year struggle with global communism. The danger of nuclear confrontation between America and the Soviet Union further added to the uniqueness of this conflict. Utilizing their commander-in-chief prerogatives, post-1945 presidents increasingly expanded the powers of their office to determine national security policy at the expense of Congress. This gave rise to the so-called imperial presidency that routinely flouted the limits of the Constitution and ultimately engaged in abuse of power. In reaction to the "presidential war" in Vietnam and the revelations of Richard Nixon's Watergate wrongdoings, Congress sought to retrench presidential power but with only partial success. In the last two decades of the twentieth century, presidents continued to push against the limits of their national security authority, most obviously in the case of the Reagan administration's illegal operations in the Iran-Contra scandal.[19]

The 9/11 attacks on New York and Washington created the conditions for the revival of the imperial presidency under George W. Bush on a scale undreamed of in its Cold War incarnation. Drawing on unitary executive doctrine developed by conservative constitutionalists in the late twentieth century, the forty-third president exploited the strategic opportunities presented by crisis to advance his national security and homeland security agendas (regardless of the consequences for civil liberties), assert the primacy of executive authority on the dubious rationale of his implied and inherent constitutional powers, and elevate government secrecy to unprecedented levels. In effect, Bush's claims of unlimited and exclusive power to conduct the war on terror sought to relegate almost to irrelevance the role of Congress and other institutions.[20]

With the increasing unpopularity of the Iraq War, a reaction set in against the new imperial presidency by the time that Bush left office. Nevertheless, America's experience in the Vietnam-Watergate era and in the early twenty-first century indicated that the presidency could be a threat to democracy as well as its guardian. In essence, therefore, the question that had troubled the founders remains unanswered: How can presidential leadership be exerted effectively but also effectively restrained?[21]

Presidents in the Movies

Until the late twentieth century, Hollywood showed little regard for the nuances of the presidency and the ebbs and flows of its power. Its representations of real presidents tended to idealize them as great leaders of the exceptional nation rather than political leaders struggling within the confines of their office. Accordingly, movies effectively wrote out of their depiction of American history and politics those presidents that did not fit the mould of heroic shapers of the nation's destiny—until the developments of the Vietnam-Watergate era forced a rendezvous with reality.

It is therefore unsurprising that cinematic representations of William Henry Harrison (1841), John Tyler (1841–1845), Zachary Taylor (1849–1850),[22] Millard Fillmore (1850–1853), Franklin Pierce, and James Buchanan are virtually nonexistent. John Adams (1797–1801), one of the less celebrated founders and a president overshadowed by his immediate predecessor and successor—Washington and Jefferson, was also overlooked by the cinema, but was rediscovered by television. The *John Adams* miniseries format was well suited for detailed examination of the political intrigues, jealousies, and quarrels of his times as well as the dedication of America's early leaders to independence, liberty, and the building of a new and unique nation.[23] Another founder undeservedly overlooked by Hollywood is James Monroe (1817–1825), perhaps because his presidency is associated with the Missouri Compromise of 1820, whose attempt to strike a balance between the number of slave and free states postponed sectional confrontation but ultimately made it inevitable. Aside from minor appearances in a handful of silent films, his only representation of note is in a quasi-documentary short feature celebrating his foreign policy achievement, *The Monroe Doctrine* (1939).

Also neglected, but with better cause, are the band of undistinguished late nineteenth-century presidents, Rutherford B. Hayes (1877–1881), James Garfield (1881), Chester Alan Arthur (1881–1885), and Benjamin Harrison (1889–1893).[24] Grover Cleveland (1885–1889, 1893–1897), generally rated a better-than-average national leader, may seem a more surprising omission from the movie pantheon. However, it is difficult to idealize a president whose primary activity in his first term was a dogged use of the veto (against protective tariffs, veterans' pensions, and public works), who ordered federal troops to break the Pullman strike of 1894, and who generally sided with Eastern financial interests against the desire of rural Populists to abandon the gold standard as an antirecession initiative in his second term. William McKinley (1897–1901), an effective leader in the Spanish-American War of 1898, also lacks cinematic presence, almost certainly because moviemakers have found greater interest in the military exploits of the more flamboyant future president, Theodore Roosevelt, during that conflict.[25] The lowly rated early twentieth-century presidents—William Taft (1909–1913), Warren Harding (1921–1923), Calvin Coolidge (1923–1929),[26] and Herbert Hoover (1929–1933)—are further nonrunners in the cinematic stakes.

Nineteenth-century presidents who have made it onto the silver screen often appear in movies about the winning of the West, usually as visionaries who dispatch agents to do their bidding. In *The Far Horizons* (1955), Thomas Jefferson (Herbert Heyes) has a small but significant role as the architect of the Meriwether Lewis and William Clarke expedition of 1804–1806 to explore and map the continental interior in the wake of the Louisiana Purchase. Andrew Jackson (Edward Ellis) appears in *Man of Conquest* (1939) as the presidential supporter of Sam Houston's drive to achieve Texan independence from Mexico. In *Lone Star* (1952) he has retired from office (Lionel Barrymore in his final role) but prevails on an influential cattle baron

(Clark Gable) to promote the annexation of Texas by the United States at a time when the independent republic's government is supposedly considering a treaty of reconciliation with Mexico. James Polk features briefly (played by Ian Wolfe and Addison Richards, respectively, in uncredited roles) in two movies about America's westward expansion to the Pacific in the 1840s, *California* (1947) and *The Oregon Trail* (1959).

Abraham Lincoln appears in several winning-of-the-West movies. The most significant of these is John Ford's silent epic about the building of the transcontinental railroad, *The Iron Horse* (1924). It shows Lincoln (Charles Edward Bull) as a visionary prepresidential supporter of this project and its presidential promoter as the signatory of the Pacific Railroad Act. The sixteenth president's status as nation builder is affirmed by the title: "More than to any other man, the nation owes gratitude to Abraham Lincoln whose vision and resolution held the North and the South, while moulding with blood and with iron the East and the West."[27] Ford also represented Lincoln (Raymond Massey in a nonspeaking role) as a national unifier in *How the West was Won* (1962).

Ulysses S. Grant is chronologically the last president to feature significantly in movies about the taming of the West. Character actor Joseph Crehan made a virtual career of playing him variously as a Union army general in *Silver River* (1948), Lincoln's transcontinental railroad legatee in *Union Pacific* (1939), and postpresidential memoir writer in *The Adventures of Mark Twain* (1944). The eighteenth president was usually portrayed as desirous of treating Indian tribes fairly as America expanded westward, as in *They Died With Their Boots On* (1941), *Sitting Bull* (1954), and *Drumbeat* (1954), movies in which he was played by Crehan, John Hammond and Hayden Rorke, respectively. Grant also appears (played by Jason Robards and Aidan Quinn, respectively) in two very expensive flops that feature law-and-order comic book heroes—as a hostage victim in *The Legend of the Lone Ranger* (1981) and as a president intent on thwarting a plot against the Union in *Jonah Hex* (2010).

For twentieth-century presidents, the cinematic equivalent of the winning of the West is displaying the vision and courage to make the world safe for peace and democracy. Theodore Roosevelt (Brian Keith) has a pivotal role as a dynamic foreign policy president dealing with a hostage crisis in the Islamic world in *The Wind and the Lion* (1975). In *Wilson* (1944), Woodrow Wilson (Alexander Knox) is portrayed as a moral idealist aspiring to create a peaceful and democratic international order in succession to the horrific bloodshed of

World War I. Franklin D. Roosevelt makes a number of appearances as an inspirational and bold commander-in-chief in World War II. He promotes patriotic values in *Yankee Doodle Dandy* (1942, played by Jack Young), rewards valor in *First to Fight* (1967, Stephen Roberts), and stiffens the resolve of America's military leaders to hit back at the Japanese aggressors in *Pearl Harbor* (2001, Jon Voight). In *MacArthur* (1977), Harry S. Truman (Ed Flanders) shows courage and determination to maintain civilian control of the military in the Korean War. The movie depicts his resistance to Douglas MacArthur's demand for a direct attack on the Chinese mainland for fear that this would lead to World War III and the great political risk he took in eventually sacking his insubordinate general. In *Thirteen Days* (2000), John F. Kennedy (Bruce Greenwood) displays not only boldness in facing down the Soviets in the Cuban Missile crisis but also wisdom in refusing to order a preemptive strike against the missile sites as urged by his more hawkish military advisers.

Far more problematic for Hollywood has been the exploration of presidents in relationship to what has been called the American dilemma, namely, the inconsistency between the nation's ideals and the reality of racial inequality.[28] Movies featuring Lincoln as president have tended to portray him as the restorer of the union rather than the emancipator of the slaves. This is particularly true of his representations (played by Joseph Henabery and Walter Huston, respectively) in the D.W. Griffith movies *The Birth of a Nation* (1915) and *Abraham Lincoln* (1930). Sectional reconciliation is also the theme of three 1930s movies in which Lincoln features in a secondary role (played on each occasion by Frank McGlynn), *The Littlest Rebel* (1935), a Shirley Temple vehicle, *The Prisoner of Shark Island* (1936), and *Of Human Hearts* (1938). *Abe Lincoln in Illinois* (1940, a.k.a. *Spirit of the People*), in which Raymond Massey plays the lead, does feature political debate on slavery, but mainly with regard to its expansion rather than abolition—in keeping with the movie's chronological focus on Lincoln's political career up to his election as president. Utterly out of step with historical reality, the biopic of Lincoln's successor, *Tennessee Johnson* (1942), with Van Heflin in the lead role, treats Reconstruction solely as a political struggle for post–Civil War reunion rather than to ensure the civil rights of former slaves in the states of the ex-Confederacy.

It is tempting to explain the surprising absence of major biopics about George Washington and Thomas Jefferson to the difficulty of squaring their heroic status with the historical reality that they were slave-owners, but this did not prevent Hollywood from celebrating other slave-owning presidents, Andrew Jackson and Andrew Johnson (without ever mentioning this particular aspect of their life). The more likely explanation in Washington's case is the difficulty of portraying someone described by actor Jeff Daniel, who played him in the television movie *The Crossing* (2000), as one of the most elusive and misunderstood men in American history.[29] For his part, Jefferson may simply be too cerebral to fit heroic movie representation.

Significantly, the one movie to explore the dichotomy between presidential ideals about liberty and the existence of slavery is not a Hollywood production but an Anglo-Indian one. The controversial Merchant-Ivory film *Jefferson in Paris* (1995) explores the alleged affair between Jefferson (Nick Nolte) and his slave, Sally Hemings (Thandie Newton), who is thought to have borne him six children. One of these, Madison Hemings—played in old age by James Earl Jones—is the narrator of the movie's story. Set against the background of the future president's ambassadorship to France in the 1780s, the film implies the clear distinction between the coming French Revolution, which abolished slavery, and the American Revolution, which did not. Harangued by his daughter (Gwyneth Paltrow) about the inequities of the "peculiar institution," the movie Jefferson seemingly recognizes its incompatibility with American ideals in his decision at the end of the film to free Sally and her brother, James (an offer that the former did not take up).[30]

Curiously, the most heroic movie representation of a president in regard to race and slavery does not feature someone conventionally lionized by historians or Hollywood. John Quincy Adams (1825–1829), at best only an average president, is depicted as a moral titan in a postpresidential real life episode as the attorney defending African slave-ship mutineers before the Supreme Court in Steven Spielberg's *Amistad* (1997). The film distorts the historical reality that the case revolved around the issue of the slave trade to make it a commentary on the domestic existence of slavery in the United States. The powerful and moving portrayal of Adams by Anthony Hopkins in an Oscar-nominated performance contrasts with the representation of President Martin van Buren (1837–1841), played by Nigel Hawthorne, as indecisive, feeble, and utterly lacking in idealism. In a unique piece of casting, former associate justice Harry Blackmun plays a judicial predecessor, Justice Joseph Story, the first time a member of the Supreme Court played another one in a movie.

In his successful plea, Adams compares the rebel slaves with the American rebels of the War of Independence. He then invokes the spirit of the founders—including that of his own father, John Adams, whose marble bust appears in shot behind him—to conclude that if a favorable verdict hastens conflict between North and South, this will be the final battle in the American Revolution.[31]

In contrast to its discomfort about presidents and race, Hollywood is far happier extolling the personal character of those it represents in film. A number of movies have highlighted the qualities they brought to office, often through exploration of episodes in their prepresidential histories. James Madison (1809–1817), a brilliant political theorist but just average as the nation's leader, features in the romantic melodrama *Magnificent Doll* (1946). Portrayed by Burgess Meredith as the epitome of unassuming patriotic goodness, he wins the hand of the vivacious Dolly Payne Todd (Ginger Rogers) in competition with the overambitious and traitorous vice president Aaron Burr (David Niven). Andrew Jackson (played on both occasions by Charlton Heston) is represented as a brave fighter defending his wife, Rachel, against Indian attack and slurs that their marriage is bigamous in *The President's Lady* (1953), and as a shrewd, resourceful, and courageous general triumphing over the might of the British army at the 1815 battle of New Orleans in *The Buccaneer* (1958).

In the most popular film about Lincoln, John Ford's mythic parable, *The Young Mr Lincoln* (1939), the future president (Henry Fonda) is depicted as the epitome of human decency in his courageous battle for justice for two brothers that an entire community wrongly believes to be guilty of murder. Andrew Johnson's rise from illiterate, runaway indentured servant to a student of the Constitution and the political leader of ordinary citizens against local elites is charted in the first act of *Tennessee Johnson*.

Theodore Roosevelt is graphically shown to combine energy, wisdom, and a dislike of materialism in *The Wind and the Lion*. In *Wilson*, the protagonist is portrayed as moral, bold, and visionary, initially through his efforts to promote reforms as New Jersey governor in defiance of the political bosses who had effectively put him in office. The physical and spiritual battle of Franklin D. Roosevelt (Ralph Bellamy) to overcome his polio-induced disability is represented as preparation for the crises he will face as president in *Sunrise at Campobello* (1960). In a movie based on his one-man stage show, James Whitmore brilliantly captures Harry Truman's candor, determination, and moral sense in his Oscar-nominated performance in *Give 'Em Hell, Harry!* (1975). In *PT109* (1963), the heroic conduct of the young John Kennedy (Cliff Robertson) as commander of a motor torpedo boat in the Pacific in World War II offers reassurance that he is similarly bold in meeting the challenges of the presidency.

"Great men" movies about Truman and Kennedy are the exception with regard to post-1945 presidents. Hollywood has steered clear of representing Eisenhower,[32] LBJ,[33] Gerald Ford,[34] Jimmy Carter, Ronald Reagan, and Bill Clinton[35] in their presidential years. One reason for this is the difficulty for cinematic image to triumph over popular memory of presidential image in modern times. From FDR's appearance on the newsreels and radio to later presidents' constant presence on television news, modern White House occupants have shaped the public's lasting perception of them. Indeed, it could be argued that Hollywood has been trumped at its own game because every president since 1963 has sought to emulate John F. Kennedy's conscious development of a heroic image, albeit never with the same success. As such, in historian Jon Roper's words, the presidency has become "a historical theatre in which the hero seeks centre stage."[36]

Another deterrent to modern presidents' filmic representation relates to their political identity in an increasingly divided polity. With the collapse of the postwar consensus in the 1960s, American politics grew more polarized and partisan.[37] Consequently cinematic celebration of a Democratic president would have caused Republican hackles to rise and the same would have been true of Democrats if a GOP president were lionized. Liberals and conservatives have also become increasingly watchful that Hollywood should not disrespect any of their champions. The controversy over a planned CBS television movie, *The Reagans* (2003), pointed to the problems. Conservatives suspected that the casting in the lead role of James Brolin, husband of prominent Hollywood liberal Barbara Streisand, signified that the film would be a hatchet job on their hero. Leaks about the contents further aroused their concern and that of Reagan family members that it was not sufficiently respectful and contained inaccuracies. In response, the network pulled the movie from its fall 2003 schedule, but aired an edited version on its Showtime cable channel. Ironically, the film proved more sympathetic to its subjects than critics had feared.[38]

Significantly, the only post-JFK presidents to have received the Hollywood treatment have been those widely deemed to have sullied their office by flouting its constitutional restraints. The rise of the imperial presidency in the era of Vietnam and Watergate and its later revival in the war on terror prompted an about turn from heroic presidential portrayals to focus on the shortcomings of Richard Nixon, in particular, and George W. Bush. The thirty-seventh president has proved an endlessly fascinating subject for moviemakers from *All the President's Men* (1976), in which the real Nixon features on news footage, to *Frost/Nixon* (2008), in which Frank Langella plays the ex-president in the story of what was in its time the most watched television interview in history. Both these films offer an optimistic view that the democratic process, with a vigilant media in a starring role, will eventually expose and rein in presidential wrongdoing. Other movies offer a bleaker message that Nixon's flaws reflected systemic shortcomings. These include the black comedies *Secret Honor* (1984) and *Dick* (1999) in which Nixon is played by Philip Baker Hall and Dan Hedaya, respectively, and the major Oliver Stone biopic, *Nixon* (1995), which features an Oscar-nominated performance by Anthony Hopkins in the main role.[39] Stone later essayed another presidential biopic *W.* (2008) that starred Josh Brolin as George W. Bush. At one level this is a dynasty story of Bush 43's struggles to live up to and eventually surpass his overachieving father, Bush 41 (James Cromwell). However, it is far less satisfactory in its fundamentally incomplete explanation of Bush's reckless invasion of Iraq on faulty intelligence and his exploitation of the opportunity afforded by crisis to expand presidential power.

The U.K. Comparison

One of the reasons why the predominantly British contributors to this volume find the subject of the American presidency in movies so fascinating is that U.K. cinema treats our national leaders in quite different fashion.[40] A number of factors account for this contrast.

The president combines the functions of the head of state and the head of government that are divided between the monarch and the prime minister, respectively, in the United Kingdom. The Shakespearean dramatic tradition, which has had a dominant influence on cultural representation of Britain's leaders, focused on the monarchy in history to allegorize the politics of the late Tudor and early Stuart dynastic eras in which William Shakespeare (1564–1616) lived and wrote. However, this portrayed some kings as heroes and others as unalloyed villains. Striking a balance, one of each kind has featured in movie recreations of Shakespeare plays. The heroic Henry V, the victor of the battle of Agincourt of 1415 against the French (a play intended to arouse patriotic emotions at a time when England was threatened by another foreign power in the shape of Spain) has had two movie outings. Laurence Olivier played the lead and directed in the 1944 World War II flag-waving version and Kenneth Branagh did the same in the 1989 version. Olivier was also the star and director of *Richard III* (1955), a Shakespearean villain who had supposedly usurped the throne by having his young nephews (the unfortunate Princes-in-the-Tower) murdered and met his end at the 1487 battle of Bosworth that led to the founding of the Tudor monarchical dynasty.

Unable to write about a living monarch, the bard of Avon never dramatized the life of Elizabeth I, but she has featured in many movies, both British and Hollywood made, because of fascination with her success in what was very much a man's world and her rallying of England to victory against the might of the Spanish Armada sent to invade the country in 1588. Her most recent representations in British movies have been in *Elizabeth* (1998) and *Elizabeth: The Golden Years* (2007), played by Cate Blanchett on both occasions. Other than Charles I (1625–1649), who lost his head and his Crown in the English Revolution, and Charles II (1660–1685), who restored the monarchy, later kings and queens have held relatively little interest for British cinema. This largely reflected the declining powers and political role of the Crown. Significantly movies about monarchs who reigned from the eighteenth century to the present have mainly featured them either during moments of institutional crisis, such as *The Madness of George III* (1994), which dealt with the mental health of the king, and *The Queen* (2006), which focused on Elizabeth II in the aftermath of the death of Diana, princess of Wales, in 1997, or in a love story, notably *The Young Victoria* (2009) and *Mrs Brown* (1997), featuring Queen Victoria's romances in youth and later middle age. Arguably the sole exception to this trend has been *The King's Speech* (2010), in which the personal struggle of George VI (played by Colin Firth) to overcome his stammer in order to address the British people by radio on September 3, 1939, the day that war was declared on Germany, symbolizes national determination to defeat Hitler.[41]

The prime minister, whose office emerged in the early eighteenth century and rose to predominance as Britain's parliamentary democracy evolved in the nineteenth century, has never held the same appeal as kings and queens to British moviemakers. Operating the more collective style of leadership associated with a parliamentary system, they are more difficult to represent in individual heroic mould. Unsurprisingly only one British film of note has featured a prime minister as its main character. William Pitt the Younger (Robert Donat) was the subject of *The Young Mister Pitt* (1942), a World War II patriotic movie that portrayed the struggles of Britain's youngest prime minister with Revolutionary and Napoleonic France as an allegory for the contemporary conflict with Nazi Germany.[42] More typically, British movies have featured prime ministers as advisers to the monarch rather than focusing primarily on their own leadership. Exemplifying this, the main role of Tony Blair (Michael Sheen) in *The Queen* is to counsel Elizabeth II about the means of restoring popular confidence in the monarchy by holding a public funeral for Princess Diana, the divorced wife of her heir apparent, Prince Charles.[43]

Nevertheless the real difference between U.S. movie representations of presidents and U.K. cinematic representations of monarchs and prime ministers is more cultural and historical than institutional. With their country lacking anything comparable to America's sense of exceptionalism, British leaders simply cannot embody the broader ideals and symbolism of the redeemer nation in the manner of the U.S. president. While they can be made to epitomize patriotism, there is no scope to link past, present, and future in their celluloid image because there was no British "founding" in the same way as there was an American one. The United States is as much an idea as a country because of the particular nature of its founding and development as a nation of liberty. In contrast, the United Kingdom evolved incrementally over time both in terms of its constitutional structures and the union of its component parts (England, Wales, Scotland, and Ireland/ Northern Ireland).

There is no equivalent of 1776 or 1787 or even 1865 in British history. The English Civil War of the 1640s only resulted in a temporary imposition of a republic that soon gave way to a restored monarchy, albeit a more constrained one. The Glorious Revolution of 1688, which placed constitutional restraints on the monarchy, simply does not have the same significance as the American Revolution in the respective history and political culture of the two countries. In other words, Britain may have a far longer history than the United States, but it has lacked the kind of enduring sense of national identity that shaped America since its founding and came to find expression in presidential leadership.

Chapter Synopses

In the chapters that follow, the contributors to this volume analyze and assess movie portrayals of presidents in relation to themes and issues outlined earlier. In the only presentation that deals with fictional as well as real presidents, Ian Scott considers how the uncanny resemblance between the rise of Barack Obama and Jimmy Santos (the presidential contender in the final series of *The West Wing*) brought the fusion of Washington and Hollywood to fruition. Using the Obama/Santos example as its starting point, his chapter examines the conceptual, historical, and cultural antecedents that have gone into the making of American presidents on screen. It explores the ways in which Hollywood and Washington have constructed increasingly mutual and advantageous agendas, and it suggests how both fictional and biographical portraits have contributed to a vision and realization of the office of the presidency that voters wish for in their choice of real occupant.

Melvyn Stokes then examines two representations of Abraham Lincoln by one of the giants of early American cinema, D. W. Griffith. In his assessment, the silent epic *The Birth of a Nation* (1915) offers not only a conventional depiction of Lincoln as a humanitarian but also an original conception of him as a symbol of national reconciliation after the Civil War. Griffith presented the same image of his subject in *Abraham Lincoln* (1930), the first major movie to deal with the martyred president in the sound era. Whereas the Lincoln imagery of the earlier film had resonated with America's need for unity in the era of the Great War, its use in the later one did not speak the needs of a nation in the early throes of the Great Depression. As Stokes shows, cinematic representations of presidents, even one as great as Lincoln, work best when they adapt their subject to their own times.

Theodore Roosevelt was the first president to have his career chronicled on a large scale by motion pictures. Brian Neve explores the interaction between Roosevelt and the new medium of film as each sought to develop his image to their own benefit. He then considers later cinematic representations of a president who expanded the power of his office at home and of his nation abroad. Most significant in this regard is *The Wind and the Lion* (1975), the John Milius epic whose dynamic representation of Roosevelt contrasted with the uncertainty and failings of America's actual leaders in the age of Vietnam and Watergate. In Neve's assessment, representations of TR raise fundamental questions about history on film, changing notions of masculinity, presidential image, and American relations with the world.

In contrast to Lincoln and TR, there is only one substantial movie representation of Woodrow Wilson. Twentieth Century Fox mogul Daryl F. Zanuck intended his biopic *Wilson* (1944) as a paean to the World War I president's internationalism and its relevance to a world once more at war. As Mark Wheeler shows, this lavish production expressed a national mythology that American "exceptionalism" endowed the United States alone with the moral authority to lead other nations into an era of wider collective security. Instead of being the major success that Zanuck expected, however, the film was the greatest flop of his career. In examining why this was the case, Wheeler points to the limitations of this presidential biopic in fusing history and entertainment, but suggests that this long-forgotten movie still has a provenance for early twenty-first-century debates about American politics, history, and film culture.

As America's leader in times of crisis at home and abroad, Franklin D. Roosevelt is one of the most frequently represented presidents in the movies. Harry Keyishian's chapter initially considers FDR as an inspirational cinematic character, both real and allegorical, in films made during his presidency and set either in the Depression era or in World War II. He then examines later films, notably *Sunrise at Campobello* (1960), that focused on his struggles to overcome his physical disability as preparation for the fulfilment of his destiny to lead the nation in times of trouble. Another FDR movie genre, typified by *Annie!* (1982), presents a more politicized image of Roosevelt as the founder of government programs that offered Americans hope of better times to come during the 1930s. Whatever the form of Roosevelt's cinematic representation, however, Keyishian argues that he always played the same part—the confidence-booster who maintained that the nation could overcome its problems.

Mark White then explores the portrayal of John F. Kennedy in *Thirteen Days* (2000), Roger Donaldson's film about the Cuban Missile Crisis of October 1962. His chapter contextualizes this in relation to the existing body of film and television representations of JFK to demonstrate its fealty to the "Camelot" view of Kennedy in American popular culture. It then contrasts the film's hagiographic approach with the growing belief among historians that Kennedy's successful management of the crisis should not obscure his role in bringing it about through his aggressive conduct toward Cuba, something not considered in *Thirteen Days*. Pointing to the problematic relationship between image and historical accuracy in presidential movies, White demonstrates that *Thirteen Days* provides only a partial view of Kennedy, one that enlarges the notion prevalent in American popular culture that he was an outstanding president.

Andrew Johnson was the first president to face impeachment proceedings and Richard Nixon was the only president to resign office to avoid impeachment. In his chapter, Iwan Morgan considers two biopics of these presidents, Metro-Goldwyn-Mayer's *Tennessee Johnson* (1942) and Oliver Stone's *Nixon* (1995), to explore the changes in Hollywood attitudes to presidential power and personality in the half-century that separated their making. In his assessment, the Johnson movie reflects traditional Hollywood's attitudes about the heroic presidency in his representation as the guardian of Abraham Lincoln's vision for sectional reconciliation and national unity against Radical Republicans intent on punishing the South for the Civil War. In contrast, the Nixon movie presents its subject as being in thrall to dark forces that threaten to undermine American democracy. As Morgan demonstrates, the two movies also testify to the different wartime impulses of patriotism in the 1940s and division in the Vietnam era.

Finally, Kingsley Marshall analyses the representation of George W. Bush in Oliver Stone's *W.* (2008), the first biopic of a living president that was released just as the 2008 presidential election reached its climax. In contrast to general expectations, the iconoclastic moviemaker did not seek to demolish Bush, whose public approval ratings had sunk to a historic low by the time the movie premiered. Instead he offered a sympathetic portrayal of his subject in relation to dynastic family pressures, but was ultimately critical of Bush's leadership in the war on terror in his first term in office. As has been the case in other presidential movies, not least those previously made by Stone, *W.* blurred and simplified the complex realities of recent history. In Marshall's assessment, therefore, the film signified that if dramatized events do not entirely subsume history, they usually serve to prevent it subsisting in its entirety.

W. is among the presidential movies that readers of this volume are likely to be familiar with from viewing in the cinema or on DVD. Other films that feature in this book, notably *Abraham Lincoln*, *Tennessee Johnson*, and *Wilson*, are less known because they have disappeared into relative obscurity since their making. Nevertheless, the contributors to this volume hope that readers will want to see or resee all the movies under discussion. Whether approached as students of the presidency or of film, each is worth viewing not only in its own right but also to assess the power of cinema to shape understanding of history and politics.

Notes

1. See, in particular, Peter C. Rollins and John E. O'Connor, eds., *Hollywood's White House: The American Presidency in Film and History* (Lexington: University Press of Kentucky, 2003); and Michael Coyne, *Hollywood Goes to Washington: American Politics on Screen* (London: Reaktion Books, 2008), especially chapters 2 and 3. Two contributors to this volume have also made valuable explorations of

presidential movies in their broader studies of films and politics: Harry Keyishian, *Screening Politics: The Politician in American Movies, 1931–2001* (Lanham MD: Scarecrow Press, 2003); and Ian Scott, *American Politics in Hollywood Film*, 2nd ed. (Edinburgh: Edinburgh University Press, 2011). For useful listings of presidential (real and fictional) representations on film, see John Shelton Lawrence, "A Filmography for Images of American Presidents on Film," in Rollins and O'Connor, *Hollywood's White House*, 383–402; and Coyne, *Hollywood Goes to Washington*, 213–21.

2. Examples include "biopics," such as *George Washington* (1984), *George Washington II: The Forging of a Nation* (1986), *Lincoln* (1988), and *Truman* (1995), and episodic movies, such as *The Missiles of October* (1974), about Kennedy's management of the Cuban Missile Crisis, and *Path to War* (2002), a sympathetic portrayal of Johnson's decision-making over Vietnam [the last movie directed by John Frankenheimer, whose credits included the political classics *The Manchurian Candidate* (1962) and *Seven Days in May* (1964)].

3. Of the twenty-seven constitutional amendments, only six have mentioned the presidency. Four of these (Amendments XII, XX, XXIII, and XXIV) deal with electoral procedures or voting rights and one (XXV) establishes succession procedures in the event of the president's removal from office, death, resignation, or incapacity to discharge his duties. Arguably, the most significant constitutional change affecting the presidency is Amendment XXII (ratified 1951) that limits the president to two terms in office.

4. Clinton Rossiter, *The American Presidency* (New York: Harcourt, Brace, 1956), 14–40.

5. James Pfiffner, ed., *The Managerial Presidency*, 2nd ed. (College Station: Texas A&M University Press, 1999); Stephen Hess with James Pfiffner, *Organizing the Presidency*, 3d ed. (Washington DC: Brookings, 2002).

6. Edward S. Corwin, *The Presidency: Office and Powers* (New York: Harcourt, Brace, 1940), 200. Corwin was specifically referring to foreign policy but his observation is also true for other policy domains.

7. Richard E. Neustadt, *Presidential Power: The Politics of Leadership* (New York: John Wiley, 1960); and *Presidential Power and the Modern Presidents: The Politics of Leadership from Roosevelt to Reagan* (New York: Free Press, 1990).

8. Edward Corwin, *The Presidency: Office and Powers* (New York: New York University Press, 1957), 29–30.

9. For presidential history, see Michael Genovese, *The Power of the American Presidency 1789–2000* (New York: Oxford University Press, 2001); Forrest McDonald, *The American Presidency: An Intellectual History* (Lawrence: University Press of Kansas, 1995); and Marcus Cunliffe, *American Presidents and the Presidency* (London: Fontana, 1972).

10. Genovese, *The Power of the American Presidency 1789–2000*, xii, 14.

11. For discussion of the pros and cons of presidential surveys, see Meena Bose and Mark Landis, eds., *The Uses and Abuses of Presidential Ratings* (New York: Nova Science, 2003); and Alvin Felzenberg, *Leaders We Deserved (And a Few We Didn't): Rethinking the Presidential Rating Game* (New York: Basic Books, 2008).

12. For a useful checklist of the rankings in the main polls from 1948 to early 2009, see "Historical Rankings of the Presidents of the United States," http://en.wikipedia.org/wiki/historicalrankingsofthepresident-softheUnitedStates. The first U.K. survey of U.S. presidents, conducted by the editor of this volume, gives top ranking to FDR over Lincoln and Washington. See http://www.americas.sas.ac.uk/research/survey/.

13. See, e.g., *C-Span 2009 Historians' Presidential Leadership Survey*, http://www.c-span.org/PresidentialSurvey/.

14. Dick Morris, *Behind the Oval Office: Getting Reelected against All Odds* (New York: Random House, 1997), 307–308.

15. Stephen Skowronek, *The Politics Presidents Make: Leadership from John Adams to Bill Clinton* (Cambridge MA: Belknap Press, 1997), 20–21.

16. Quoted in Thomas E. Cronin, *The State of the Presidency*, 2nd ed. (Boston: Little, Brown, 1980), 1.

17. Peggy Noonan, "Ronald Reagan," in Robert A. Wilson, ed., *Character Above All* (New York: Simon, 1995), 202. For insightful analysis of the character issue, see James Pfiffner, *The Character Factor: How We Judge America's Presidents* (College Station: Texas A&M Press, 2004).

18. Fred Greenstein, *The Presidential Difference: Leadership Style from FDR to Clinton* (New York: Free Press, 2000). See too "Taking the Temperature," October 16, 2008, http://www.time.org.

19. Arthur M. Schlesinger, Jr., *The Imperial Presidency* (Boston: Houghton Mifflin, 1973); Andrew Rudalevige, *The New Imperial Presidency: Renewing Presidential Power after Watergate* (Ann Arbor: University of Michigan Press, 2005).

20. Arthur M. Schlesinger, Jr., *War and the American Presidency* (New York: Norton, 2005); James Pfiffner, *Power Play: The Bush Administration and the Constitution* (Washington DC: Brookings Institution, 2008).

21. Michael Genovese and Lori Cox Han, *The Presidency and the Challenge of Democracy* (New York: Palgrave, 2006).

22. Taylor appears in his prepresidential career as an army general in *Distant Drums* (1951), a Raoul Walsh movie about the Seminole War of 1840 in Florida, which stars Gary Cooper.

23. The HBO series *John Adams* ran to seven episodes, only one of which dealt with his presidency. It was based on David McCullough's best-selling study, *John Adams* (New York: Simon & Schuster, 2001). The second president had also featured in a thirteen-part examination of his life and times, *The Adams Chronicles* (1976), made by New York's WNET to coincide with the bicentennial. Highly popular because it focused on Adams as a family man as much as a political leader, it was widely credited with creating the television miniseries boom of the late 1970s and

1980s. See Scott F. Stoddart, "*The Adams Chronicles*: Domesticating the American Presidency," in Rollins and O'Connor, *Hollywood's White House*, 30–49.

24. Hayes is briefly represented to exemplify William F. Cody's celebrity status in *Buffalo Bill* (1944), while Arthur is featured in *Silver Dollar* (1932), which chronicles the rise and fall of a Colorado silver baron loosely based on H.A.W. Tabor, and in a western, *Cattle King* (1963, a.k.a. *Guns of Wyoming*).

25. McKinley has a secondary but still significant role in *This is My Affair* (1937), a drama about the travails of his secret agent, played by Robert Taylor. He only has a minor part in the John Milius made-for-television movie *Rough Riders* (1997), which focuses on Theodore Roosevelt.

26. Coolidge featured briefly in *The Court Martial of Billy Mitchell* (1955) about an early advocate of American air power.

27. For discussion, see Andrew Piasecki, "Abraham Lincoln in John Ford's *The Iron Horse*: Both Trumpets and Silences," in Rollins and O'Connor, *Hollywood's White House*, 62–75.

28. Gunnar Myrdal, *An American Dilemma: The Negro Problem and Modern Democracy* (New York: Harper & Bros., 1944).

29. For discussion, see Stuart Leibiger, "George Washington, *The Crossing*, and Revolutionary Leadership," in Rollins and O'Connor, *Hollywood's White House*, 19–29. The movie, about Washington's decision to cross the Delaware river to attack the Hessian garrison at Trenton in December 1776, was based on Howard Fast, *The Crossing* (New York: Morrow, 1971; reprint New York: Simon & Schuster, 1999).

30. For a critique, see Jim Welsh, "Jefferson in Love: The Framer Framed," in Rollins and O'Connor, *Hollywood's White House*, 50–61.

31. For the historical inaccuracies of *Amistad*, see Eric Foner, "The Amistad Case in Fact and Film," March 1978, http://historymatters.gmu.edu/d/174/.

32. Eisenhower (played by Robert Beer) had a small role in *The Right Stuff* (1983), a movie about the early days of America's manned space program. The thirty-fourth president has featured more significantly in television productions. Robert Duvall played him in the miniseries *Ike* (1979) and Tom Selleck took his part in the telefilm *Ike: Countdown to D-Day* (2004).

33. LBJ, played as something of a buffoon by Donald Moffat, featured as a senator in *The Right Stuff*, but is more significantly represented, played respectively by Randy Quaid and Michael Gambon, in the television movies *LBJ: The Early Years* (1987) and *Path to War* (2002).

34. Ford (Josef Sommer) was the second lead character in the tele-movie *The Betty Ford Story* (1987), which focused on his wife's battle with alcohol dependency.

35. Clinton is the model for Governor Jack Stanton (John Travolta) in the Mike Nichols movie *Primary Colors* (1998), based on the novel of that name by Clinton campaign aide Joe Kline.

36. Jon Roper, *The American Presidents: Heroic Leadership from Kennedy to Clinton* (Edinburgh: Edinburgh University Press, 2000), 220. See also the same author's "The Contemporary Presidency: George W. Bush and the Myth of Heroic Presidential Leadership," *Presidential Studies Quarterly* 34 (March 2004): 132–42.

37. For discussion, see Iwan Morgan, *Beyond the Liberal Consensus: A Political History of the United States since 1965* (New York: St Martin's Press, 1994); and Rick Perlstein, *Nixonland: The Rise of a President and the Fracturing of America* (New York: Scribner, 2008).

38. "CBS Pulls Reagan Miniseries," November 5, 2003, CNN.com/ Entertainment; "The Reagans," http://en.wikipedia.org/wki/The_ Reagans.

39. For fuller discussion, see Mark Feeney, *Nixon at the Movies: A Book about Belief* (Chicago: University of Chicago Press, 2004).

40. For good discussion of British history in film, see Claire Monk and Amy Sergeant, eds., *British History Cinema: The History, Heritage, and Costume Film* (London: Routledge, 2002). For readers seeking to learn more about British cinema in general, useful websites include: "The British Cinema History Project" (University of East Anglia) at http://www.uea.ac.uk/ftv/bchip; and "British Cinema Greats" at www.british-cinemagreats.com/.

41. Movies about British monarchs have had considerable success in the competition for Motion Picture Academy Awards. Laurence Olivier received an Honorary Academy Award "for outstanding achievement as actor, producer, and director in bringing *Henry V* to the screen," a recognition of the problems of making this epic in the wartime conditions of 1944. Helen Mirren received the best actress award for her performance as Elizabeth II in *The Queen* and Judy Dench received the best supporting actress award for playing Elizabeth I in *Shakespeare in Love* (1995). In addition, the following received Oscar nominations: Lawrence Olivier and Kenneth Branagh for their performances in their respective versions of *Henry V*, Olivier for *Richard III*, Cate Blanchett for *Elizabeth*, Nigel Hawthorne as George III in *The Madness of George III*, and Judy Dench as Victoria in *Mrs Brown*. Presidents do not provide such good dramatic material if judged on the relative lack of Oscar success for actors playing them. Five actors have been nominated for playing real presidents but none has won: Anthony Hopkins as John Quincy Adams and Richard Nixon, Alexander Knox as Woodrow Wilson, James Whitmore as Harry Truman, and Frank Langella as Nixon (in *Frost/Nixon*).

42. Two films have also represented future prime ministers: *The Iron Duke* (1934) deals with the military campaigns of the Duke of Wellington against Napoleonic France; and *Young Winston* (1972) deals with the early life and military exploits of Winston Churchill. Paradoxically, one of Hollywood's early sound movies, *Disraeli* (1929), featured Victorian-era prime minister Benjamin Disraeli as an empire builder. Made by Warner Brothers, it was a critical and commercial success—far more so

than the near contemporary D.W. Griffith biopic of America's sixteenth president, *Abraham Lincoln* (1930). George Arliss won the best actor Oscar for his role as the main character.

43. This film was the second in a loose "Blair trilogy," each scripted by Peter Morgan and starring Sheen, but the other two were made-for-television movies that were not theatrically released. *The Deal* (2003) dealt with Blair's pact with Gordon Brown, who agreed not to stand against him in the Labour Party leadership election of 1994. *The Special Relationship* (2010), which was shown on HBO in the United States, explored Blair's dealings with President Bill Clinton (played by Dennis Quaid).

Chapter 1

Transition: The Making of Screen Presidents

Ian Scott

As the 2008 presidential primary election season took off, the campaign for the Democratic Party nomination attracted even more attention than usual. With Senators Barack Obama of Illinois and Hillary Clinton of New York as frontrunners, it appeared likely to produce an African American or female nominee, either of whom would be a historic first. Despite this, the contest also generated a feeling of déjà vu among pundits and the public alike. Here was an election that seemed very familiar, but this sense of recall did not emanate from another time in American history. This was not a rerun of any previous presidential contest. Instead, the historical antecedent came from television, specifically the seventh and final season of the acclaimed NBC political drama *The West Wing*. In this, the aspiring but largely inexperienced Latino congressman Matthew Santos (Jimmy Smits) beat Vice President Bob Russell (Gary Cole) to the Democratic nomination and went on to be elected president by a narrow margin over a moderate Republican from the West, Arnold Vinick (Alan Alda).

At first glance the story appears as one of those felicitous connections that the news media seizes upon when looking for new angles on political events as an election season gets under way. If this were nothing more than the coincidental coming-together of art and life, it would be of momentary interest but little else. The fact that one drew direct and acknowledged inspiration from the other, however, shows the reality of the Hollywood/entertainment/Washington nexus within American political culture in the early twenty-first century. When Elie Attie, a former speechwriter for Al Gore in 2000 and later a writer and producer on *The West Wing*, asked Obama aide David Axelrod in the summer of 2004 about the background and life of his boss, the two men set in train a sequence of events that saw the fictitious show uncannily predict the real-life politics that unfolded two years after the final season of the series had been screened in the United States. "We're living your scripts," joked Axelrod in an e-mail to Attie as the gathering momentum of Obama's campaign encouraged hope that it would emulate Santos's success.[1]

Using the Obama/Santos example as its starting point, this chapter considers the conceptual, historical, and cultural antecedents that have gone into the making of American presidents on screen. In addition, it examines the ways in which Hollywood and Washington have constructed increasingly mutual and advantageous agendas. Finally, it suggests how both fictional and biographical portraits have contributed to a vision of the presidency that voters wish for in their choice of the real White House occupant.

It was Obama's speech at the 2004 Democratic convention in Boston that first inspired Attie to use the prospective senator's tone, style, and rhetoric as a basis for his construction of Matt Santos in *The West Wing*. As he put it, "After that convention speech, Obama's life changed. He was mobbed wherever he went. He was more than a candidate seeking votes; people were seeking him. Some of Santos's celebrity aura came from that."[2]

Of course, Attie is not the first former political speechwriter to make his way to Hollywood and rewrite at least some piece of political reality for the big or small screen. He was following in the wake of people such as Jeremy Larner, Gary Ross, and even Dee Dee Myers—a long time script/story adviser on *The West Wing* and former press secretary in the Clinton White House. All these individuals had drawn on their insider experience to pen political stories. However, the real impact of this fictional/reality crossover was not just in highlighting the long tradition of politics on screen, nor in underlining the links between politics and speechwriters who had made their way into film and television. The true importance of this tale lay in the long-standing success of *The West Wing* as a political drama that could convey a credible, if wishful, portrayal of the inner workings of executive politics to its audience in the late twentieth and early twenty-first centuries. In what was a rapidly changing era for cultural representations of politics in general and the presidency in particular, few could have predicted at the turn of the millennium what an outstanding success *The West Wing* would become. While the series was first screened during Bill Clinton's presidency, its mythos was garnered on George W. Bush's watch through presenting a very different picture of White House procedure from that going on in the real Oval Office at the time. As cultural critic David Hepworth observed:

> The fact that the TV presidency has been occupied by President Sheen and his team of handsome, well-read, clubbable young people, while the real presidency has been gifted to an individual incapable of forming a thought that hasn't been prepared by the sinister committee who call the shots, is more than one of those amusing little things.[3]

The juxtaposition of these two personalities (Martin Sheen's Jed Bartlet and Bush 43) riding side-by-side through their own presidential years in the new century, respective journeys that culminated in the Santos/Obama successions, reminds us that the nature of presidential representation on big and small screen has often been a tricky historical and cultural endeavor. Whether in regard to biographical portraits from filmmakers such as John Ford and Oliver Stone or fictional recreations by Rob Reiner and Barry Levinson, critics, scholars, and audiences alike have more often than not been gripped by the "authenticity" question: is that fact correct, did this event happen at that moment, does that actor look right in the role?

According to political scientist Myron Levine, only by reviewing "the vast literature, written by both presidential scholars and former White House insiders, that has traced the growth and transformation of the modern White House...can we gauge the degree of *accuracy* or *inaccuracy* [my emphasis] of the portrait of the American presidency provided by Hollywood film."[4] This suggests that only through the proximity of presentation to the real thing—the office or occupant—can we get to any positive evaluation of screen presidents, implying that approval is based solely on such accreditation. In short, conventional wisdom presupposes that when the life of a presidential figure—real or imagined—is portrayed on screen, there is automatically an agenda being followed by the filmmaker in conceiving the central character in a certain way because it conveys traits and attributes sympathetic to his or her own ideology or vision. As one such auteur said of himself in an interview promoting *W.* (2008), his movie about Bush 43: "To be 'Oliver Stone,' whoever that is, is to provoke feelings in people before they've even met me."[5] But can and should authenticity really be the only watchword for the efficacy of presidential representation and its impact as a cultural force on society?

This chapter examines the evolution of presidential portrayals on screen, tests the sustainability of Levine's theory, and suggests that audiences have become increasingly enamored by the small-screen incarnations of chief executives in particular, with the consequence that these characterizations have become the template for the kind of leaders that many Americans would like to see replicated in their real counterparts. If all of this sounds largely superfluous to the question of authenticity, it is because, increasingly, real presidents, just like screen ones, must "look and feel right" to attain credibility in the modern age. In short, now that Barack Obama has assumed the reins of the most high-profile job in the world, the question we might contemplate is the degree to which the presidency has finally become an amalgam of historical construction and Hollywood superimposition.

Hollywood Presidents Past and Present

Prior to the success of Bartlet and Santos in *The West Wing* and the consequent morphing between real and reconstructed occupants of the White House, fictional presidents did not cause anything like the same kind of headaches for filmmakers as the real thing. Indeed the history of these Hollywood presidents is one of wildly different social, moral, and ideological standpoints that suited the generic form of the movie being made. Political melodramas usually had strong and resolute chief executives, exemplified by *Gabriel Over the White House* (1933), *Fail Safe*, *Seven Days in May* (both 1964), *Deep Impact* (1997), and *The Contender* (2000). Conversely, paranoia or conspiracy thrillers offered up duplicitous leaders, as in *Absolute Power* and *Murder at 1600 Pennsylvania Avenue* (both 1997). Light-hearted comedies and satires, such as *My Fellow Americans* (1996) and *Head of State* (2003), featured humorous presidents. Finally, action blockbusters constructed presidents as heroic figures, notably in *Independence Day* (1996) and *Air Force One* (1997).

The constant in each of these portrayals was some tangible reference point to previous real incumbents. Of course, a minority of films featuring fictional presidents tried hard to dodge their real parallel but still failed. Examples include the obvious and acknowledged construction of JFK masquerading as President James Cassidy in *The Greek Tycoon* (1978), and the rendition of Bill Clinton through the personification of Jack Stanton in the Mike Nichols film based on presidential aide Joe Klein's novel, *Primary Colors* (1998). Far more commonly, however, portrayals of fictional presidents have referenced the personality, politics, or policy of a real counterpart—or represented composites of several ones.

Rather like the example of *Primary Colors*, the Obama/Santos construction does not work easily for a straight rendition of presidential politics. Santos was a fictional character chasing the biggest prize in politics, but virtually the whole of this final season of *The West Wing* was devoted to his character and through him the electoral process, rather than to any embodiment of the presidency. In this regard, one might make the point that electoral movies in general have often been an easier subgeneric form in which to play with, and recount, past political actions and personalities as preparation for the office rather than having to document a time when such characters inhabited the White House. In Franklin Shaffner's *The Best Man* (1964), for example, Henry Fonda's William Russell partly resembles Adlai Stevenson with a touch of charismatic Kennedy. *Man of the Year* (2006), directed by Barry Levinson, features Robin Williams as a talk show host, endowed with elements of Larry King and Jon Stewart as well as certain Kennedy-esque values, who winds up getting involved in electoral politics against his better judgment. In *Primary Colors*, moreover, Jack Stanton mirrors the trials and tribulations of the Clinton campaign in 1992 to portray a victory against the odds for a flawed but still inspiring candidate.

These films have therefore taken their license to create a potential chief executive in very broad brush stokes of personality and character while attempting to nudge the memory bank of audiences into recognizing some flicker of familiarity in their protagonists. In films portraying real presidents, from early examples such as *Abraham Lincoln* (1930), *Tennessee Johnson* (1942), *Wilson* (1944), *The President's Lady* (1953), and *Sunrise at Campobello* (1960), to recent ones such as *Nixon* (1995) and *W.*, however, such artistic license has never been easy. Each of these biographical films found their treatment of the central character questioned—and often criticized—precisely for taking such liberty with the historical record and personality, despite attempts by some of the filmmakers involved to do exactly the opposite.

Overall then it is this differential between the two types of presidential portrayal in Hollywood—biographical presentation as reality, fictional recreation as idealized amalgam—that really gives us a clue to the reception, success, and historical realization of the presidency on screen. As Terry Christensen and Peter Hass have observed with regard to two relatively successful comedies of the mid-1990s, the light-hearted and affable portrayals of fictional presidents are often the most interesting for their measure of sympathy with and comprehension about the office. In their view, "Neither *Dave* nor *The*

American President may have had any measurable impact on movie-goers: conjointly with many other movies that have also embodied a simplistic view of the presidency, however, they may have helped mould our expectations of the office."[6]

It is not a startling revelation that audiences by-and-large like their fictional presidents far more than their biographically reheated ones, and probably more than the current incumbent as well. Nevertheless the public can fuse together the characteristics of fictional chief executives with the actors playing them into an appealing political entity. A poll during the 2004 presidential contest suggested that if *The West Wing's* President Bartlet were running for office, he would have handily beaten both the actual candidates, George W. Bush and John Kerry. A body of opinion also preferred Martin Sheen himself as the candidate over the real ones. This prompted conservative "shock-jock" Michael Savage to rubbish Sheen's chances of ever being president and excoriate Hollywood liberals for meddling in politics. Far from being an expression of ideological self-confidence, this was more a sign of American conservatives' vexation at the popularity of progressive values associated with the fictional television program and its players.[7]

What does all this prove—that presidents need to be boiled down to generic and positive character traits; that Americans sometimes mistake their fictional leaders as somehow having the tone and convictions of the actors playing them; or that the electorate has been both flattered and deceived by the rich personalities that have preceded modern leaders and thus search in their films for a new Kennedy, new FDR, a new Lincoln even? Seeking to understand the success of *The West Wing*, Michael Coyne confirms as much in suggesting that "part of the show's appeal is that Bartlet is as close as the world will ever come to getting Jack Kennedy back."[8] In contrast, Myron Levine asserts—only half-jokingly—that the failure of what he dubs simple and uncritical hagiographies, such as *Wilson* and *Sunrise at Campobello*, to ignite audiences is their lack of a human dimension. For him, the empathetic portrayal of FDR in John Huston's *Annie!* (1982), though interjected into a patently fictional storyline, offered far better characterization of presidential leadership and capacity to uplift the national spirit.

There is something of a contradiction in this judgment. *Wilson* and *Sunrise at Campobello* strove for authenticity and accuracy. Indeed director Henry King and producer Daryl Zanuck, together with historian Ray Stannard Baker, went well beyond the call of duty to do so in the former. Of course, this was the benchmark on which they expected presidential movies to be judged. In reality, however, the impact of such films has more to do with character, rhetoric, and style rather than reality.

Despite some admirable traits in the Wilson and FDR biopics, cinematic representations of real presidents work best when they are not rewrites of history or reassembled artifacts of a president's life and times. Instead, films that have tried to move away from the strictures of historical authenticity have found resonance in projecting presidents as the embodiment of national hope and mission and, in some instances, of divine guidance. John Ford's *Young Mr. Lincoln* (1939) and John Cromwell's *Abe Lincoln in Illinois* (1940, also known as *Spirit of the People*) were righteous, mythic tales about America's anointed greatest leader. They were every bit as symbolic and full of predestination as the apparitions of Lincoln in Ford's earlier *The Iron Horse* (1924), Frank Capra's *Mr. Smith Goes to Washington* (1939), or even Stone's *Nixon*. It was not the actual story of Lincoln that was important (and indeed Ford and Cromwell took early life, semi-apocryphal tales and made them metaphoric), but the mystique and the reverence surrounding him that won people over to his representation in these films and hence in history itself. Indeed for a director like John Ford, Lincoln became the emblem of not just politics, but the whole American experience of westward expansion and maturity as a nation. Hence his usage of portraits and other images of Lincoln in numerous movies, including *The Prisoner of Shark Island* (1936), *Sergeant Rutledge* (1960), *How the West was Won* and *The Man Who Shot Liberty Valance* (both 1962), and *Cheyenne Autumn* (1964).[9]

Of course, we might say that Lincoln is an exception in the presidential pantheon as a leader towering above mere politics to represent something tangible about the whole of the American experience. The reworking of the Lincoln image, or at the very least the image that is etched on the minds of Americans and others around the world by his representation at the memorial in Washington, D.C., has thus been appropriated for a mixture of movies that range from *The Firm* (1992) to the remake of *Planet of the Apes* (2001). The spirit of John Kennedy and even further back of Thomas Jefferson have been similarly utilized as symbolic of a grander, purer political age, wherein rhetoric, fierce intellect, and urbane manners were better appreciated and great men could rise through their talent. Nevertheless Lincoln remains the template for political grandeur, heroic leadership, personal sacrifice, and martyrdom.

It is very interesting, therefore, that so many commentators should be so taken by the reverence of the Lincoln spirit in these movies, and yet so revile Oliver Stone's similar treatment of Kennedy in *JFK* (1991). Criticizing the latter as "unctuous, disingenuous and excruciatingly long," Michael Coyne commented, "Assuredly the worst element...(totally unsubstantiated by the historical record) was Kevin Costner as New Orleans District Attorney Jim Garrison delivering an interminable and woefully indulgent closing speech to the jury."[10] At the moment of the film's release, *Newsweek* slapped the now infamous headline across its front cover, "The Twisted Truth of *JFK*: Why Oliver Stone's Movie Can't be Trusted."[11] Reflecting on such criticism and similar condemnation of Stone's later biopic of Nixon, David Belin insisted that filmmakers had a "moral obligation to avoid major distortion of the facts."[12]

The furor brings us back to the "authenticity" debate and whether critics are justified in focusing on this issue. Whatever its shortcomings, *JFK* remains visceral filmmaking that places it apart from any recent Hollywood political movie. Though it can be criticized for factual inaccuracy, polemics, and misrepresentation, charges also laid against Michael Moore's documentaries, this movie undeniably generated great debate and interest in galvanizing so many people— hitherto little engaged with cinema, let alone politics—into some realization of their nation's political culture and the machinations of governmental agencies. Film historian Robert Rosenstone may be pushing the point too far in claiming that "the Hollywood historical film will always include images that are at once invented and yet may still be considered true."[13] Even if this contradiction were possible, it is doubtful that the symbolism and intent of a picture can carry it through a multitude of sins, including erroneous material passing for accurate historical reflection. However, Rosenstone's corollary assertion that *JFK* remains one of the most important works of American history to appear on screen is more persuasive in insinuating the ability of film to capture a zeitgeist like no other medium. This is no small achievement and perhaps it is all that Hollywood need be capable in its depictions of the presidency.

That said, it should be acknowledged that Lincoln is also a common enough reference point for criticism—or at least pointing out the limitations—of what the representation of cinematic presidents can offer. The sixteenth president's "story" as the backwoods poor boy who taught himself the law and became the savior of the nation is an enduring myth that almost no amount of minor factual error can contradict. As Richard Shenkman observes, the eponymous hero of Ford's *Young Mr. Lincoln* is honorable, innocent, and folksy, but what of the Lincoln "who was so hungry for power and influence that he ran for public office at age twenty-three, married a woman 'above his station,' and represented rich corporations [as an attorney]?"[14]

Shenkman's point is important here, and not just as a counterweight to arguments about Lincoln's persona. What he also critiques is the way in which historical figures can be inserted into dubiously acknowledged "real" events in movies and then emerge as mythical overlords of their own destiny, sprinkled with foresight, intuition, and some intangible exceptionalism that naturally signals their future greatness. This is the essence of the mythic narrative that Hollywood has helped construct over time and is the key to all manner of portrayals that have followed in the footsteps of a film such as *Young Mr. Lincoln*. In other words the arc of the storyline is the thing that has to be right; historical fact becomes secondary. Indeed neither Ford nor Stone in their respective times set the tone for the reception of the two presidents they rebuilt on screen. The likes of Isaac Newton Arnold in Lincoln's case and William Manchester in Kennedy's had already begun that process on paper many years before. But, as Shenkman comments:

> If Hollywood's power to shape our perception of individual presidents has been limited, its power to shape how we think about presidents in general has been great. Hollywood, more than any other force in society, has determined how people think a president should act and look. Hollywood has given us a standard by which to measure the actual people holding the office.[15]

Cinematic biographies of presidents have, therefore, fallen into two very neat divisions throughout Hollywood's existence. They are either denounced for their lack of attention to the historical record, or they are lauded for their ability to capture the social, philosophical, and idealistic character of the person, if not the times in which he lived. More often than not, however, the most successful emblems of this ability to capture the stylistic signature of a chief executive are not reassembled figures from history, but the made-up presidents who have appeared out of imagination, such as Dave Kovics (*Dave*, 1993), Andrew Shepherd (*The American President*, 1995), and Jed Bartlet.

Hollywood and Presidential Political Culture

So presidential movies, perhaps fictional ones far more than the portentously inferred biographical ones, can offer us a picture of executive performance, and provide a facsimile of appearance that shows Americans what they would really like to see in their president. But have Hollywood portrayals really made any serious attempts to account for and counter the trends and issues in the real political culture at large; to offer a critical vision of how the American polity in general, and the presidency in particular, works, exists, and declaims? And if they have, how might this have been done?

Ben Dickenson in *Hollywood's New Radicalism* (2006) is clear that the presentation of politics in the 1990s in particular manifested an ideological bent. This was tied up, he believes, with the failing liberal ethos emanating from both Hollywood and the Clinton White House. Left-leaning activists in the film community craved change, enlightenment, and a return to the hope and optimism of the 1960s. Their equivalents in Washington saw in Clinton a candidate who could fulfill that kind of pledge. Both, argues Dickenson, were destined for disappointment. In explaining the causes of this failure, he draws a parallel between the political movies of the era and former Clinton economist Joseph Stiglitz's book *The Roaring Nineties: The Seeds of Destruction* (2003), which indicted *inter alia* the president's promotion of film industry deregulation, financial services deregulation, fiscal conservatism, and free trade. In his assessment, "Contemporary progressives were fooled by the liberal rhetoric that shrouded the third way."[16] Whereas Stiglitz voiced the disillusion felt in academic and intellectual circles with a four-hundred-page critique of Clinton's market-oriented economic policies, Dickenson sees movies such as *Wag the Dog* (1997), *Bulworth* (1998), and especially *Primary Colors* as the Hollywood equivalent of this. The latter showed the "dangerous capitulation of power...and the damaging practice of progressive activists hanging their hopes of change on one man." This was embodied in the central relationship between the hopeful and idealistic Henry Burton (Adrian Lester) and aspiring candidate Jack Stanton (John Travolta). For Dickinson, their interaction was a metaphor for Hollywood and Clinton's courting of each other during the 1990s.[17]

John Shelton Lawrence offers another conceptual analysis of Hollywood influence centered on what he calls the "hard-boiled" presidents of the 1990s, the action heroes James Marshall and Thomas Whitmore (Harrison Ford and Bill Pullman, respectively, in *Air Force One*, 1997, and *Independence Day*, 1996). In his view, these portrayals helped condition a new generation of young voters into believing that their presidents should be dynamic, gung-ho, and capable of saving the world single-handedly, in a metaphoric if not literal way. Both films had huge box-office appeal to younger moviegoers, a group with little interest in "conventional" political cinema, and thereby had the capacity to influence their expectations of the presidency.[18]

In like fashion, Jean-Michel Valantin contends that so-called national security cinema, in which "on-screen dramas can be fables," illuminate the burdens of responsibility and discuss the legitimacy of U.S. power.[19] His principal examples are less presidential movies than they are diplomatic or international adventures, including *Crimson Tide* (1995), *Rules of Engagement* (2000), and *Black Hawk Down* (2001). In also citing *The American President, Independence Day,* and *Thirteen Days* (2000), however, Valantin couches his thesis of military engagement propagandized within Hollywood narratives as an endorsement of executive actions. For him, crucial evidence of the convergence of Hollywood and the White House on this score was the now notorious meeting between the head of the Motion Picture Association of America Jack Valenti and George W. Bush's Senior Adviser and Deputy Chief of Staff Karl Rove in Hollywood on November 11, 2001, two months to the day after the terrorist attacks on New York and Washington. As Valenti related it, Rove insisted that propaganda was not the goal of the administration, especially in the aftermath of 9/11, merely "clear and honest" information that should be disseminated through movies. Hollywood should not seek to pitch the war on terrorism as a "war of civilizations" in the manner of Harvard academic Samuel Huntington's controversial thesis. On the other hand, the White House was anxious for its assistance in promoting America's image as a force for global freedom, prosperity, and security in a dangerous international environment.[20]

Whether Valenti and Rove reached an agreement on this score was never clarified. However, the deferral of two major movies featuring actual or threatened terrorist attacks on America, respectively *The Sum of All Fears* and *Collateral Damage* (both eventually released in 2002) together with the release of a small but interesting coterie of contemporary and historical military pictures, *Spy Game* (2001), *We Were Soldiers* (2002), and *Tears of the Sun* (2003), confirmed that some sort of understanding and ideological presence, if not pressure, was being mapped out in the film industry in the wake of 9/11. What role the White House and its incumbent, fictional or otherwise, were likely to play in that arrangement was never made clear. In fact only on the small screen, in shows such as *Commander-in-Chief, 24,* and a special episode of *The West Wing* at the outset of season three in late 2001, was there any contemporary reference to 9/11. On the big screen, presidents largely disappeared from view until Oliver Stone brought out *W.* in the twilight of the Bush era.

Conclusion

If Bill Clinton provided the template for Hollywood pictures about the presidency at the close of the 1990s in the likes of *Primary Colors* and Rod Lurie's *The Contender* (2000), in which Jeff Bridges played Jackson Evans as an astute, if food obsessed, Democratic president looking to replace a dead vice president, the changes that occurred subsequently and the provocative assault on the political senses by a whole slew of films in the new century is something few could have anticipated as the forty-second president left office. Despite a flurry of movies that delved into what at first seemed ludicrous conspiracy plots involving sex, murder, and national security within the Oval Office itself, notably *Absolute Power, Murder at 1600,* and *Shadow Conspiracy* (all released between 1996 and 1998), revelations of Clinton's sexual adventures in the real White House proceeded to surpass anything a Hollywood scriptwriter could come up with. The ongoing suspicions at the heart of the Whitewater inquiry into Bill and Hillary Clinton's land deals in 1980s Arkansas were superseded by the Monica Lewinsky revelations in 1998. What could possibly top the president's indiscretion with a White House intern right there in the Oval Office? But then nobody had anticipated the disputed 2000 presidential election, 9/11, the wars in Iraq and Afghanistan, and the economic meltdown to follow in 2008. And yet it was not just what was to come, but what had passed that seemed to indicate a watershed in Hollywood political films at the end of the Clinton years.

The sheer number of presidential portrayals in the 1990s suggested that the genre had reached saturation point. Thereafter Hollywood appeared far less inclined to continue producing chief executive portrayals and storylines. Excluding made-for-TV movies and certain independent features, forty films that appeared in the 1990s had some sort of presidential character in them, set against a total of ninety that had real or fictional presidents in their narratives over the entire course of Hollywood's history up until 1990.[21]

Yet the film industry's response to events in the early twenty-first century was not a total surprise. Hollywood has often followed political and military crises with a raft of concerted features based around prevailing moods, ideas, and characters throughout its history. It did so in the 1930s as a counterpoint to the Wall Street Crash and the onset of the Depression, and again in the early-to-mid-1970s in the wake of Vietnam and Watergate. So it was in the middle years of the new century's first decade that Hollywood found a way to reengage with the countervailing moods of the electorate, though not without criticism and controversy. For all the efforts made by the White House to reach out to the leading powerbrokers within the industry in the months after 9/11, Hollywood's new approach to presidential and political filmmaking after the commencement of the second Iraq War was very different from the more unassuming, patriotic, or gently mocking tone of 1990s movies.

Michael Moore's *Fahrenheit 9/11* arguably paved the way for such a bold reimmersion in political and social subject matter with its scathing indictment of Bush's approach to office, the 9/11 response, and the administration's relationship with Saudi Arabia where a number of the 9/11 plane hijackers had originally resided. The movie's influence and notoriety owed much to its enthusiastic reception in Europe, which shocked many Americans. When *Fahrenheit 9/11* went on to win the *Palme d'Or* at the Cannes Film Festival in the spring of 2004 and subsequently become the highest grossing film of its type in American box-office history, it sealed a triumphant return for the political documentary in no uncertain terms.[22]

If Moore single-handedly turned around the fortunes of agit-prop filmmaking, he also highlighted something else that different Hollywood eras have in common and is critical to the way political movies operate within the film industry. The early twenty-first century witnessed the emergence of another new generation of socially engaged filmmakers working in Hollywood. From Frank Capra, Gregory La Cava, Orson Welles, and Preston Sturges in the 1930s and 1940s, to Sidney Pollack, Alan J. Pakula, and Robert Altman in the 1970s, each new phalanx of political movies has been predicated upon a wave of emerging filmmakers with fresh ideas being brought into the fold.

In addition to Moore, the likes of Paul Haggis, Peter Berg, Paul Greengrass, and Kevin MacDonald feature in the early twenty-first-century roster of newer filmmakers. Moreover, key screenwriters such as Mathew Michael Carnahan, Haggis, and Stephen Gaghan formed a "brat pack" of politically engaged and intellectually curious filmmakers intent on bringing ideas, debate, and controversy to the screen. Movies such as *Crash* (2004), *Silver City* (2004), *Syriana* (2005), *Goodnight and Good Luck* (2005), *United 93* (2006), *Lions for Lambs* (2006), *The Kingdom*, *Rendition*, and *In the Valley of Elah* (all 2007) have little to do with presidential politics but offer broader perspectives on the state of America.

The irony of Hollywood presidents in mainstream film in the first decade of the twenty-first century is that while the politics has been ratcheted up, the chief executives have been paraded on screen as rather empty vessels, lacking precise motivations and exact policies. Whether deliberate and ironic or not, a range of newly revived assassination thrillers, such as *The Manchurian Candidate* (2004), *The Sentinel* (2006), *Shooter* (2007), and *Vantage Point* (2008), reinterpreted the genre but made the president little more than a target for a set of conspiracies only half-articulated at best, and whose motivations were deeply buried in cliché and stereotype. As such they were pale imitations of forerunners such as *Suddenly* (1954), *The Parallax View* (1974), *In the Line of Fire* (1993), *Enemy of the State* (1998), and especially the original production of *The Manchurian Candidate* (1962). Movies characteristic of the early twenty-first-century wave of political assassination thrillers allude to militaristic policies in the Bush era and the threat of a terrorist network, Middle-Eastern or otherwise, either working outside America or—in *The Sentinel* (2006) and *Vantage Point* (2008)—within its institutional fabric. The central conceit of each plot is to bring about the removal of a vaguely defined and politically indistinguishable president for reasons that are never made very clear beyond the need for a central hero to stop it all happening.

On the other hand, *Fahrenheit 9/11*, the (UK) Channel 4/Film 4-backed *Death of a President* (2006), and *W.* controversially deal with real presidents. Moore's film made headlines around the world, earning praise and denunciation in equal measure. Following its success at the Toronto Film Festival, *Death of a President* came under attack from such disparate sources as the Texas Republican Party Committee and Senator Hillary Clinton. Somewhat against the odds, Stone's *W.* ranked fourth at the American box office after an opening weekend's take of $10.5 million in the autumn of 2008.[23]

With no major studio willing to fund *W.*, much of its money came from Canadian and European backers. Eventually distributed in the United States through Lionsgate, it made a respectable twenty-five million dollars in domestic box-office takings and a further thirty million dollars around the world. And yet, hand in hand with the difficulties of actual production goes the auteurist reputation and preconceptions over Stone's ideological outlook that this chapter began with. Almost every review acknowledged "surprise" that *W.* was not a character assassination of Bush, just as critics had done earlier with *Nixon*. In many ways it is a classic embodiment of the presidential biographical picture. In common with the staple elements of such movies in Hollywood's past, themes of familial relations, oedipal complexes, and early life engagements form the backbone of *W.*'s take on a complex individual, driven by inner demons, whose destiny stretches out before him.

Whether this film bucks the trend of recent disappointing realizations of real presidents on screen to breathe new life into an old movie genre remains to be seen. The overwhelming success of *John Adams* (2008), the Golden Globe and Emmy Award winning HBO miniseries about the life and times of America's second president, confirms that there is both a critical and commercial audience for the representation of the presidency on the small screen at least. Made with the scope and scale of a big screen presentation and benefiting from astounding central performances from Paul Giamatti and Laura Linney as John and Abigail Adams, this combined the history of the nation's founding with the intimate reflections of personal endeavor and sacrifice under the shrewd direction of Tom Hooper. Its grand sweep and attention to detail hold the audience's attention in a manner Hollywood has found increasingly difficult to achieve in a two-hour movie construct. *John Adams* is unlikely to spawn the revival of Hollywood presidential movies for that very reason. It is difficult to envisage studio executives supporting projects of comparable scope and depth for the big screen.

What is more likely in the future, and the representations of Bush in documentary, docu-drama, and (with *W.*) conventional biographical pose presume this, is that Hollywood will make the presidency, whatever the incumbent might have to offer, an even more irresistible celebrity force than it has been over the last forty years or so. In Mark Wheeler's words: "[T]he relations between Hollywood and politicians have been a two-way street as the political classes have realised that stars can help them to appeal to a wider constituency."[24] As he notes, no one showed greater mastery in the use of the entertainment industry to develop his image than John F. Kennedy. The thirty-fifth president placed himself at the center of celebrity culture and the world of the rich, well-heeled, and famous in a fashion little imitated since the time of that other savvy publicity machine, Franklin D. Roosevelt This was instrumental in making the Kennedy presidency into what scholar Hugh Brogan has termed "a magical episode," both during his lifetime and in the eyes of history.[25]

Since JFK, White House occupants have been caught up in the wave of iconic reference points that make their candidacy for office and then their presidency a rich potency of imagery and myth. In historian Jon Roper's account of "heroic leadership" in presidents, he refers to the photograph of Kennedy shaking hands with a young Bill Clinton in 1963 as a "timeless gesture...that resonates with symbolic significance," almost as though Hollywood had invented the scene for its own dramatic purposes.[26] Such a "timeless" moment is the sort of exercise in mythic public relations that George Bush sought to copy with his landing aboard the USS *Abraham Lincoln* aircraft carrier in May 2003 to declare the end of major combat operations in Iraq. Of course the subsequent insurgency against the U.S. occupation ensured that the historic effect of this image would be ironic rather than iconic.

Bush's experience also underlines the new reality that no president can any longer pass into history unnoticed.[27] Whether they are unpopular or otherwise, whether the public desires closure from their tenure in office or not, the circumstances of media influence, global communications, and cultural and artistic mediums cannot allow it. Accordingly, the presidency is naturally set to fall in step with the next mythic realization of its feats and foibles on TV, in film, or book form. This traditional Hollywood exercise even stretches beyond American politics in the twenty-first century in the case of Roman Polanski's adaptation of Robert Harris's Blair-ite fable, *The Ghost* (2010). With cinematic and televisual examination and reenactment a certainty, the presidency has become not only a political office but also reality TV. The Obama/Santos connection that struck such a chord in 2008 is not the natural conclusion of ninety years of respective posturing and mutual courting on the part of the White House and Hollywood. It is only the start of symbiotic storylines and fantastic fables that will continue to trace the movements of incumbents and their personalities from the Oval Office to TV series and films for the foreseeable future and beyond.

Notes

1. Jonathan Freedland, "From West Wing to the Real Thing," *Guardian*, February 21, 2008, at http://www.guardian.co.uk/world/2008/feb/21/barackobama.uselections2008/.

2. Ibid.

3. David Hepworth, "The Pretenders," *Word*, 47 (January 2007): 83.

4. Myron Levine, "The Transformed Presidency," in Peter C. Rollins and John E. O'Connor, eds., *Hollywood's White House: The American Presidency in Film and History* (Lexington: University Press of Kentucky, 2005), 351.

5. Oliver Burkeman, "W and I," *Guardian Weekend*, October 4, 2008, 19.

6. Terry Christensen and Peter J. Hass, *Projecting Politics: Political Messages in American Films* (London: M.E. Sharpe, 2005), 212.

7. Michael Savage, *The Enemy Within: Saving America from the Liberal Assault on our Churches, Schools and Military* (New York: Nelson, 2005), 104.

8. Michael Coyne, *Hollywood Goes to Washington: American Politics on Screen* (London: Reaktion Books, 2008), 71.

9. Ibid., 42.

10. Ibid., 72, 73.

11. See Michael L. Kurtz, "Oliver Stone, JFK, and History," in Robert Brent Toplin, ed., *Oliver Stone's USA: Film, History, and Controversy* (Lawrence: University Press of Kansas, 2000), 167.

12. David J. Belin, "History According to Hollywood," *Wall Street Journal*, February 14, 1996. See also Robert Brent Toplin, *Reel History: In Defense of Hollywood* (Lawrence: University Press of Kansas, 2002), 10.

13. Robert A. Rosenstone, "JFK: Historical Fact/Historical Film," *American Historical Review*, 97 (1992), 50.

14. Richard Shenkman, "Foreword," in Rollins and O'Connor, *Hollywood's White House,* x.

15. Ibid., xiv.

16. Ben Dickenson *Hollywood's New Radicalism: War, Globalisation and the Movies from Reagan to George W. Bush* (London: I.B. Tauris, 2006), 82; Joseph Stiglitz, *The Roaring Nineties: Seeds of Destruction* (New York: Norton, 2003) .

17. Ibid., 80.

18. John Shelton Lawrence, "The 100 Million$ Men: Presidential Action/ Adventure Heroes of *Independence Day* (1996) and *Air Force One* (1997)," in Rollins and O'Connor, *Hollywood's White House*, 223–33.

19. Jean-Michel Valantin, *Hollywood, The Pentagon and Washington: The Movies and National Security from World War II to the Present Day* (London: Anthem Press, 2003), xi.

20. Ibid., 90. For the Huntington thesis, see Samuel Huntington, "The Clash of Civilizations?" *Foreign Affairs* 72 (Summer 1993), 22-49, and *The Clash of Civilizations and the Remaking of World Order* (New York: Simon & Schuster, 1996).

21. This total excludes very early one-reel silent movies, roughly pre-1915, that often had leaders to the fore, sometimes shot as documentary footage, other times with actors playing out the roles. Lincoln was frequently represented in such motion pictures. See Lawrence, "The 100 Million$ Men," 225.

22. Moore's film became the highest grossing documentary ever at the U.S. box office, taking more than $120 million. For an account of the controversies over it and the debates between Moore, the Disney corporation, and eventual distributors Miramax, see Daniel P. Franklin, *Politics and Film: The Political Culture of Film in the United States* (Oxford: Rowman and Littlefield, 2006), 1–3.

23. "Wahlberg's 'Payne' Maxes out at $17.6m Debut: Stone's 'W' pulls in $10.5m," at http://www.startribune.com/entertainment /movies/31285649.html?elr=KArksD:aDyaEP:kD:aUnc5PDiUiD3aPc: _Yyc:aUU.

24. Mark Wheeler. *Hollywood Politics and Society* (London: BFI Publishing, 2006), 139.
25. Hugh Brogan, *Kennedy* (Longman: London, 1996), 2.
26. Jon Roper, *The American Presidents: Heroic Leadership from Kennedy to Clinton* (Edinburgh: Edinburgh University Press, 2000), 1.
27. Bill Minutaglio, "The Afterlife of George W. Bush," *Newsweek*, May 16, 2009, At http://www.newsweek.com/id/197811/output/print.

Chapter 2

D.W. Griffith's Abraham Lincoln

Melvyn Stokes

David Wark Griffith was born on January 22, 1875, in Oldham County in the north of Kentucky, about twenty miles east of Louisville. Abraham Lincoln had been born slightly less than sixty-six years earlier in the southeastern part of Hardin County, Kentucky, approximately sixty miles due south of Louisville and two counties removed from Griffith's birthplace. While Griffith only entered the world a decade after Lincoln's assassination, the two men would be tied together by more than the geographical accident of their birth. Griffith would contribute to the historical construction of Lincoln's memory and reputation by representing him in two major motion pictures: the silent-era *The Birth of a Nation* (1915) and the biopic "talkie" *Abraham Lincoln* (1930).

Many influences went into the construction of Griffith's view of Lincoln. Although Kentucky itself finally declared for the Union in the American Civil War, pro-slavery sentiment was strong in the part of the state where the Griffith family lived. Griffith's father, Jacob, fought in the Confederate Army, rising to the rank of lieutenant colonel. Jacob and his reminiscences of the war were a seminal influence on the outlook of his son. Although evidence on the point is lacking, it may have been Griffith's father who passed on to him in boyhood a respect for the "magnanimity and wisdom" of the man who had defeated the Confederacy—a sentiment, Richard Schickel remarks, "not uncommon" in the South.[1]

D.W. Griffith's schooling was not very thorough: he attended local country schools until 1889, four years after the death of his father, when he moved with his family to Louisville. After only one year in high school there, Griffith felt obliged to leave and take up a job to help support his family. He was largely self-educated, making use of the Louisville public library and Flexner's bookstore, where he worked for a time.[2] There is no record of what, if anything, Griffith read about Lincoln during these years.

The future movie director took his first step toward his ultimate career by going on the road with a traveling stock company of actors in 1896. Two years later, he had a major success with his depiction of Abraham Lincoln in William Haworth's play *The Ensign*. Based on a real incident of November 1861—the seizure of two Confederate emissaries to Europe, James M. Mason and John Sliddell, on the high seas by Captain Charles Wilkes of the USS *San Jacinto*—the play revolved around the attempts of two British officers to pick a quarrel with Wilkes in order to prevent him from sailing to intercept the *Trent*, the ship bearing the two Southerners. Convicted of the killing of one of these officers, Wilkes escaped execution only through the direct intervention of President Lincoln himself.[3] Griffith's portrayal of Lincoln reflected one aspect of the image of the martyred president that emerged during these years: his compassionate character.

The attempt to "humanize" Lincoln was partly a response to his construction as an ideal hero and semimythical character by John Nicolay and John Hay, formerly his private secretaries. Their monumental biography of the sixteenth president had been published in installments over two and a half years by the *Century Magazine* in the late 1880s and subsequently as a ten-volume book in 1890, both relatively expensive forms of output that appealed mainly to an upper-class readership. The Nicolay and Hay view of Lincoln was challenged in plays such as *The Ensign* that reached a wider audience. It was also undercut in two forms of media that appeared for the first time in the 1890s. The first was the arrival of the cheap monthly magazine. Some of these, such as *Munsey's* and *Cosmopolitan*, had been founded in the late 1880s or early 1890s, but had not immediately captured a wide readership. This changed with the publication of the first issue of *McClure's Magazine* at a sale price of just ten cents in 1893. Its appearance prompted a price war among the newer magazines that led to the emergence of the ten-cent "monthly." Huge numbers of people now began to buy and read magazines. Frank Munsey, one of the founders of the new medium, estimated that between 1893 and 1899 "the ten-cent magazine increased the magazine-buying public from 250,000 to 750,000."[4] With the arrival of the cheap monthly, the United States gained its first truly national media and took a major step toward the inauguration of a mass culture.

One major reason for the success of the new magazines was the salience they accorded biography. Ida Tarbell's serial life of Napoleon ran from November 1894 to April 1895 in *McClure's*, and this period saw the circulation of the magazine double. Rejecting the conventional wisdom that Nicolay and Hay's biography had exhausted interest in Lincoln, editor-proprietor Sam McClure subsequently assigned Tarbell to write a new and more popular life for his magazine. Within three months of the publication of the first installment, *McClure's* had signed up another 100,000 subscribers.[5] Clearly, there *was* continuing interest in Lincoln, but Tarbell's biography was astutely positioned to differentiate it from that by Nicolay and Hay. It owed more to the three-volume life of Lincoln published in 1889 by William Henry Herndon, Lincoln's friend and former law partner. Herndon had attacked the perception of Lincoln as a heroic legend to present him as a characteristic westerner—plain, frank, and sometimes crude. However, this interpretation was deeply unappealing to the reading public, with the consequence that his biography was either reviled or simply ignored. Tarbell's genius was to present Lincoln—not as Herndon had done—as a great man *in spite of* his background but mainly *because* of it. She created a folk myth of Lincoln as the conscious descendant of generations of western pioneers. Such a representation of "indigenous greatness" clearly caught the popular imagination of the 1890s. Disturbed by the impact of the economic depression of 1893–97 and highly conscious of the changes in their society as a result of industrialization, urbanization, and immigration, many native-born Americans found in Tarbell's Lincoln a reaffirmation of the values of an older America at a time when these seemed under threat from social change.

The first part of Tarbell's serialized life of Lincoln appeared in the November 1897 issue of *McClure's*. Eighteen months earlier, cinema had been born in the United States with the first commercially successful showing of motion pictures at Koster and Bial's music hall in New York. The movies, the second new form of mass media to emerge in the 1890s, would soon emulate popular magazines in presenting to mass audiences an image of Lincoln that emphasized his democratic and accessible qualities. Early twentieth-century films frequently represented him as a homely and compassionate figure, happy to make time to see ordinary citizens and discuss their concerns. In such motion pictures as *The Reprieve* (1908), *Abraham Lincoln's Clemency* (1910), *One Flag at Last* (1911), *The Seventh Son* (1912), *When Lincoln Was President* (1913), and *The Songbird of the North* (1913), the screen "Lincoln" saved the life of a sentry who had fallen asleep at his post or that of a convicted spy by issuing a presidential pardon. Perhaps the most fanciful of all these films was *The Toll of War* (1913), in which Lincoln freed a Southern girl sentenced to death for spying against the North. After her release, she was present at Ford's Theatre and witnessed his assassination. The mortally wounded president was carried to her room, which was nearby, and died in her bed while she knelt beside him in prayer.[6]

In the summer of 1914, therefore, when Griffith began to shoot a film called *The Clansman*, based on a novel by Thomas Dixon, Jr., there was already a culturally dominant view of Lincoln as a humane and merciful figure. In some respects, *The Clansman* (soon renamed *The Birth of a Nation*) closely followed this view. When Lincoln (played by Joseph E. Henabery) signs the call for volunteers to subdue the South's rebellion, he is shown wiping away tears with a handkerchief. When the main Southern figure in the story, Col. Ben Cameron (Henry B. Walthall), is unjustly condemned to be hung as a guerrilla, his mother (Josephine Crowell) and Elsie Stoneman (Lillian Gish), the daughter of Radical Republican leader Austin Stoneman (Ralph Lewis), visit Lincoln to plead for a presidential pardon. After some hesitation, the compassionate Lincoln—hailed as "Great Heart" in an intertitle—agrees. Mrs. Cameron, resisting with difficulty the urge to embrace the president, goes to see Ben in hospital and tells him, "Mr. Lincoln has given back your life to me."

In addition to showing Lincoln's compassionate side, *The Birth of a Nation* portrays him as a Moses figure: he will never reach the promised land of the "coming nation" he has done so much to create. That nation will be born only after the Reconstruction process has ended and Southern whites have succeeded in subordinating all blacks and excluding them from political power. *The Birth of a Nation* suggested that if Lincoln had lived, this new (all-white) American nation would have emerged much sooner. A Lincoln admirer, Griffith plainly believed that if he had not been murdered, Reconstruction generally (and specifically the Radical Reconstruction from 1867) would not have happened. With the war over, *The Birth of a Nation* depicts a confrontation between Lincoln and Austin Stoneman, a fictional character based on Representative Thaddeus Stevens of Pennsylvania, one of the real Republican architects of Radical Reconstruction. Stoneman protests the presidential policy of clemency for the South, insisting that Confederate leaders must be hanged and their states treated as "conquered provinces," a phrase actually used by Stevens. True to the spirit of the real Lincoln's second inaugural address delivered on March 4, 1865, Griffith's screen version insists that he will deal with the seceded states with great generosity. To underline the director's belief in the wisdom of this benign approach, his film shows the South cheerfully beginning the work of rebuilding under its aegis, a process interrupted by Lincoln's unexpected murder.

The depiction of Lincoln's assassination at Ford's Theatre—including fifty-five shots and nine intertitles, and lasting nearly five minutes—is one of the longest sequences in *The Birth of a Nation* (figure 2.1). The intertitles emphasize the essential truthfulness of the reconstruction by giving a series of precise historical details: the play being presented is *Our American Cousin*, starring Laura Keene; the presidential party arrives at 8:30 P.M.; Lincoln's bodyguard deserts

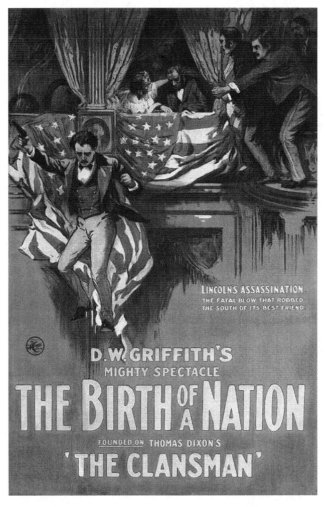

Figure 2.1 *The Birth of a Nation* poster illustrating Abraham Lincoln's assassination.

his place outside the presidential box to get a better view of the play; the shooting takes place at 10:13 P.M., during act III, scene 2; and John Wilkes Booth (Raoul Walsh), having fired the fatal shot, leaps onto the stage shouting "*Sic semper tyrannis!*" Lincoln's assassination is crucial in narrative terms: it sets the scene for the second half of the film. On hearing the news, Stoneman's mulatto mistress, Lydia Brown (Mary Alden), gleefully informs him that he is "now the greatest power in America." The pathway is open to a much more radical postwar Reconstruction than Lincoln would ever have countenanced.

In reality, what Griffith was offering was a further development and refinement of the Lincoln legend. He presented the sixteenth president as a symbol of reconciliation between the sections, the first signs of which had appeared in the mid-1870s. In 1875, Confederate veterans marched in a commemorative parade in Boston, Massachusetts. The formal ending of Reconstruction in 1877, when Republican president Rutherford B. Hayes withdrew the last federal troops from the South, laid the political ground for further gestures of reunion. The early 1880s saw a number of joint Union and Confederate parades, and when Union commander and former president Ulysses S. Grant died in 1885, several Confederate generals acted as his pallbearers. However, it was the Spanish-American War of 1898 that truly set the seal on this renewed sense of intersectional amity. It was commonplace for newspapers at the time to observe that "the blue and the gray" were marching together for the first time in decades against a common foe.[7]

Against this background, Lincoln began to emerge as a symbol of national unity around the turn of the century. In *The Birth of a Nation*, Griffith projected this idea backward in time to the closing moments of the Civil War. Its most direct manifestation was in the depiction of Lincoln's confrontation with Stoneman. In addition, it was visually represented in a key scene near the movie's end when Northern and Southern whites take refuge together against marauding blacks in a log cabin, the most famous icon associated with the Lincoln legend.[8]

Lincoln did indeed hope to treat the South with considerable leniency but had not developed a coherent policy for the region by the time of his assassination. In reality the South experienced very little of what an intertitle in the Griffith movie called "Lincoln's fostering hand" to encourage the process of reconciliation. Consequently, the reaction of Ben Cameron's father (Spottiswood Aitken) to the news of Lincoln's assassination—"Our best friend is gone. What is to become of us now?"—is frankly absurd in its attempt to represent Lincoln as a hero to the hostile Southerners that he has spent the last four years trying to subdue.

The release of *The Birth of a Nation*—in the year commemorating the fiftieth anniversary of the ending of the Civil War and Lincoln's death—arguably had greater impact than any other contemporary interpretation in representing Lincoln in American popular culture. While there are no accurate audience figures, Everett Carter estimated that three million people had seen it between March 1915 and January 1916 in the Greater New York area alone. Carl E. Milliken, secretary of the Motion Picture Producers' Association, guessed that fifty million people in all had "probably" seen it by 1930.[9] *The Birth of a Nation* propagated the view of Lincoln as a man of compassion to a broad popular audience. It also offered him as a symbol of national unity and reconciliation at a moment when the United States was probably more conscious of its own divisions than at any time since the Civil War. The outbreak of World War I in August 1914 had underlined America's ethnic disunity. One-third of all U.S. residents were either immigrants or the children of immigrants, and many retained residual loyalties (or antipathies) to the nation from which they or their ancestors had originated.[10] Later in the war, the consciousness of the large numbers of "hyphenated Americans" (particularly those of German and Austro-Hungarian origins) would lead to demands for enforced "100 per cent Americanization."[11] But to concerned American audiences of 1915, *The Birth of a Nation* offered a reassuring vision of national unity on the basis of ethnicity (a constructed, inclusive whiteness) and Lincoln as a unifying iconic hero.

In foregrounding a discourse of Lincoln as an advocate of reunion and sectional reconciliation, Griffith carefully avoided any reference to what might have been an alternative discourse: Lincoln as emancipator of the slaves. *The Birth of a Nation* begins with two shots that suggested the possibility of such an approach. The first, introduced by the intertitle "The bringing of the African to America planted the first seed of disunion," implies that secession and Civil War derived from the introduction of blacks into a land meant to be an Eden for whites.[12] It features a minister praying over manacled slaves who are going to be auctioned. The second shot is of "Abolitionists of the Nineteenth Century demanding the freeing of the slaves." Spectators, at this point, may have thought they were about to see a film *about* emancipation. However, the focus of the film suddenly switches to the Northern Stoneman family and the Southern Camerons. When slaves on the Cameron plantation do appear, they are well-treated

("The two-hour interval given for dinner, out of their working day from six till six") and contented. They happily put on a dancing show for their masters and visiting friends, Phil and Tod Stoneman, whose untroubled reaction to the display seemingly belies their status as the sons of the Radical Republican leader.

Immediately after the plantation sequence, the Civil War is shown to be imminent: an intertitle suggests that the "new administration" threatens "the power of the sovereign states" and a newspaper headline announces, "If the North carries the election, The South will secede." Lincoln's first appearance in the film is in a tableau showing him reluctantly signing a proclamation for 75,000 volunteers to suppress the Southern threat to the Union—a shot suggesting that the *North* was the actual aggressor in the Civil War. Thereafter, Lincoln is presented entirely as a figure of compassion and reconciliation. There is no reference whatever to his provisional Proclamation of Emancipation in September 1862 or to the Thirteenth Amendment that abolished slavery. The only evidence of these momentous developments comes shortly after the start of the second half of the film, when a real-life character, Senator Charles Sumner of Massachusetts, is improbably shown visiting his fellow Radical Republican, Stoneman, to urge "a less dangerous policy in the extension of power to the freed race."

Fifteen years after the release of the silent classic that made his name as a movie director, Griffith reengaged with Lincoln, now as the main character in another film but one made amid very different circumstances—personal, economic, and cultural—from those of 1915. When shooting *The Birth of a Nation*, he had been young (thirty-nine) and ambitious, both for himself and for his medium. By 1930 he was in his mid-fifties and his career had been in the doldrums for years. He had failed to sustain his own studio, which had been sold off in 1924. Thereafter, he worked successively for Adolph Zukor's Famous Players-Lasky and Joseph Schenck's United Artists (ironically the company he had cofounded with Charlie Chaplin, Douglas Fairbanks, and Mary Pickford in 1919). Griffith's independent spirit and his reputation for profligacy as a director made him an uneasy participant as a contract director in Hollywood's new studio system. *Abraham Lincoln*, his first "talkie," was an unsuccessful attempt to revive a declining career by returning to the period and part of the subject-matter of his greatest success. It would be the last film he made for a major studio. Indeed he would only direct one other movie after this biopic.

Whereas Griffith's earlier motion picture had been released at a time when America was emerging as the world's leading industrial nation and was increasingly confident about its economic future, the Lincoln biopic appeared at the early stages of the Great Depression. Caught up in his own understanding of Lincoln, the director never adjusted the representation of him to address the new circumstances of the film's reception by audiences. This may well also have reflected the fact that the severity of the downturn was not fully evident at the time of its making. As such the Griffith movie looked outdated and out of touch when compared to films about Lincoln that appeared later in the 1930s.

In cultural terms, however, the movie was attuned to the consolidation of Lincoln's reputation since his 1909 centennial. By 1920, observes Barry Schwartz, the sixteenth president had become "a demigod."[13] One symbol of this was the erection of the Lincoln Memorial in Washington, DC. After many previous failures, Congress finally agreed in 1910 to build a national monument to Lincoln in Potomac Park. His sacred status was reflected both in the geographical isolation of the monument dedicated to his memory and in the style of its construction. Building began in March 1914, just over three months before Griffith started shooting *The Birth of a Nation*, and the Memorial was opened in 1922. Designed by architect Henry Bacon, it resembled a Greek temple (echoing "the ancient Greek practice of placing statues of gods in enclosed temples to secure their separation from the mortal world").[14] From the point of view of filmmakers, however, the most visually significant part of the memorial was the huge statue of Lincoln by Daniel Chester French. This would become a key feature in most subsequent filmic treatments of Lincoln. Griffith's 1930 movie itself ends with a cut from the mortally wounded president to a stormy, wintry shot of the log cabin in which he was born and then segues directly into a shot of the Lincoln Memorial in which the camera slowly tracks forward to pass through the Greek columns to focus on French's statue (which has a pronounced halo effect) as a choir sings "The Battle Hymn of the Republic."

If the inauguration of the Lincoln Memorial represented the godlike attributes of Lincoln's greatness, other developments in the 1920s emphasized his alternative historical reputation as a common man. A major influence in this regard was the publication of the first two volumes of Chicago poet Carl Sandburg's biography of Lincoln in 1926. In *The Prairie Years*, Sandburg advanced a view of Lincoln as a folksy Westerner that was very similar to the one originally propounded by Ida Tarbell. He greatly expanded it, however, to include many mythical features. Sandburg, as David Turley writes, "expressed a profound empathy with Lincoln such that he felt licensed to make use of

folkloric and legendary material in pursuit of 'the spirit of Lincoln.' "
Lincoln was portrayed as a true product of the Western frontier, a
"man of the people" who was at the same time conscious of America's
divinely ordained mission as the world's foremost champion of freedom and democracy.[15] So impressed was Griffith by this biography
that he originally wanted the author himself to write the script of his
new film, but United Artists balked at the $30,000 fee demanded
by Sandburg.[16] In the end, the script was written by another poet,
Stephen Vincent Benét.

In choosing the subject for his new film, Griffith was also aware
that the flood of "Lincoln" movies had by no means receded after
The Birth of a Nation.[17] The sixteenth president remained an ever-
present representation as the new movie industry went from strength
to strength. Benjamin Chapin played him in a series of movie shorts
(*The Lincoln Cycle*) that continued until 1917; Ralph Ince did so in
Vitagraph's *The Battle Hymn of the Republic* (1917) and Louis J.
Selznick's *The Land of Opportunity* (1920); and Meyer F. Stroell
performed the role in Artcraft's 1919 version of Augustus Thomas's
play *The Copperhead* (1919).[18] In 1924, Phil Rosen directed George
A. Billings as the protagonist in *The Dramatic Life of Abraham
Lincoln*, a long and pedestrian biopic that left audiences considerably
underwhelmed.

Lincoln films during these years broadly fell into two categories.
The first comprised didactic, historical pieces. These tended to be
the least successful in box-office terms, especially those among them
that concentrated on the *whole* of Lincoln's career—notably *The Life
of Abraham Lincoln* (1915), a Thomas Edison production, and *The
Dramatic Life of Abraham Lincoln*.[19] The other category of Lincoln
movies, which generally enjoyed greater commercial success, con-
sisted of features that often emerged from other forms of popular
entertainment. Charles E. Bull, for example, played the president in
Warner Brothers' *The Heart of Maryland* (1927), the second version
of David Belasco's 1895 melodrama to be made into a film.

Probably the most commercially successful picture featuring
Lincoln between 1915 and 1930 was John Ford's *The Iron Horse*
(1924). This reshaped the image of Lincoln, again played by Charles
E. Bull, to fit the outlook of 1920s audiences. Ford managed this in
part by extending the focus of Herndon and Tarbell on Lincoln as a
Westerner. *The Iron Horse* endeavored to associate Lincoln with the
myth and folklore that had come to surround Western movies—an
increasingly popular genre, as demonstrated by the great success of
The Covered Wagon a year earlier. Much of *The Iron Horse* is about

ordinary construction workers and engineers, as they fight Indians, nature, and corrupt landowners to finish the first transcontinental railroad. Lincoln appears as a major character in the story line of the film—first in his hometown of Springfield and subsequently when, as president, he signs the Pacific Railroad Act of 1862 into law. An intertitle praises "the far-seeing wisdom of the great rail-splitter President" who had tied the American East more closely with the West. The film begins and ends with a shot of Lincoln's bust and is dedicated "to the ever-living memory of Abraham Lincoln, the Builder—and of those countless engineers and toilers who fulfilled his dream of a greater nation." By disseminating a heroic myth about the building of the first transcontinental railroad—and associating Lincoln closely with it—*The Iron Horse* offered the business civilization of the 1920s a new symbol for its own belief in technological innovation and the unifying effects of material progress.

In constructing his own Lincoln film, Griffith determined to make a biopic that covered, albeit highly selectively, the whole of his protagonist's career.[20] As was the case with Phil Rosen's 1924 film, this approach abbreviated some sequences to the point of semicomedy. The Lincoln-Douglas debates of 1858 are summarized in a series of onesentence exchanges. The Civil War is effectively reduced to the first battle of Bull Run, the subsequent attempts to defend Washington, and Phil Sheridan's ride during the Shenandoah campaign of 1864. Lincoln spends much of the film muttering "The union must be preserved" to various audiences. Arriving at Ford's Theatre, he is asked to make a speech. Beginning with the useful phrase "Again I say," he simply repeats unconnected phrases from his second inaugural ("with malice towards none, with charity for all") and the Gettysburg Address ("government of the people, by the people, for the people" ').

The fact that Lincoln would be speaking in his movie greatly influenced Griffith's choice of actor to play him. Among the candidates who received consideration were those who had played the role in the past (George A. Billings and Frank McGlynn) or would in the future (Charles Middleton). Although many of these actors bore an uncanny resemblance to the Lincoln shown in photographs, the casting in a sound picture raised different issues. There could be no question of verisimilitude—Lincoln had died well before the introduction of recording equipment, so no one really knew what his voice had sounded like. Nevertheless, this made it all the more important that the actor finally selected could impress audiences as a credible speaking Lincoln. After much hesitation, Griffith finally gave the part to Walter Huston, already well-known as a vaudeville and stage actor but a comparative newcomer to the movies. As a successful actor from the "live" theater, of course, Huston could be relied upon to have the "voice" to carry Griffith's first talking picture.

With the advent of the talkies, Griffith was compelled to adapt to the new medium. One effect of the coming of sound was to make movies themselves more "stagey." According to French film critic André Bazin, silent cinema had reached an artistic peak by 1928. Mainly through editing techniques—such as montage, in which Griffith was highly gifted—it had mastered the art of telling stories without words. Even intertitles setting the scene or representing dialogue were used less and less by the mid-1920s.[21] For several years, while directors learned how to produce the new sound films and technology was further developed to solve some of the basic problems, movie quality went backward. Owing to the size and unwieldiness of early microphones and the need to soundproof booths from which the dialogue was recorded, films became much more static. This in itself had an impact on the filming of *Abraham Lincoln*, which lacked the fluidity of *The Birth of a Nation* and Griffith's other previous works. Much of the film was obviously stage-bound, though Richard Schickel argues that the palpable falsity of some of the settings "actually worked for the picture, imparting a stylized quality to it, lifting it out of the merely realistic towards the mythic level."[22] Sound itself only rarely succeeded in conveying something particularly new in terms of plot or character. One of the few times that it did was in John Wilkes Booth's declamation of "*sic semper tyrannus*" from the stage after shooting Lincoln. These words and the way they are delivered convincingly evoke the ham actor that the assassin had once been.

It remains an open question how much of *Abraham Lincoln* was really due to Griffith. In the negotiations for the financing and budgeting of the film, Joseph Schenck of United Artists was so tough and parsimonious that Richard Schickel concludes he "was doing his best to drive Griffith into quitting." Even when a grudging agreement was finally reached between Griffith and the studio, there is a distinct possibility that Schenck deliberately set out to sabotage the production. The effective producer he selected for the picture, John Considine, Jr., through his constant interference turned the two-month shooting of the film into what Griffith himself called a "nightmare of mind and nerves."[23] Much of Griffith's earlier genius as a director had been due to his close supervision of the editing process (cutting 150,000 feet of film stock down to 12,000 for *The Birth of a Nation*), of intertitles, and of the scoring (including the invitation to Joseph Carl Breil to compose for *Birth*, the first ever full musical score for a long American picture).[24] Once principal photography of *Abraham Lincoln* was over, he simply handed the editing of the film, together with its dubbing and scoring, to Considine. Other than some retakes, Griffith's only subsequent involvement with the picture was to suggest rearranging some of the material after seeing a finished print three weeks before the première in August 1930, a proposal that cut no ice with the producer.[25]

There were consequently reasons, other than Griffith's unfamiliarity with sound and his adoption of a fairly straightforward biographical approach to *Abraham Lincoln*, why the film failed at the box office. However, its failure to provide a mass audience with a means of connecting more closely with Lincoln's life was his own doing. Griffith's major problem in his epic films, Vlada Petric has argued, was to integrate the individual story line (usually a love conflict) with the historical or social events and environments that he wanted to be "more than mere background."[26] Griffith and Benét had thought of doing something on these lines in *Abraham Lincoln*. Instead of having a Mrs. Cameron visiting Lincoln to plead for her son's life or Elsie and Phil Stoneman present at Ford's Theatre at the time of Lincoln's assassination—which had personalized the link between film characters and president in *The Birth of a Nation*—they had conceived the notion of having in the foreground of the film two fictional lovers whose story would parallel that of Lincoln. In the end, the young man would be revealed as the sentry saved by presidential pardon from a sentence of death for being asleep at his post. Whether Considine vetoed the idea or Griffith and Benét never managed successfully to work out how to deploy it, the characters were absent from *Abraham Lincoln*. In retrospect, Griffith felt this had been a mistake: it would have created a human perspective on Lincoln's career and given the film a degree of suspense that a simple biography (everybody knew the story of Lincoln's fate) could never do.[27]

It is unusual in the history of cinema to have the same director shoot sequences about a historical event with a fifteen-year time lag in between. Yet this is precisely what Griffith did: *The Birth of a Nation* and *Abraham Lincoln* each included reenactments of Lincoln's assassination. While both lasted exactly the same amount of time (four minutes and forty seconds) and included some very similar shots (Booth leaping onto the stage to speak to the audience, Lincoln pulling a shawl over his shoulders to ward off the cold immediately before he is shot), the scene in *Abraham Lincoln*, notes Anthony Slide, "has none of the sparkle or emotion of the same scene in *The Birth of a Nation*."[28] Part of this can be explained by the lack of a personal element to the sequence. Elsie and Phil Stoneman are not only present in Ford's Theatre: they stand up to applaud Lincoln when the president arrives and are shown jumping up with the rest of the audience after the shooting (Elsie is also the first one to notice John Wilkes Booth, pointing at him with her fan). As Vlada Petric comments, such camera work makes the viewer "identify with the shot's point of view—it is as if we were in the position of Elsie and Phil, attending the performance."[29] The inferior quality of the scene in the 1930 biopic was also partly attributable to the bland way in which sound was used—Lincoln repeating his famous lines, Mary Lincoln's staid compliments to her husband, the dialogue of the actors in the play, John Wilkes Booth's remark—with only one moment (the unseen firing of the fatal shot) when sound actually replaced rather than simply reinforced an image. Considine's unimaginative editing was doubtless another factor in this outcome.

However, there was also an emphasis on narrative at the cost of dramatic tension in *Abraham Lincoln*. One of the features of the assassination sequence in *The Birth of a Nation* was the depiction of Lincoln's personal detective, whose irresponsible decision to leave his post to get a better view of the play left the door of the presidential box unguarded. The detective does not appear in the 1930 version. In *The Birth of a Nation*, the gun in Booth's hand is foregrounded in an iris shot; in *Abraham Lincoln*, the pistol is never seen. Even the actual assassination itself is much more mundane and less dramatic than in *The Birth of a Nation*. It shows Lincoln sitting in his box, there is the sound of an off-screen gunshot, and Lincoln slumps in his chair. In *Birth*, by contrast, Booth appears behind Lincoln, the camera heightens suspense by cutting to the play, Booth shoots at Lincoln's back, the president flings up his arms before slumping forward, and Booth jumps from the next-door box onto the stage. Since this scene in *Abraham Lincoln* is supposedly the climax of the film, it feels curiously flat, particularly in comparison to the parallel silent movie scene.[30]

Griffith's Lincoln of 1930 is a folksy Sandburgian hero: he wrestles with one of his neighbors, is physically strong (one character calls him "the best rail-splitter in the country"), has a fund of stories to meet all occasions, wears a stove-pipe hat, and, as played by Walter Huston, has a suitably rangy look. He is once again shown as humane and compassionate: as in *The Birth of a Nation* he uses his handkerchief to wipe away tears after signing the proclamation calling for volunteers and issues a presidential pardon (this time to a young soldier about to be executed for cowardice). He is instinctively a peaceful man, but he resists the town bully in New Salem—beating him in a fair fight—and later bluntly refuses to countenance any further extension of slavery.

Abraham Lincoln begins, like *The Birth of a Nation*, with a sequence dealing with African enslavement. In a very early representation of the horrors of the Middle Passage, a ship is shown at sea, full of chained blacks. One who has died is unceremoniously thrown overboard. Later, in a major change from *The Birth of a Nation*, slaves themselves are given some agency. A chain-gang of African Americans is shown pulling ropes at a dockside and, despite the presence of a white overseer, singing a song demanding freedom.[31] This is immediately followed by a shot of Lincoln reading a draft of the provisional Proclamation of Emancipation to his cabinet (figure 2.2). In contrast to *The Birth of a Nation*, Griffith's biopic did embrace a discourse of emancipation, but this was still subordinated to the discourse of union and sectional reconciliation.

Without doubt *Abraham Lincoln* is consciously more balanced in its treatment of North and South than *The Birth of a Nation* had been. It shows that the Civil War really began when the Confederates fired on Fort Sumter on April 12, 1861. This sequence now precedes Lincoln's call for volunteers to suppress the rebellion. Also unlike the earlier movie, which only showed Confederates marching off to

Figure 2.2 The great emancipator: Lincoln (Walter Huston) signs the provisional Emancipation Proclamation in *Abraham Lincoln*.

war, it depicts the troops of both sides doing so. Yet when a sleepless Lincoln paces the White House at night, it is not slavery he is really thinking about but "the blood it takes to hold this Union together." As his thoughts begin to shift toward the end of the conflict, he is principally concerned not with the plight of freed blacks but with the need for reconciliation between whites. The president will not agree to have General Robert E. Lee shot after his surrender, vetoes the idea of confiscating Southerners' horses since they will need them for spring ploughing, and suggests allowing Confederate president Jefferson Davis to escape. He finishes by outlining a magnanimous policy toward the defeated Southern states, declaring—in exactly the same words as in *The Birth of a Nation*—that he plans to take them back "as though they had never been away."

Griffith was determined, according to studio manager Raymond Klune, "that *Abraham Lincoln* shall be a great picture."[32] Many critics believed that he had succeeded in this endeavor.[33] But the movie was not a commercial success. Some of the reasons for that failure— the episodic structure of the film, the failure to dilute its "epic" quality with the addition of some personal element, the politics surrounding the production, the technical difficulties in making sound films, and Griffith's own unfamiliarity with the new format—have been outlined earlier. Moviegoers may also have resisted the didacticism of what Merrill Peterson would later call "the first major historical film of the sound era."[34] Perhaps the greatest problem, however, was that the film did not speak in any convincing way to contemporary concerns.

In 1915, *The Birth of a Nation* had caught the mood of its time by presenting Lincoln as a symbol of national unity and reconciliation. During the 1930s, Lincoln would emerge in other movies as a potent symbol of American resilience in face of the Depression. As featured in John Ford's *Young Mr. Lincoln* (1939) and John Cromwell's *Abe Lincoln in Illinois* (1940), his early struggles and the energy he displayed in overcoming adversity could be identified with the difficulties confronting ordinary Americans in the Depression. In their different ways, too, both these movies convey an intertwining of personal and national destinies in their depiction of Lincoln. The Ford film, which shows Lincoln as a young attorney battling for justice on behalf of two brothers wrongly accused of murder, ends with him walking to the top of a hill (to symbolize his journey to the presidency) amid a gathering storm (symbolic of the Civil War). The Cromwell movie, scripted by FDR-admirer Sherwood Anderson from his own play, draws clear parallels between Lincoln's values and those of the New Deal to renew America's promise for all its peoples. Even Griffith's use of the Lincoln Memorial to signify his subject's almost Christlike quality was surpassed by its far more imaginative dramatic usage as a populist image in Frank Capra's *Mr. Smith Goes to Washington* (1939), which had greater resonance for Depression-era audiences.

More than any other occupant of the office, Abraham Lincoln is a president that moviemakers can relate to their times. D.W. Griffith had demonstrated this to great effect in *The Birth of a Nation* but not in his later biopic. *Abraham Lincoln* did move beyond the portrayal of the sixteenth president in the silent masterpiece by adding his role in freeing the slaves and the notion of black agency. Nevertheless, it remained largely fixated with its precursor's themes of sectional unity and reconciliation. In view of the significantly different historical contexts in which the two movies were made, however, *Abraham Lincoln* had nothing of major importance and relevance to say about its subject to moviegoers of Depression-era America.

Notes

1. Richard Schickel, *D. W. Griffith and the Birth of Film* (London: Pavilion, 1984), 551.
2. Melvyn Stokes, *D. W. Griffith's "The Birth of a Nation": A History of "The Most Controversial Motion Picture of All Time"* (New York: Oxford University Press, 2007), 59–62.
3. Griffith also played Lincoln on at least one other occasion: at an Elk's Club minstrel show in Indiana, the trade press reported, he "made his famous Lincoln pose in the tableau finale and received deserved praise." See Schickel, *Griffith*, 51.
4. Cornelius Regier, *The Era of the Muckrakers* (Chapel Hill: University of North Carolina Press, 1932), 13–14, 17, 20–21.
5. Ray Stannard Baker, *American Chronicle: The Autobiography of Ray Stannard Baker* (New York: Charles Scribner's Sons, 1945), 96–7; Ida M. Tarbell, *All in the Day's Work: An Autobiography* (New York: Macmillan, 1939), 161; Mary E. Tomkins, *Ida M. Tarbell* (Boston: Twayne, 1974), 38; Harold S. Wilson, *"McClure's Magazine" and the Muckrakers* (Princeton, NJ: Princeton University Press, 1970), 73–4.
6. Jack Spears, *The Civil War on the Screen and Other Essays* (South Brunswick, NJ: A. S. Barnes, 1977), 65, 67–70; Robert C. Roman, "Lincoln on the Screen," *Films in Review*, 12 (February 1961): 87–90; Barry Schwartz, *Abraham Lincoln and the Forge of National Memory* (Chicago: University of Chicago Press, 2000), 180.
7. Joseph Smith, *The Spanish-American War: Conflict in the Caribbean and the Pacific 1895–1902* (London: Longman, 1994), 102; Frank Freidel, *The Splendid Little War* (Boston, MA: Little, Brown, 1958), 33.

8. See Michael Rogin, "The Sword Became a Flashing Vision: D. W. Griffith's *The Birth of a Nation*," in Robert Lang, ed., *The Birth of a Nation: D. W. Griffith, Director* (New Brunswick, NJ: Rutgers University Press, 1994), 281.

9. Everett Carter, "Cultural History Written With Lightning: The Significance of *The Birth of a Nation*," *American Quarterly* (Fall 1960), reprinted in Fred Silva, ed., *Focus on "The Birth of a Nation"* (Englewood Cliffs, NJ: Prentice-Hall, 1971), 133–4; Carl E. Milliken to Will W. Alexander, August 9, 1930, National Association for the Advancement of Colored People Papers, Library of Congress.

10. Maldwyn A. Jones, *The Limits of Liberty: American History, 1607–1980* (New York: Oxford University Press, 1983), 412.

11. See John Higham, *Strangers in the Land: Patterns of American Nativism, 1860–1925* (New Brunswick, NJ: Rutgers University Press, 1955), 204–207, 212–19; Frederick C. Luebke, *Bonds of Loyalty: German-Americans and World War I* (DeKalb: Northern Illinois University Press, 1974).

12. The first Africans to arrive in the British colonies in America were seemingly the twenty blacks who landed at Jamestown, Virginia, from a Dutch frigate in 1619—twelve years after the founding of Jamestown itself and a year before the Pilgrim Fathers sailed on the *Mayflower*. The idea of the existence of a white "Eden" before the arrival of Africans is consequently near-unsustainable. See John Hope Franklin and Alfred A. Moss, Jr., *From Slavery to Freedom: A History of African Americans*, 7th ed. (New York: Alfred A. Knopf, 1994), 56.

13. Schwartz, *Abraham Lincoln and the Forge of National Memory*, 264.

14. Ibid., 286.

15. David Turley, "A Usable Life: Popular Representations of Abraham Lincoln," in David Ellis, ed., *Imitating Art: Essays in Biography* (London and Boulder, CO: Pluto Press, 1993), 59–60.

16. Spears, *The Civil War on the Screen*, 75; Roman, "Lincoln on the Screen," 96.

17. One study lists forty-four films that featured Lincoln between Griffith's *The Birth of a Nation* and his 1930 biopic. See Frank Thompson, *Abraham Lincoln: Twentieth-Century Popular Portraits* (Dallas: Taylor Publishing Co., 1999), 194–204.

18. Roman, "Lincoln on the Screen," 90–5.

19. Ibid., 95.

20. Richard Schickel sardonically comments that it might more accurately have been titled "Beloved Moments With Mr. Lincoln." See Schickel, *Griffith*, 557.

21. André Bazin, "The Evolution of the Language of Cinema," in Bazin, *What Is Cinema?*, vol. 1, trans. Hugh Gray (Berkeley: University of California Press, 1971), 23–4.

22. Schickel, *Griffith*, 558. Schickel also argues that some action scenes, notably Sheridan's ride and semispectacular ones such as Lincoln's

nomination, "hinted…that the range of the sound film was greater than had as yet been apprehended, that it might encompass something more than backstage musicals and drawing room dramas, for the most part taken over directly from the theatre."

23. Ibid., 552–5.
24. See Stokes, *D. W. Griffith's "The Birth of a Nation,"* 102–109.
25. Schickel, *Griffith*, 555–6.
26. Vlada Petric, "Two Lincoln Assassinations by D. W. Griffith," *Quarterly Review of Film Studies* 3 (Summer 1978): 347.
27. Schickel, *Griffith*, 558–9.
28. Edward Wagenecht and Anthony Slide, *The Films of D. W. Griffith* (New York: Crown, 1975), 252.
29. Petric, "Two Lincoln Assassinations," 350.
30. Ibid., 353.
31. Singing blacks, of course, emerged as one of the earliest tropes of sound-era cinema. King Vidor had directed an all-black musical, *Hallelujah*, for MGM in 1929.
32. Schickel, *Griffith*, 553.
33. See ibid., 556–7; Thompson, *Abraham Lincoln*, 175–6.
34. Merrill Peterson, *Lincoln in American History* (New York: Oxford University Press, 1994), 344.

Chapter 3

The "Picture Man": The Cinematic Strife of Theodore Roosevelt

Brian Neve

Introduction

Theodore Roosevelt (1858–1919) was the first U.S. president to have his career and life chronicled on a significant scale by motion picture companies. William McKinley may have been the first occupant of the Oval Office to be filmed and Calvin Coolidge was the first to speak on film, but neither matched the sheer volume of TR's celluloid imagery. The first part of this chapter explores Roosevelt's interaction with the new medium, from his emergence as a major public figure during the Spanish-American War of 1898, to his presidency (1901–1909) and subsequent public life. Consideration will also be given to the impact of Roosevelt's writing and experience on the origins of two staple genres of American cinema—the Western and the war film. The nascent film industry, before or at the very beginning of the nickelodeon era (generally seen as dating from 1905), not only conveyed moving pictures of this highly distinctive leader to the public, but also produced early satires of his presidency. The developing film medium further recorded Roosevelt's eventful postpresidential decade, including his epic hunting trips in Africa and Brazil (in 1909–10, and 1913), his European tour, his 1912 Progressive Party campaign, and especially his controversial last hurrah as a campaigner for preparedness and Americanism before and during U.S. involvement in World War I.

In addition to his contemporary significance, Roosevelt pioneered important aspects of the modern presidency that formed a core element of his historical legacy: notably expanding the "White House" (this official name for the president's Washington home dates from the 1902 refurbishment); using the office as a moral "bully pulpit" to directly address the public; and establishing a proactive tradition of American foreign policy intervention. In light of his significance to

American history through the entirety of the twentieth century and beyond, the second part of the chapter explores later cinematic representations of a president that range from the comic to the reverential.

While Theodore Roosevelt's stock has remained high as one of the "near greats" of the office, contradictions have remained, a product in part of the uneasy fit between his values, exemplified by his late Victorian thinking about race, nation, and gender, and his concern with building a tradition of public regulation and social citizenship. As historian Sarah Watts has argued, he was "the man who identified with the past yet embodied modernity, the patrician with an affinity for workers, the conservationist who proudly killed animals, the bodybuilder who loved poetry, and the civilised Easterner who made it in the barbaric West."[1] TR was also a gift to political cartoonists, who influenced early filmmakers. One of his biographers has referred to the difficulty of getting behind his caricature, a larger-than-life Mount Rushmore image that has at times resembled a cartoon character "remembered more for his frenetic visual kinship with Charles Chaplin and the Keystone Cops than for his real personality."[2] Nevertheless, Roosevelt also provided a historical benchmark of strong leadership at times when modern America was in crisis. Movie brat John Milius was his most enthusiastic chronicler on film in *The Wind and the Lion* (1975). Released when the public agenda was dominated by Watergate and failure in Vietnam, this offered a nuanced but still affirmative portrait of the twenty-sixth president.

Prepresidential Roosevelt and Film Genre: The Westerner and the Citizen Soldier

Roosevelt's life after he graduated from Harvard in 1880 included a two-year period as a rancher in the Dakota Badlands, following the sudden deaths in 1884 of his first wife and his mother. On his first trip west the previous year, the patrician Easterner had purchased a ranch and killed his first buffalo. He saw his life there as a test of his manhood, and wrote of how "strenuous" frontier life could revive the spirit of the American leadership class, and ultimately of America itself, as it faced new international challenges. His best-selling book *Ranch Life and the Hunting-Trail* was first published in 1888 and included illustrations (apparently from photographs taken by Roosevelt) by his friend and fellow Easterner Frederic Remington. Among the drawings in the 1902 edition are those titled "A Fight in the Street" (outside the saloon), "Painting the Town Red," and "The Round-Up," scenes that became familiar motifs of the Western film genre that slowly emerged from early shorts, including *The Great Train Robbery* (Edwin Porter, 1903), *The Life of a Cowboy* (Porter, 1906), and the first Tom Mix film, drawing on the title of Roosevelt's book *Ranch Life of the Great Southwest* (1909).[3] The duel outside the saloon in Roosevelt and Remington's book, for example, suggests a key scene in John Ford's *The Man Who Shot Liberty Valance* (1962), while Remington's paintings are reflected in other Westerns from Ford's Technicolor *She Wore a Yellow Ribbon* (1949) to William Fraker's *Monte Walsh* (1970). The first epic Western film, *The Covered Wagon* (James Cruze, 1923)—originally ten reels—was dedicated to the memory of Theodore Roosevelt, and Kevin Brownlow has seen it as capturing something of the former president's spirit.[4]

Roosevelt and Remington were two of three key Easterners who helped to discover and project Western life and who made it central to their own vision. The cowboy experience had generated a wave of dime novels, but it was Owen Wister who wrote the first serious Western novel, *The Virginian* (1902), and dedicated it to both Roosevelt and to William F. Cody, star and entrepreneur of the Wild West shows that had become a major domestic and overseas attraction since 1883. Roosevelt returned east in 1887 and began his political ascent to the governorship of New York and beyond via spells as New York police commissioner, U.S. civil service commissioner, and assistant secretary of the Navy in the McKinley administration. Meanwhile, he also produced between 1889 and 1896 four volumes of a history, *The Winning of the West*, which paid tribute to the self-sacrifice of those who had wrested the Western lands by violence and bloodshed, and welcomed the civilizing advance of the English-speaking peoples over the "world's waste space."[5] Roosevelt's Anglo-Saxon view on American Indians in his many writings during this period would come to dominate Western films for much of the first half of the next century. As he avowed in 1886, "I don't go so far as to think that the only good Indians are the dead Indians, but I believe nine out of every ten are, and I shouldn't like to inquire too closely into the case of the tenth. The most vicious cowboy has more moral principle than the average Indian."[6]

The Western shows (called the "Wild West") that Cody managed and starred in were a huge commercial success from 1883 to 1916. They provided spectacles of the recent history of the frontier, including stagecoach chases and cavalry charges, designed as both entertainment and education. The shows also began to stress reconciliation with the Indians, as the battles of Little Big Horn (1876) and Wounded Knee (1890) passed into history. The term Rough Rider, used in dime novels even before 1880, was adopted by Cody, and the shows from 1892 offered a parade of the "Congress of Rough Riders of the World," an internationalization that reflected the way elite figures, including Roosevelt, saw a stronger American presence in the world as a natural legacy of the closing of the domestic frontier. Several performers from the shows, including sharpshooter Annie Oakley, were filmed by the Edison Company in 1894, and the brief scenes, shot in its "Black Maria" studio in New Jersey, were exhibited in the peepshow machines of the day.[7]

The Spanish-American War of 1898 both transformed the status and public visibility of Theodore Roosevelt, a committed expansionist, and provided a much needed impetus to the growth of the early cinema industry. When an explosion sunk the American battleship *Maine* in Havana, TR resigned as assistant secretary of war to form his own regiment with Colonel Leonard Wood. William Randolph Hearst, pioneer of "yellow journalism," sent cameramen to Cuba, and Roosevelt himself ensured that room on the crowded ships was made for two men from Vitagraph, one of the world's first motion picture companies.[8] Roosevelt and Wood's regiment comprised volunteers, from Eastern friends to Western types and Indian fighters he had met in Dakota (Wood himself was a veteran of the wars against Apache chief Geronimo). One film crew, dispatched to Washington in the wake of the crisis, took the first moving pictures of Roosevelt, before he resigned as assistant secretary of the Navy.[9] The shots of the wreck of *Maine*, together with various views of flags, Cuban volunteers, and U.S. troops disembarking (often "edited" by exhibitors in sequence to make up a "war" program) provided a suitably patriotic account of the war to home audiences. In essence, the Spanish-American War revived interest in moving pictures, while the projected images helped further a new pro-imperial public philosophy.[10]

Roosevelt was full of enthusiasm for the war and its benefits for American expansionism. In line with this, friendly journalists cast him in heroic mode when he and the Rough Riders, along with other regiments, captured the hills before Santiago, leading to the Spanish defeat. Roosevelt's July 1898 charge was actually up neighboring Kettle Hill, but it was the related battle of San Juan Hill that became his "crowded hour," the central legend of his life. To Watts, the Rough Riders were the "true inheritors of the cowboy tradition of white, aggressive, nationalist manhood." Roosevelt wrote his own book and commissioned Remington to paint the charge in heroic form, while the Edison "Wargraph" Company advertised the "best views of the Spanish-American War."[11] Short films (usually around one minute in length) that were made and exhibited in 1898–99 included documentary "actualities," faked reenactments, and early story films about those involved in war. *U.S. Troops Landing at Daiquiri, Cuba* (1898), *Roosevelt's Rough Riders* (1898; showing a charge at the camera), and *Love and War* (1899) were examples of these three film types, which together helped establish the main conventions of what would become the war film genre.[12] Roosevelt emerged as a national hero from the engagement, and later that year, accompanied by fellow Rough Riders, he mounted a victorious campaign for the governorship of New York. Cody's Wild West adapted to these events by integrating the new ideology of imperialism into the traditional frontier spectacles. "Custer's Last Fight" was replaced by the "Battle of San Juan Hill," celebrating in particular the heroism of Theodore Roosevelt.[13]

While Roosevelt's time in the Badlands was no more meant to be an electoral tactic than his formation of the Rough Riders and his going to Cuba in 1898, both contributed to his selection as the Republican vice presidential candidate in 1900 and to his celebrity status and political capital as an unelected president, when succeeding the assassinated McKinley in September 1901.

Captured on Film: Roosevelt as President and After

Capitalizing on public and media interest in his military exploits in Cuba, Roosevelt cultivated good relations with journalists from the outset of his presidency and established a White House press room for the first time. He was the "past master of the leak, the trial balloon and the unattributed source," not to mention the sound-bite, and was said to have regularly allowed reporter Lincoln Steffens to interview him as he was being shaved.[14] Beyond that, a number of early short films in the pre-nickelodeon days showed him in presidential and military mode, often reviewing troops or part of a parade. A two-minute actuality shows him on the quayside at Shooters Island, walking with Prince Heinrich of Prussia during a state visit, at the head of a long line of their respective dignitaries and underlings. Another, from 1903, shows him at the dedication ceremonies of the St Louis Exposition, while a ten-minute sequence records the stately dance of diplomatic meetings and greetings at the quayside at Portsmouth, New Hampshire, attendant to the Russian-Japanese peace conference in 1905, for which the president later gained the Nobel Peace Prize. In 1906, cameras showed TR's visit to the future site of the Panama Canal, the first time that an American president had visited a foreign country while in office.

Even before he became president, Roosevelt's reputation for showmanship invited criticism and parody. Edwin S. Porter (1869–1941) was a key figure in the history of American cinema prior to the development of the nickelodeon around 1905. The inventor of electrical devices for the U.S. Navy, from 1900 he ran a new film studio that Thomas Edison had built, and began making films based on news events and political cartoons of the day. An early example of the latter was *Terrible Teddy, the Grizzly King* (1901), a film described by a contemporary Edison advertisement as a "burlesque of Theodore Roosevelt hunting mountain lions in Colorado."[15] This was released in February 1901, following the November election but before Roosevelt was inaugurated as vice president on March 4, 1901.

Porter's film, which runs for just over a minute and contains only two shots, linked by one cut, was based on a cartoon in Hearst's *New York Journal* of February 4, 1901, lampooning the then vice president elect.[16] It begins with a country scene with snow on the ground: three men are seen coming clambering down a hill in the background toward a large tree in the foreground. The first is the TR figure in what looks like Rough Rider uniform, brandishing a rifle and waving to the other two to follow. When he reaches the tree "Roosevelt" aims his rifle and fires upward into the upper branches; when an animal drops to the ground, it is not a "grizzly" but seemingly a domestic cat. Nonetheless TR lifts it up in triumph, demonstrating his prowess to the two observers, one carrying a placard with "My Press Agent" written on it, the other holding the sign "My Photographer." One sets up his tripod and the other makes notes, while Roosevelt gets to work with a bowie knife. In the second, longer shot of the forest, TR, now on horseback, leads his two publicity men who are on foot. They seem ever present and ever ready to serve their political master and, in the words a half century later of the newspaper editor in *The Man Who Shot Liberty Valance*, "print the legend." John Ford, of course, exposed the legend in his 1962 film, as Porter does here. It was a succinctly made point about a new political phenomenon, and also an early demonstration of how satirical awareness of what would later be called "spin" could help disarm it.

Film was used in a presidential election for the first time in 1904 to exploit Roosevelt's controversial friendship with African American leader and educator Booker T. Washington. Their 1901 White House dinner provoked an explosive reaction from Southern newspapers and politicians. Keen to break down the Democrats' hold on the "solid South," TR subsequently became more discreet about their relationship, but cinema made it an issue in the election of 1904. Blackface vaudevillian minstrel Lew Dockstadter played Washington in a skit shot by the ubiquitous Edwin S. Porter for the Edison Kinetoscope Company, in front of the capitol, with actor Harry Ellis playing the president. The film generated much press discussion and some agitation in the White House. Although no one involved in making the film was overtly connected to the Democratic Party, it was eventually seized and destroyed by the police on grounds of being a political "fakery."[17]

Porter's cinematic interactions with Roosevelt continued apace with a five-minute story film shot in December 1904, and entitled *The Strenuous Life: or Anti-Race Suicide*. TR had spoken in Chicago in April 1899 about his notion of the "strenuous life" that he associated with vigorous masculine behavior. This address had endorsed and reinforced the dominant gender perceptions of the day, from the virile man engaging in the "stern strife of actual life" to the woman as housewife, "helpmeet of the homemaker, the wise and fearless mother of many healthy children." Adding that "no race has any chance to win a great place unless it consists of good breeders as well of good fighters," Roosevelt decreed it a moral imperative for American families to produce four children. More controversially he later used—as early as 1903—the term "race suicide," originally coined by sociologist Edward A. Ross, in voicing concern that white Americans would come to be outnumbered by other racial and immigrant minorities unless they maintained adequate birthrates.[18] Satirizing these views, the Porter film shows a well-off man being called home from his workplace to attend his wife, who is about to give birth. In long shot but with a telling close-up, it observes the father's joy turn to something more complex as not one, but two, and then three, and eventually four babies are presented to him by the nurse. The wife's own strenuous life upstairs is kept discreetly off-screen.

Roosevelt was the subject of another Porter-directed "topical" film in his second term. *The "Teddy" Bears* (1907) is a thirteen-minute film that, as Scott Simmon has argued, is part "charming fairy tale, part violent political satire, and part accomplished puppet animation." The film drew on the craze for teddy bears that was apparently a commercial response to a 1902 incident during Roosevelt's bear-hunting vacation in Mississippi. An African American scout led the hunt to look for suitable prey, but by the time the president was called to the scene the bear intended for his gun was injured and tied up. Following the sporting code, TR refused to make the kill, but exaggerated stories about the incident caused him political embarrassment. In particular a Clifford Berryman cartoon showed him declining to shoot a much smaller and "cuter" bear. First published in the *Washington Post* on November 17, 1902, this was entitled "Drawing the Line in Mississippi," a caption that may also have referenced the president's opposition to a recent spate of racial lynching in the South. All of Berryman's subsequent Roosevelt cartoons kept the incident in the public mind by including a representation of the small bear.[19]

The "Teddy" Bears begins with a telling of the Goldilocks tale that shows a young girl visiting the bears' house. After a short but elaborate sequence of animated teddy bears, which took a full week to film, there follows a rather shocking change of tone. Goldilocks is chased by the bears, now played by actors in bear suits, through a snowy park exterior, and a figure appears, dressed in familiar Roosevelt military attire and carrying a rifle, to rescue the damsel in distress. "Roosevelt" is prompted by Goldilocks to spare Baby Bear but only after he kills its parents. In other words, what begins as fairy tale ends as with a rather grim and adult mix of satire, topical reference (to the president hunting in Mississippi), and realism.[20] Something of this ambivalence, between the comic and the serious, between TR as harmless caricature and as a more threatening warrior figure, has remained a pattern in representations of him.

Roosevelt left office in 1909 to honor his much regretted pledge to reporters four years previously that he would not seek another term. Testifying to his concern with publicity during his White House tenure, the film industry in 1910 saluted the former president's impact on camera by referring to him as "more than a picture personality—he is A PICTURE MAN." There was an immediate sense that footage of the great man should be conserved; an article in *The Moving Picture World* concluded that Roosevelt "was such an overmastering personality that we go to the length of expressing the hope that moving pictures of him may be preserved in safe custody for future reference."[21]

Roosevelt also became the subject of political satire in the form of film animation, which is generally seen as dating from 1906. When he embarked on his extended African safari in 1909, a short animated sequence parodied his obsession with hunting. What seems to be an excerpt from the line-drawn cartoon can be seen in David Grubin's 1996 PBS documentary discussed later: the sequence shows a Teddy Roosevelt figure, brandishing a rifle, emerging over the brow of an African hill to see a comic tableau: a host of animals, including elephants, clinging precariously to a tree for safety. This tone was repeated in a better-known animated film from 1913, the first in a series created by the newspaper cartoonist turned pioneer animator John Randolph Bray. Most reports suggest that this cartoon, *Colonel Heeza Liar in Africa*, was widely seen as a satire on Roosevelt's big-game hunting expeditions.[22]

Much surviving footage records TR's postpresidential life, from his flight in a plane (in 1910) to his African safari and subsequent European tour, to his speeches during the Progressive campaign, his meeting with "suffragists" (1917), and his interventions on the subject of the war in Europe. The earliest compilation of all this material, amounting to the first real film documentary on the man, was assembled by archivist and filmmaker Caroline Gentry in the 1920s.[23] Yet the series of short newsreels that most vividly captured his return to public prominence concerned the war in Europe. Compared to the early long shots, most of these later films show Roosevelt in medium or close-up shots.

TR had originally supported President Woodrow Wilson's neutrality policy, but shifted his position after hearing of German atrocities in Belgium to become an ever more strident supporter of "preparedness" after the sinking of the Lusitania in May 1915. A Paramount Pictures sequence from 1916 shows him speaking (with intertitles) about preparedness for war with the editor of the *Metropolitan* magazine. He also became interested in ways of shifting public opinion toward his position. To this end, the former president assisted (mainly by encouraging friends to participate) in the making of a Vitagraph fiction film by Oyster Bay neighbor J. Stuart Blackton that showed Germany invading an unprepared America. Although peace sentiment remained strong outside of the Eastern cities, *The Battle Cry of Peace* (1915) drew large crowds. One of the top-grossing films of the war years, it was an early disaster movie, showing an espionage threat and a Teutonic enemy besieging New York from the sea and reducing skyscrapers to ruins.[24]

Other newsreels of Roosevelt's speeches followed. He spoke out about hyphenated Americans whom he felt were serving the Kaiser. Later emulated by Wilson, super-patriotic rhetoric of this ilk led to several cases of mob action against pacifists.[25] After involvement in further preparedness parades in 1916, Roosevelt began a prowar speaking tour the following year despite failing health. A Universal

Animated Weekly newsreel shows him waving to large crowds from a car in Chicago, in a sequence followed by this title card:

> The war must not end until Germany is whipped. It cannot terminate unless there is an end of the militarized Prussianism that directs the course of our enemies!
>
> *Theodore Roosevelt.*
>
> *American—For America ALWAYS*

A further sequence, from 1917, shows TR, described by a title card as "America's citizen extraordinary," speaking to a large, flag-bedecked crowd in St. Paul, Minnesota. A Hearst-Pathe newsreel from the same year reviews several Roosevelt events, from receiving "the Envoys of Bleeding Belgium" at his Sagamore Hill home, to a speech in Forrest Hills, Long Island, in which he is recorded as saying: "Put down the Shadow Huns within our gates. There can be no fifty-fifty Americans." A further intertitle records another Roosevelt visit, in Billings Montana, and invokes the spirit of 1898: "The famous 'Rough Riders' in another drive—Colonel Roosevelt tours the West to help put the Liberty Loan over the top."

There are also newsreel scenes of Roosevelt with sons Quentin and Archie at Sagamore Hill, and then shots from 1918 of the sons' regiments in France, indicating the degree to which the ex-president's family was still central to his public persona. Popular support for Roosevelt revived as America entered the war, and he still maintained hopes of gaining the Republican nomination for 1920, but ill health, and in particular the death in action of his son Quentin wore him down, and he died in January 1919.

The 1940s and Popular Front Perspectives

Various films helped to keep the story of 1898 alive, not least the Paramount production of *The Rough Riders* (Victor Fleming) in 1927, while TR's presidency was commemorated by the completion of his Mount Rushmore sculpture in 1939, joining the granite pantheon of George Washington, Thomas Jefferson, and Abraham Lincoln. There followed a significant revival of cinematic invocations of the first President Roosevelt in the 1940s, in part as filmmakers invoked his memory in support of American participation in the war against fascism.

Significantly, too, Orson Welles made several oblique references to TR in *Citizen Kane* (1941), one of the masterpieces of cinema. First, a figure with Roosevelt's familiar profile appears beside Charles Foster Kane, a thinly veiled representation of William Randolph Hearst, on the platform of a campaign train in the "News on the March" sequence. A further scene draws on stories of a reportedly unproductive trip made by Frederic Remington to Cuba in 1897, before the sinking of the *Maine* sparked the Spanish-American War. As Kane, newly established editor of the *New York Inquirer*, responds to an overseas cable received from a reporter, we see that the main headline on that day's *Inquirer* is "Galleons of Spain off Jersey Coast!" and that a secondary story, under a prominent picture of Theodore Roosevelt, is "Teddy Raps Boss Rule." The cable concludes with "THERE IS NO WAR IN CUBA," and Kane, to the exasperation of his ex-guardian, Mr. Thatcher, immediately dictates his reply: "DEAR WHEELER. YOU PROVIDE THE PROSE POEMS, I'LL PROVIDE THE WAR." It has also been suggested that "Boss" Jim Getty, who sabotages Kane's subsequent attempt to run for office, owes something to Roosevelt, who is said to have leaked information damaging to Hearst during the tycoon's unsuccessful 1906 race for the New York governorship.[26]

Actor Sidney Blackmer played TR in a number of films in the period 1937–48, most notably in the 1940 biographical short *Teddy, The Rough Rider* (Warner Bros., Ray Enright), and in two features, *War of the Wildcats* (*In Old Oklahoma*, Albert S. Rogell, 1943) and *My Girl Tisa* (Elliott Nugent, 1948). In the first two Blackmer contributes rather superficial impersonations that mainly entail declaiming, as if constantly giving a speech even when engaged in conversation. The color short provides a brief summary of Roosevelt's career, identifying him at every step with the people against the special interests, bosses, and politicians. There is also a brief action sequence recreating the charge at the Battle of San Juan Hill. The film concludes with the great man, near to death, extemporizing a speech. Although this begins by his declaring that there "cannot be, there must not be, a repetition of the crime against Belgium," it continues in a way that mixes the politics of 1940 with those of 1918. Roosevelt asserts that little nations have the right to live, and that great nations must respect this; he calls for world peace, but also for preparedness, warning against Americans seeking to promote "foreignisms"; and he affirms that the country has room for only one flag, one language, and one loyalty. The twenty-minute short ends patriotically with a fade to the stars and stripes.

In Republic's *War of the Wildcats,* set in 1905, John Wayne and Albert Dekker play rival claimants for a contract to exploit oil reserves in Indian lands. Blackmer as President Roosevelt makes a fleeting appearance when the two men go to Washington to argue their cases. Although Dekker is the more experienced businessman, Wayne, as a cowboy, has the special advantage of being an ex-Rough Rider with experience of the campaigns in Cuba and the Philippines. When they meet, Roosevelt asks him, "How did you manage to get to the top of San Juan Hill ahead of us?" Ultimately he decides the issue in favor of the Wayne character on the grounds that his proposal is far more generous to the Indians. Roosevelt's decision is thus supportive of the grassroots Western farmers in a way that associates the president with the Popular Front "people's war" notion of World War II.

The most appealing of Blackmer's cameo appearances in this period is in the fantasy ending of *My Girl Tisa*, the sentimental Warner Bros. period drama of struggling and striving immigrants in 1905 New York (adapted for the screen by left-wing writer Allen Boretz). Tricked by a corrupt ticket agent, Tisa Kepes (Lilli Palmer) is to be unfairly deported. Boyfriend, immigrant, and would-be lawyer Mark Denek (Sam Wanamaker) can seemingly do nothing. However, there is a nearby harbor parade for President Roosevelt, who is meeting a disembarking foreign crown prince. In an off-camera encounter Denek somehow persuades TR to reverse the course of the law. Without any explanatory dialog, the two immigrants are suddenly seen in the president's carriage, on their way to American success. Theatrical and unbelievable as this ending is—the screenplay was originally a play—there is a warmly populist feel to the piece. Appearing as bewildered by the ending as the couple, Roosevelt provides an affirmative finale, strengthened by the performances of future blacklist victims Palmer and Wanamaker (the latter, ironically, was to leave America for the "old country," in 1951, when named a communist). The real TR was less keen on immigrants in 1918, of course, but here the Roosevelt figure ends with something near to a joke against himself, telling the couple that he "cannot keep the Crown Prince waiting—(it) might lead to war."

John Milius and the Homage to TR's Martial Spirit

Writer-director John Milius (born 1944) brought his own distinctive mix of political and cultural concerns to a series of films that deal directly or obliquely with Theodore Roosevelt. Although Milius described TR as "flawed" and "overzealous," he was nonetheless a consistent admirer, as well as being a director who brought his hero's "strenuous" perspective to the process of filmmaking, which he described as "like going to war without suffering casualties." He was one of a group of young, cine-literate, and film-school educated "movie brats," seen in the late 1970s as inheriting the mantle of the old studios. After writing an early script for *Apocalypse Now,* he directed his first film, *Dillinger* (1973), for American Independent Productions.[27] Before that he had written another original screenplay for *The Life and Times of Judge Roy Bean* (1972), for director John Huston, but felt that the commercial tone and Paul Newman's casting in the central role had sentimentalized his vision of the making of a Western legend. As in the later *The Wind and the Lion*, the Huston film reflects Milius's admiration for self-made Western heroes who become the victim of the "materialist civilization" that they make way for. The film also contains a sequence that is a direct tribute to Theodore Roosevelt as the "finest President in the history of the country" and the one closest to the values of the old West.

The Wind and the Lion is an epic, an imperial adventure based on a real event of 1904 when an elderly American and his stepson were kidnapped and held hostage by a local Berber chief, Raisuli, on land nominally controlled by the Sultan of Morocco. President Roosevelt responded strenuously, diverting warships to Tangier and successfully demanding the release of the hostages. Milius draws loosely on the facts, making the main hostage a (much younger) woman, and actually engaging the marines, creating an elaborately choreographed set-piece of gunboat diplomacy. For all its desert romance, the film has most political and psychological depth in its portrait of Roosevelt, as played by Brian Keith. It provides an unusually respectful and nuanced perspective of a vigorous American presidency at a time when the contemporary presidency had been much weakened by the Watergate scandal and the final, humiliating loss of Vietnam.

Milius's film is a kind of Victorian adventure, and the director has made reference to the comparison with such Kiplingesque film adaptations as *The Drum* (1938) and *The Four Feathers* (1939). Less than a quarter of the movie is set in Washington, with the rest of the story taking place in the desert, and in and around the palaces and fortresses of Morocco. In fact all the scenes, including the Washington ones, were filmed in Franco's Spain. The catalyst for the story is the capture of an American, Mrs. Pedicaris (Candice Bergen), and her two young children by the "brigand" chief Mulay Ahmed al-Raisuli (Sean Connery). While Milius clearly admires Roosevelt's decisiveness

in the international arena, he presents him here as a reflective, sometimes melancholy figure, in conflict with both diplomats and the
"interests." We hear the often withering commentary of Secretary
of State John Hay (John Huston) on his commander in chief's disin-
terest in diplomatic and constitutional niceties. Nevertheless, several
scenes also highlight Roosevelt's decisive moral vision and assertion
of a strong presidential prerogative in relation to the selfish politics of
bosses and special interests.

Although the real historical events are represented only loosely
and the film is far more critical of European than American meddling, the Berber figure is made into an unusual Muslim hero, albeit
one played by a Scotsman. Milius has claimed that the film gained
an Islamic following, and one can certainly point to the prominence
of broadly Islamic style, in the opening credits, dress, and architecture, and to the fact that Raisuli, and not Roosevelt, is the star. By
making the hostage an attractive woman the director also plays on
familiar sexual tensions in the tradition established by the Rudolph
Valentino silent film *The Sheik* (1921). Yet he also tries to ground his
romance in the desert imagery and texture of David Lean's *Lawrence
of Arabia* (1962), and provides, in the Washington scenes, an unapol-
ogetic view of a president's imperial stance. There is nothing of the
way T.E. Lawrence, in Lean's film, mediates between two cultures.
Milius brings the historical events forward in the election year of
1904, emphasizing the way in which TR was persuaded to play up
the issue for political purposes. In reality the U.S. Marines did not
intervene, as they do in the film. Milius's historical research—unlike
that of Lean's screenwriters—was never more than an important
stepping off point for his greater enthusiasm for depicting imperial
"derring-do," audacious presidential command, and swashbuckling
military intervention.[28]

President Roosevelt is first pictured being photographed, his hand
on a large globe, as we hear the report of the U.S. Consul General
in Tangier concerning the kidnapping. He mulls over his response
while first boxing and then practicing on the archery range. When
Secretary of State Hay suggests that Roosevelt's plan to send the
Atlantic Squadron to Morocco is illegal, the president replies: "Why
spoil the beauty of a thing with legality?" This is a line adapted from
Attorney General Philander Knox's tongue-in-cheek response to TR's
defense of his support for the Panamanian revolution that he should
not "let so great an achievement suffer from any taint of legality."[29]
Indeed the film is constantly dotted with inaccurately sourced quota-
tions from the historical record: for example, Hay calls Roosevelt a

"damned cowboy," a phrase actually used by one of his prepresidential Republican critics Senator Mark Hanna of Ohio.

The second American scene is an elaborate set-piece showing TR campaigning from the observation car of a train at a station packed with enthusiastic supporters. There are Rough Riders in the crowd, and one banner proclaims "Remember the Maine & Remember San Juan Hill." Beside the president on the train is Apache chief Geronimo, while behind him we see petty politicos making deals. Roosevelt announces his policy: "America wants Pedicaris alive or Raisuli dead," a phrase actually used in a diplomatic cable at the time (figure 3.1). In the film, the incident is designed to influence the electorate; in reality, it was intended to provide some excitement at the earlier Republican Convention.

The third presidential scene shows TR at a camp on the Yellowstone River, returning from a hunting trip and characteristically talking to reporters who hang on his every word. "We're the intruders here," he tells them when pointing to the bear that he has killed. He argues that the American grizzly is more emblematic of America's character than the nation's official symbol, the American eagle, because it is occasionally blind and reckless, but lonely and full of "audacity." A fourth scene depicts a White House birthday party for the president at which he symbolically makes the first cut (across the line of the proposed Panama Canal) to a huge cake decorated by a map of the Americas. After the meal he talks with enthusiasm of the American Winchester gun, and poses to demonstrate for a camera the "fighting

Figure 3.1 "America wants Pedicaris alive or Raisuli dead": Theodore Roosevelt (Brian Keith) spells out his hostage policy in *The Wind and the Lion*.

stance" that he wants used for the bear to be stuffed for exhibition at the Smithsonian.

The penultimate American sequence shows TR at the shooting range, with an image of the Russian Czar as a target. Commenting that the president has "gone cowboy again," Hay remarks that he might even consider "a declaration of war would be a joke too." Finally, as the desert melodrama subsides, the film returns a last time to "Washington," where Roosevelt communes alone with "his" bear and reads a meditative letter from Raisuli. Here is a film about the presidency in which the president is the supporting player: the American scenes are deliberately made as a low key contrast to the "Indiana Jones" tone of the desert story. Milius himself turns up in the latter, playing—in jokey reference to his right-wing political reputation—a one-armed arms salesman. In the more sober Washington scenes TR contrasts himself to the bureaucrats and politicos, and instead sees himself as a "pirate," a mixture of Raisuli, the grizzly bear, and J.P. Morgan, "enemies" that—as we hear him explain to his children—he prefers to his friends. For all the scholarly discussion of the modernity and innovation of Roosevelt's presidency in the history books, Milius's picture is of an anachronistic American, at a time before the institutionalized executive, the military-industrial complex, and Oliver's Stone's "the Beast" became motifs of American foreign policymaking.

In the 1980s Milius went on to write and direct *Red Dawn* (1984), which presents a group of young Americans as citizen-soldiers supposedly in the tradition of the Rough Riders defending America from Soviet invasion. An early scene shows a main street statue of TR in Rough Rider uniform, in the Colorado small town where the highly implausible parachute attack begins. The inscription is from an 1899 Roosevelt speech paying tribute to those who dare to accomplish "mighty things." Reflecting early Reagan-era anxieties about Soviet militarism, *Red Dawn* shows its rebels adopting frontier strategies to combat the invading force.[30] The TR motifs—including scenes displaying the Arapaho National Forest, founded by Roosevelt in 1905—are clearly Milius creations, but the heavier political references (notably the reeducation camps) reflect the powerful influence of MGM CEO Frank Yablands and President Reagan's recently retired secretary of state Alexander Haig on the final screenplay.[31]

Milius returned to the TR theme with a nearly four-hour television miniseries, *Rough Riders*, made for Turner Network Television (TNT) for 1997 transmission. The overall tone, and the emphasis on the action rather than causes of the 1898 war, is suggested by a statement at the beginning:

> To the American citizen soldier
> Who answered the call
> Climbed the hill
> Paid the price
> And never let us down.

The film appeared at a time of intense conflict between President Bill Clinton and the fiercely partisan Republican majority in Congress and in the same year as Barry Levinson's cynical satire on presidential war-making, *Wag the Dog*. Theodore Roosevelt (Tom Berringer) is second-in-command of the Rough Riders regiment, fighting alongside professional soldier Captain Bucky O'Neill (Sam Elliot) and overall commander of the Santiago assault, the ex-Confederate general Joe Wheeler (Gary Busy). Milius stresses regional, multicultural, and class unity as the disparate group come together and tries to balance what he sees as the ultimate glory of the enterprise with some sense of the chaos of war. Compensating for its hero's less-than-sterling record on race, more stress is put on the role of the black Buffalo Soldiers regiment than in Roosevelt's own accounts. There is also some attempt to capture both TR's bluster and the myth-making apparatus that elevated him to fame, represented by the appearance of Remington and journalists Edward Marshall and Stephen Crane. William Randolph Hearst, reputed to have been in Cuba at the time, is also shown making a visit to the battlefield.

A TR for All Times?

Archive footage of Theodore Roosevelt has also been used in two significant documentaries. In his celebrated twelve-minute film *A Movie* (1958), artist and avant-garde filmmaker Bruce Connor connected a montage of sound footage—mostly of chases, death, destruction and disasters, and the atomic mushroom cloud—to a brief silent close-up of Theodore Roosevelt in mid-address. This short provides a scatter-shot critique of the "stock shot" narratives and motifs that overlapped American public life and B-movies in the first half of the twentieth century, implying through the inclusion of the Roosevelt clip that this particular president had done a good deal to both reflect and propagate such mayhem. In more conventional fashion Harrison Eagle put together a ninety-three-minute film biography that was aired on television in 1983 and shown at the White House. The account, narrated by screen actor George C. Scott, sticks to the well-established story, and spends as much time on Roosevelt's family life—recreated with actors in sentimental soft focus—as on public policy. The tone of the film is also set by the rousing John Philip Sousa marching music that accompanies most of it. In short, little debate is invited. To the reviewer for *Film and History* the documentary compressed the life story of a complex man into a "hero tale for children," providing a "frothy, celebratory film fit for a network attempting to ingratiate itself with the Reagan administration."[32]

David Grubin produced a fuller and more sophisticated documentary account of both man and president for WGBH Boston and American Experience in 1996. This drew on the advice and "talking head" participation of a number of distinguished historians, including John Morton Blum, John Milton Cooper, William Harbaugh, Walter La Feber, David McCullough, and Jean Strouse. The 225-minute production uses their expertise, together with the testimony of Roosevelt family members, to paint a sympathetic but at times critical portrait. This film biography deals thoroughly with the private and public lives, while rightly suggesting that this distinction evaporated as Roosevelt and his family became national and international celebrities. It weaves together period photographs, newspaper stories, and cartoons, and the ephemera of the time, and provides adequate coverage of the more frustrating later presidential and postpresidential years, when TR was opposed by Congress and much of the Republican Party. Most illustrated by archive film material are Roosevelt's wartime speeches of 1918, as his jealousy of Woodrow Wilson seemingly led him to take increasingly extreme and demagogic positions on hyphenated Americans. The documentary concludes in a melancholy fashion as son Quentin's death in action in the new and hellish kind of twentieth-century-warfare on the Western front seemed finally to undermine TR's lifetime confidence in manliness and the martial spirit.

Conversely, references to Roosevelt's life as a subject for humor—in *Arsenic and Old Lace* (1942) through to Robin Williams' wax impression, mounted and in mid-charge, in *Night at the Museum* (2006)—indicate that this larger-than-life figure continues to be seen by some as ridiculous as well as heroic. In Frank Capra's film version of Joseph Kesselring's play, two old ladies murder their suitors while mad Uncle, Teddy Brewster, charges up the stairs, sword aloft, and digs the Panama Canal in the cellar. Although it is Brewster (played by John Alexander—Capra originally wanted Andy Devine) who is the infant-lunatic, the film captures a recurring contemporary perception of Roosevelt as a grown-up child. Historian and novelist Henry Adams, a frequent guest at TR's White House, took to referring to him as "Theodorus I, Czar Rooseveltoff," a title that suggests something of the frenetic atmosphere of a presidential court attended by politicians, advisors, journalists, and children.[33]

For the most part, however, the heroic image of Roosevelt has overshadowed other cinematic portrayals of him. J. Tillapaugh, a student of all the TR film representations, has argued convincingly that "caricature on occasion resulted while revisionism never did." The trend toward accepting Roosevelt's interpretation of his own life has made rethinking him in visual and dramatic terms all the more difficult.[34]

Accordingly, Roosevelt's presidency remains a ready reference point for those who have, at certain times, bemoaned the weakness of both national will and the presidency. The political Right has been most enamored by the recurring myth of him as a dynamic figure on the world stage, but the Left has also seen him as a cautious critic of materialism, a conservationist, an intellectual (albeit one with some unpalatable views), and (in the doomed campaign of 1912) the Progressive pioneer of health insurance.

Roosevelt stands out as a liberal Republican, a political type that is all but extinct in the early twenty-first century. He challenged the monopolies of the day, if only as a reformer and regulator, and resisted the Wall Street wing of the Republican Party. To Richard Hofstadter he "despised the rich, but he feared the mob" and stood for "the aggressive, masterful, fighting virtues of the soldier." More recent students of his presidency have argued for a reassessment of Roosevelt as a "naturalist president," someone who challenged the "myth of inexhaustibility" as the frontier was closed by setting aside 230 million acres of wild America for posterity. The issues relating to hunting and conservation are still debated: *In the Blood* (1989), a film directed by George Butler, 35 mm footage of Roosevelt's 1909 trip to East Africa is used to support a view of contemporary hunters as conservationists and nature lovers.[35] In general terms the photographs and films of Roosevelt the naturalist now have more currency than the cartoon image of him as the great white hunter, although both were part of the story.

Theodore Roosevelt represented contradictory impulses at a time when new aspects of American identity were being forged. Yet his image and legend remain powerful signifiers for liberals, conservatives, and radicals alike (with few of the latter having much purchase on the cinema). Like Ronald Reagan, TR forged a degree of consensus admiration by welding an international peacemaker role on to his earlier "happy warrior" rhetoric.[36] Cinema, early and late, has often printed the legend: the myth of Roosevelt the self-made Westerner and the Rough Riders acted as a catalyst for the early cinema industry, but Porter's satires helped provide the emerging medium with a degree of critical edge. Others have used the squinting, iconic figure for their own purposes, and *The Wind and the Lion* is perhaps the most distinctive single portrait, giving us a leader forever confident of America's global role (as the American century began), but also one whose individualism seemed somehow innocent of the corporate and bureaucratic tides that engulfed later presidencies.

A Note on Film Sources

A total of 104 early motion picture actualities and newsreels of the period 1898–1919 are available online at the "Theodore Roosevelt on Film" collection, American Memory at the Library of Congress, http://memory.loc.gov/ammem/collections/troosevelt_film/, while 87 are from the Theodore Roosevelt Association Collection; the others are from the Paper Print Collection, Library of Congress. *Terrible Teddy, the Grizzly King* (1901) is available on the BFI DVD of *Before the Nickelodeon* (Charles Musser, 1982) and also on *History of US Presidents: Teddy Roosevelt* (DVD), A2ZCDS.com (2004); *The Strenuous Life: or Anti-Race Suicide* (1905) and *The "Teddy" Bears* (1907) are available on the Kino Video DVD box set *Edison: The Invention of the Movies* (MOMA, 2005). *A Movie* (1958) is available at http://www.tudou.com/programs/view/3-9tCeFX0Eo/.

Notes

1. Arthur M. Schlesinger, Jr., "Rating the Presidents: Washington to Clinton," *Political Science Quarterly* 112 (1997): 182; Sarah Watts, *Rough Rider in the White House: Theodore Roosevelt and the Politics of Desire* (Chicago: University of Chicago Press, 2003), 4.
2. Kathleen Dalton, *Theodore Roosevelt, A Strenuous Life* (New York: Vintage Books, 2002), 9.
3. Theodore Roosevelt, *Ranch Life and the Hunting-Trail* [first edition, 1888] (London: T. Fisher Unwin, 1902), 87, 92.
4. Kevin Brownlow, *The War, The West and the Wilderness* (London: Secker & Warburg, 1979), xv–xvi, 381.

5. Theodore Roosevelt, *The Winning of the West* (an abridgement edited by Christopher Lasch; New York: Hastings House, 1963), 21.

6. Roosevelt (1886), quoted in Richard Hofstadter, *The American Political Tradition, And the Men Who Made It* (London: Jonathan Cape, 1967), 209.

7. Watts, *Rough Rider in the White House*, 142; Richard Slotkin, "Buffalo Bill's 'Wild West' and the Mythologization of the American Empire," in Amy Kaplan and Donald E. Pease, eds., *Cultures of United States Imperialism* (Durham, NC: Duke University Press, 1993), 176; Scott Simmon, film notes in *More Treasures from American Film Archives, 1894–1931* (San Francisco: National Film Preservation Foundation, 2004), 60.

8. Edmund Morris, *The Rise of Theodore Roosevelt* (New York: The Modern Library, 2001), 658–9; Louis Pizzitola, *Hearst over Hollywood: Power, Passion and Propaganda in the Movies* (New York: Columbia University Press, 2002), 63.

9. Charles Musser, *The Emergence of Cinema: The American Screen to 1907* (Berkeley: University of California Press, 1990), 245–7.

10. Kristen Whissel, "Uncle Tom, Goldilocks, and the Rough Riders: Early Cinema's Encounter with Empire," *Screen* 40 (1999): 384–404.

11. Watts, *Rough Rider in the White House*, 165; J. Tillapaugh, "Theodore Roosevelt and the Rough Riders," in Peter C. Rollins and John E. O'Connor, eds., *Hollywood's White House: The American Presidency in Film and History* (Lexington, Kentucky: University of Kentucky Press, 2003), 98. Roosevelt's book on the war was first published in 1899; see *The Rough Riders* (Blacksburg VA.: Wilder Publications, 2008).

12. Robert Eberwin, *The Hollywood War Film* (Chichester: Wiley-Blackwell, 2010), 4–6, 11.

13. Slotkin, "Buffalo Bill's 'Wild West,'" 176.

14. Daniel J. Boorstin, *The Image* (Harmondsworth: Penguin Books, 1963), 41; Nathan Miller, *Theodore Roosevelt, A Life* (New York: William Morrow, 1992), 421.

15. *Before the Nickelodeon: The Early Cinema of Edwin S. Porter* (Charles Musser, 1982), BFI DVD.

16. Pizzitola, *Hearst over Hollywood*, 86–7.

17. Willard B. Gatewood, "Theodore Roosevelt and the 'Kinetoscope Fakes': An Incident in the Campaign of 1904," *Mid-America* 49 (1967): 190–9.

18. Holly Jackson, "'So We Die before Our Own Eyes': Willful Sterility in The Country of the Pointed Firs," *The New England Quarterly* LXXXII (2009): 284–5.

19. Simmon, film notes in *More Treasures*, 59–63; Douglas Brinkley, *The Wilderness Warrior: Theodore Roosevelt and the Crusade for America* (New York: Harper Collins, 2009), 439–43.

20. Whissel, "Uncle Tom, Goldilocks, and the Rough Riders," 400–403.

21. "Theodore Roosevelt—the Picture Man," *The Moving Picture World*, October 22, 1910, quoted in Karen C. Lund, "The First Presidential Picture Man," Library of Congress Information, September 1999, http://www.loc.gov/loc/lcib/9909/tr.html.

22. Richard Schickel, *The Disney Version* (London: Pavilion Books, 1986), 99.

23. Veronica Gillespie, "Theodore Roosevelt on Film," Theodore Roosevelt on Film Collection, Library of Congress, http://lcweb.loc.gov/ammem/collections/trooosevelt_film/trffilm.html.

24. Dalton, *Theodore Roosevelt*, 457, 634; Leif Furhammar and Folke Isaksson, *Politics and Film* (London: Studio Vista, 1971), 9.

25. Dalton, *Theodore Roosevelt*, 501.

26. Pizzitola, *Hearst over Hollywood*, 60, 393.

27. "John Milius," in Patrick McGilligan, ed., *Backstory 4: Interviews with Screenwriters of the 1970s and 1980s* (Berkeley: University of California Press, 2006), 307; Michael Pye and Lynda Myles, *The Movie Brats, How the Film Generation Took Over Hollywood* ((London: Faber and Faber, 1979), 171–87.

28. Frances Poole, "*The Wind and the Lion*: Myth versus Reality in the Life and Times of Moulay Ahmed al-Raisuli," in Kevin R. Lacey and Ralph M. Coury, eds., *The Arab-African and Islamic Worlds* (New York: Peter Lang, 2000), 279–88.

29. Dalton, *Theodore Roosevelt*, 256.

30. Stephen Prince, *Visions of Empire, Political Imagery in Contemporary American Film* (New York: Praeger, 1992), 56–7.

31. Peter Bart, "'Red Dawn': Shooting the McVeigh Way," *Daily Variety*, June 16, 1997, 34.

32. Anonymous review, *Film and History* 16 (May 1986): 46–8.

33. Joseph McBride, *Frank Capra: The Catastrophe of Success* (New York: Simon & Schuster, 1992), 445; Miller, *Theodore Roosevelt*, 413.

34. Tillapaugh, "Theodore Roosevelt and the Rough Riders," 111; Dalton, *Theodore Roosevelt*, 8.

35. Hofstadter, *The American Political Tradition*, 205–206; Robert P. Harrison, "A Great Conservationist, by Jingo," *New York Review of Books*, LVI, November 5, 2009, 44; Robert V. Hine and John Mack Faragher, *Frontiers, A Short History of the American West* (New Haven CT: Yale University Press, 2007), 178; Barbara Moes, "Hunters as Conservationists, 'In the Blood,'" *Image Technology* 71 (1989): 501–502.

36. John Dos Passos, *U.S.A.* (1938; Harmondsworth, UK: Penguin Books, 1976), 455.

Chapter 4

Darryl F. Zanuck's Wilson

Mark Wheeler

Introduction

Wilson, the biographical film (biopic) about America's twenty-eighth president, Woodrow Wilson, was produced by the studio mogul Darryl F. Zanuck at Twentieth Century Fox in 1944. Costly and ambitious, the movie was a prestige production for the studio and a personal crusade for Zanuck. *Wilson* marked the first time Hollywood had tackled the life of a recent president and its cast of characters included many real-life principals who were either still alive or remained vivid in popular memory.[1]

Zanuck's World War II experience as a colonel in the U.S. Signal Corps was one source of inspiration for his decision to produce a biopic of the World War I president who was frustrated in his effort to bequeath a legacy of lasting peace in the form of an effective League of Nations. His previous service in the Great War—he saw action in France as a sixteen-year-old after deceiving recruitment officials about his real age—had further endowed him with great admiration for his former commander-in-chief. Zanuck's commitment to the Wilson project also reflected his strong ties to Wendell L. Willkie, the Republican candidate for president in 1940 and author of the best-selling *One World*. Published in 1943, this memoir was based on Willkie's world trip the previous year as President Franklin D. Roosevelt's special envoy.[2] It spoke out against isolationism and advocated international peace through a form of world governance. Zanuck was particularly attracted to Willkie's contention that World War II could have been avoided had Wilson's vision of the League of Nations become reality.

At the time of its making, *Wilson* was Hollywood's most expensive film with a total production and marketing expenditure of $5.2 million. This was some 25 percent higher than the $4.2 million budget spent by David O. Selznick and Metro-Goldwyn-Mayer (MGM) on *Gone with the Wind* (*GWTW*; 1939). Like *GWTW*, *Wilson* was shot in the expensive three-strip Technicolor process and included sequences of mass crowds in historical settings. The movie was also very long, running to 154 minutes in its episodic coverage of Wilson's political career.

Unlike *GWTW*, however, *Wilson* is an almost forgotten film that merits scant mention in the biographies of Zanuck despite its lavish budget, cinematography, vast sets, crowd scenes, and the expensive marketing. Hailed by studio publicity as "The Most Significant Event in the Fifty Years of Motion Picture Entertainment," *Wilson* was one of Zanuck's greatest follies.[3] Instead of being the entertaining, uplifting, and profitable film that he had intended, the biopic of the twenty-eighth president did not resonate with audiences because of its inability to make its subject a relevant hero for current times.

This essay examines the film's production history, narrative, principal themes, and reaction to it, both critical and commercial. It also assesses the movie's representation of Woodrow Wilson and what this demonstrates about America's sense of "exceptionalism." Finally it considers how *Wilson* provided a template for other films about U.S. political engagement. As such, the analysis casts the spotlight on a largely forgotten film that still has a provenance in current debates about American politics, history, and film culture.

Production History

Although the "auteur" theory has placed the director at the center of the filmmaking process, *Wilson* can only be viewed as Darryl F. Zanuck's film rather than that of its scriptwriter Lamar Trotti or director Henry King. Reflecting his position in the Hollywood hierarchy of the times, Zanuck alone had both the financial and creative acumen to get the film made. In the 1930s and 1940s, the outputs of the studio system were invariably determined by the studio moguls or heads of production. Zanuck, along with Irving Thalberg at MGM and Selznick at RKO, became one of the youngest heads of production in the early 1930s, originally making his name at Warner Brothers. One of the film industry's producer geniuses, he had a keen eye to match projects with actors and directors.[4]

As second-in-command at Warners, Zanuck had been responsible for the career of the famous canine star Rin-Tin-Tin, was instrumental in the introduction of sound with *The Jazz Singer* (1927), inaugurated the gangster movie with *Little Caesar* (1930), and presided over the early Busby Berkeley musicals. In many respects, he transformed Warner Brothers from a small, struggling company into a major studio and set the house style for its production output. He was noted for his social consciousness; his interest in prison reform, for example, inspired his production of *I was a Fugitive from a Chain Gang* (1932), for which he ultimately provided an uncredited rewrite of the shooting script.

On being told by Jack Warner that he would never be anything more than a highly paid employee at Warner Brothers, Zanuck left the company in 1933 to form a new studio, Twentieth Century. Backed by Joseph Schenck and William Goetz (Louis B. Mayer's son-in-law), this enterprise released its films through United Artists. In 1935 it took over the ailing giant Fox, thereby enhancing its production capacity and distribution power.

As vice president in charge of production at Twentieth Century Fox, Zanuck differed in several respects from other moguls. He was the only one to identify with the production of his films by retaining dual credit as film producer and production chief. His status and authority as both a "creative" producer, whose pictures reflected his overall vision, and as head of Fox's production roster was total and unquestioned. As he put it, "Every creative decision was either authorised, or okayed, or created by me...I decided whether we made something or didn't make it. I was a One-Man Show."[5] Zanuck was also the only non-Jewish mogul and Twentieth Century Fox was known as the "Goy" studio. Less concerned than their Jewish counterparts to assimilate into American society, Zanuck and Fox made their reputations by developing a varied portfolio of films.[6] Zanuck was the principal force behind a number of "message" films, notably the John Ford–directed classics *Young Mr Lincoln* (1939) and *The Grapes of Wrath* (1940), and lavish historical dramas, including *Les Miserables* (1935) and *Call of the Wild* (1935). Fox also developed a specialty in biographical films, such as *The House of Rothschild* (1934), *The Mighty Barnum* (1934), *Clive of India* (1935), and *Stanley and Livingstone* (1939). Zanuck looked to develop a prestigious big-budget movie that combined all three genres of entertainment, message, and biography.[7] In the late 1930s, he considered a film about labor and politics focusing on the craft union leader Samuel Gompers but rejected the project as too controversial amid the growing union militancy of the time. However, the appearance of Woodrow Wilson within its outline engaged his attention owing to his growing interest in world affairs.[8]

Zanuck's Ambitions for Wilson

Zanuck's ideas for *Wilson* began to take concrete form as a result of his return to military service after Pearl Harbor. He had frequent discussions with other army officers and enlisted men about America's role in world affairs after the war. In these conversations, the former "doughboy" increasingly brought up Woodrow Wilson's vision of world peace and the tragedy of his failure to make this a reality.

Zanuck's ties with Wendell Willkie, whose presidential campaign he had actively supported, also shaped his thinking on this score. The two men were drawn together again by the Senate investigations held by Republican Gerald Nash of North Dakota and Democrat Burton Wheeler of Montana, both prominent isolationists, into the pro-British and interventionist bias of Hollywood films in 1941. During these hearings Zanuck was one of the chief defendants and Willkie acted as the film industry's legal counsel. Impressed with the latter's performance, the mogul subsequently invited him to become chair of Fox's board in 1942, but this initiative fell foul of studio politics.[9] After being demobbed in 1943, Zanuck considered making a semi-fictional film titled *One World* with a Willkie-like main character. Commenting of his friend, he declared, "He's such a decent man. He's the only pol I know who doesn't fill the basin with muck every time he washes his hands."[10] However, he decided to focus on the sections in Willkie's text that argued the war could have been averted had Wilson been able to realize a truly effective League of Nations. In spite of their Republicanism, both Zanuck and Willkie admired the Democratic Wilson as a visionary internationalist in his quest for world peace.

Instead of producing a small-scale message film aimed at a limited audience, Zanuck insisted that *Wilson* should be a lavish spectacle with appeal to a wide range of cinemagoers. Owing to the commercial failure of some recent message movies, notably the antilynching film *The Ox-Box Incident* (1943), he faced considerable opposition within the studio. Nevertheless, Zanuck remained adamant that Wilson's battles over the League of Nations ensured a combination of dramatic entertainment and political relevance that would win large audiences.[11]

To develop the project, Fox bought the rights to the Howard Koch–John Huston play *In Time to Come* (1941), which had focused on Wilson's losing battle to establish a potent League of Nations. Its portrayal of the president set him against his congressional opponents, such as Republican senator Henry Cabot Lodge of Massachusetts, self-interested European allies, his own failing health, and the

American public's preference for postwar disengagement and "normalcy." Ominously for Zanuck's hopes regarding *Wilson*, the stage production enjoyed only a short run. According to its director Otto Preminger, nobody had wanted to see the play just as the United States was entering World War II. Adjudging the stage version of Wilson to be as ' "austere and detached" as the real one, theater critic Richard Lockridge issued a further warning that "it is hard to make such men into the heroes of drama."[12] Nevertheless, a defiantly optimistic Zanuck asserted that his biopic would benefit from new interest about the shape of the post–World War II world and its more human representation of Wilson. Convinced that the movie would prove the doubters wrong, he declared: "I am doing it because I think it's the right thing to do at this time. I think that it will serve a tremendous purpose for our company, our industry, and for our country, and furthermore, I will not start shooting it until I am completely satisfied that I have the opportunity of making it a popular entertainment." For good measure, the mogul proudly avowed, "We are producing *Wilson* because we believe in it. It is, by far, the biggest undertaking of the Twentieth Century Fox studios."[13]

Preproduction Scripting: Trotti and Zanuck's Shaping of the Screenplay

Zanuck employed studio writer-producer Lamar Trotti to write the script and top Fox director Henry King to make the film. Zanuck supervised Trotti, who had previously written *Young Mr. Lincoln, The Story of Alexander Graham Bell* (1939), and *The Ox-Bow Incident*. To ensure authenticity, Trotti extensively researched Wilson over a two-year period with the aid of the president's biographer, journalist-historian Ray Stannard Baker, who worked as a consultant on the film for five months in 1943. Moreover, Wilson's widow Edith Galt Wilson reviewed each draft and her comments were incorporated into the final shooting script.

Throughout the writing process, Trotti and Zanuck focused on the personal aspects of the rather austere Wilson. They sought to highlight his essential decency and commonality with the people and to provide an upbeat cinematic ending to what was essentially a downbeat historical finale. As annotations on transcripts of screenplay conferences confirm, Zanuck's hand was evident in efforts at character fine-tuning to make Wilson audience friendly. He wanted the twenty-eighth president to be dignified but also human and non-elitist. To this end, the film is dotted with scenes designed to show Wilson the man in a sympathetic light. In Zanuck's reasoning, the president's impassioned promotion of the League of Nations in the later stages of the motion picture would more likely find acceptance if moviegoers had already seen him as "plain" Woodrow Wilson.[14]

Casting and Characterization

The choice of actor to play the lead role was a critical decision. At first Zanuck considered stars such as William Powell, Tyrone Power, and Ronald Coleman, but he decided a little-known actor would provide a more convincing representation of Wilson. He eventually opted for Alexander Knox (figure 4.1). Blessed with a mellifluous voice, this Canadian Scottish character actor won praise for a sympathetic and accurate rendition of Wilson. His performance also drew on the Scotch Presbyterian religious upbringing that he shared with Wilson, the son of a pastor in this church. This was an enormous role for Knox, who was required to appear in nearly all of the film's 294 scenes and to recite over 1,124 lines, including 338 based on Wilson's real-life oratory. As he himself acknowledged, playing someone who existed in the living memory made the challenges of performing such a large part even greater.[15]

Figure 4.1   Alexander Knox as Woodrow Wilson.

Sir Cedric Hardwicke provided a mercurial rendition of Senator Henry Cabot Lodge, the Republican chairman of the Senate Foreign Relations Committee and the main opponent of Article X of the League of Nations, which required member nations to preserve each other's independence and take concerted action when any member was attacked. For Wilson this was "the heart of the covenant," but Lodge and his allies feared that it entailed a surrender of U.S. foreign policy sovereignty and an abrogation of the congressional war power decreed in the Constitution. Zanuck received the go-ahead for Lodge's portrayal in the movie from his grandson Henry Cabot Lodge Jr., himself now the Republican senator for Massachusetts. Ironically the latter would ultimately serve from 1953 to 1960 as U.S. ambassador to the United Nations, the successor organization to the League of Nations. The only proviso that Lodge made about his grandfather's representation was that he should be shown as honest and sincere. Zanuck, Trotti, and King duly aimed for a "balanced" portrayal but firmly made Lodge Sr. the main adversary to Wilsonian internationalism. Hoping to preempt accusations of political bias, they took his lines from the official government records. However, some Republicans would later claim that the film's "distortion" of the Massachusetts senator was a propaganda triumph for FDR's fourth-term presidential campaign and aided his victory in the 1944 election.[16]

Ruth Nelson and Geraldine Fitzgerald played Wilson's respective wives, Ellen Axson and Edith Galt Wilson. The rest of the extended cast was filled out by Fox contract players and well-known characters actors, including Charles Coburn as a composite fictional character called Professor Henry Holmes, Thomas Mitchell as Wilson's secretary, Joseph P. Tumulty, and Vincent Price as William Gibbs Adoo, the secretary of the treasury and Wilson's son-in-law. The final film included 126 speaking parts and 96 permissions were granted for either living or dead real-life figures to be portrayed in it. None of the parts were played by recognized stars, whose presence in the movie might have enhanced its prospects at the domestic and international box office.

Production, Direction, and Shooting

Henry King was one of Fox's most reliable directors in keeping to budget while turning out hits for the studio. His filmography included *Jesse James* (1939), *The Song of Bernadette* (1943), *Twelve O'Clock High* (1949), and *The Gunfighter* (1950). Unlike other more independently minded directors such as Ford or Preminger, King was amenable to allowing Zanuck onto the set. Recognizing that *Wilson* was Zanuck's film, he also tolerated the mogul's micromanagement that littered the production process with constant rewrites and a barrage of memos.[17]

Wilson was given a lavish ninety-day shooting schedule from November 22, 1943, until February 16, 1944. In total 126 sets were constructed to represent the White House, Versailles' Hall of Mirrors, and other localities. The enormous 1912 convention scene was filmed in the Los Angeles Shrine Auditorium, requiring 1,500 extras and 34 trucks of props and gear. The same venue was used to recreate the joint session of Congress in 1917 when Wilson gave his war speech.[18]

The decision to film *Wilson* in Technicolor increased the size of the budget. It also rendered useless much of the hundreds of feet of old black and white newsreel of Wilson that Fox had bought up at considerable cost. The only footage eventually used was incorporated into the scenes covering World War I and Wilson's trip to Versailles. Typified by this extravagance, Zanuck's no-expense-spared approach drove the production budget from an original estimate of just under two million dollars to more than four million.[19]

The highly experienced King skillfully marshaled the elaborate production throughout the shoot, while also dealing with inevitable logistic problems and Knox's personal aloofness, which caused difficulties with the film crew technicians. Without doubt, the production costs would have been even greater but for his efficiency. Moreover, it was King who came up with the idea for the movie ending that Zanuck and Trotti had long puzzled over. In this an obviously weakened Wilson walks off into the sunset with his ideals intact—symbolizing that the fight for world peace, far from being over, is just beginning.[20]

Themes and Narrative

Zanuck wanted to establish that Wilson's greatness was a reflection of America's values. Accordingly, the film begins with a declaration:

> Sometimes the life of a man mirrors the life of a nation. The destiny of our country was crystallized in the life and times of Washington and Lincoln and perhaps too in the life of another president...that's the story of America and the story of a man...Woodrow Wilson, twenty-eighth president of the United States.

The musical accompaniment to these words, a rendition of "Hail to the Chief" and "God Bless America," reinforces the link between great man and great nation. The opening sets up the overarching theme of the movie that Wilson was a wise leader of a peaceful society seeking to understand its new status as a great power in the world order. The film's patriotism was also evident in its closing statement accompanied by a chorus (to the tune of "America the Beautiful"):

> Long may our land be bright,
> With freedom's holy light,
> Protect us by thy might,
> Great God our King.

The narrative featured a series of chronological episodes that demonstrated Wilson's political life and values. The film begins when Wilson as the president of Princeton University is approached by Senator "Big Ed Jones" (in reality New Jersey boss James E. Smith) to stand as the governor of New Jersey in 1909. It then focuses on the short governorship, the riotous 1912 Democratic Convention where Wilson finally gained the presidential nomination on the forty-sixth ballot, Wilson's electoral success, his first-term presidency, the death of his first wife, his remarriage in office, his reaction to the German U-boat sinking of the British Cunard liner, *Lusitania* (124 U.S. citizens were among the 1,198 casualties), his popularity in keeping the country out of the war, and his reelection in 1916.

Scenes in the second act show Germany reneging on its agreement not to attack the merchant marine of the neutral United States and Wilson's critique of its imperial ambition. This establishes the context for Wilson's reluctant decision to enter the war and his address before a joint session of Congress on April 2, 1917, to request a declaration of war against Germany.[21] With the nation now at war, Wilson and his second wife are seen serving troops refreshments at a posting station. In this scene, the president outlines his vision for world peace in front of the "doughboys." Knowing they will soon be caught up in the carnage on the Western Front, Wilson pledges that the conflict America is entering will be the war to end all wars. This is followed by a newsreel montage of the American troops going into action and then a scene in which a distressed Wilson receives information about the number of U.S. deaths and casualties. Soon after, the president receives news of the Armistice and Germany's agreement to his Fourteen Point peace plan.

The final act deals with the triumph and tragedy of Wilson's last two years in office. Though respectful of his idealism and commitment, modern historical scholarship has also criticized his inflexibility and almost messianic determination to establish the League of Nations, which he regarded as his personal creation.[22] Had Wilson possessed a more pragmatic mindset, he might have achieved most of what he wanted through compromise and persuasion. However, the closest the movie comes to questioning his unyielding stance concerns his decision not to include Cabot Lodge in the American delegation that goes to Europe to negotiate the peace in talks at Versailles. Advised to take the senator because he is a "practical man," Wilson insists in response that the time for pragmatic consideration is gone and only a visionary solution can ensure world peace.

Like the real one, the cinematic Wilson establishes an uneasy but ultimately effective working relationship with representatives of the victorious allies and finally gains acceptance of his core aims in the Treaty of Versailles. On his return home, however, he faces opposition to the League of Nations from the Republican-controlled Congress, particularly in the Senate that has the ultimate power to ratify the peace treaty. In reality, the predominantly Republican opposition to the League in the upper house was hardly monolithic—being composed of fourteen "irreconcilables," twenty-three "strong reservationists," and twelve "mild reservationists." A political comprise might have been negotiated to gain votes from the latter two groups but the president insisted that the treaty had to be approved without changes or "reservations." Eschewing representation of the complex politics of the situation, the film boils the fight for the League down to a titanic struggle between Wilson and Lodge.[23] Embarking on a whistle-stop tour to take his case to the people, an exhausted president suffers a stroke and spends his final year in office as an invalid, effectively dependent on his wife to act as de facto president on his behalf.

The Private Man

A key theme of the film focused on the interplay of the "private" and "public" Wilson. In this regard there is clear similarity in his depiction with that of Lincoln in the previous Zanuck-Trotti collaboration, *Young Mr Lincoln*. In both films the fundamental human decency of the main character lies at the heart of the story. In the latter, Lincoln exudes warmth, charm, and accessibility in contrast to his real-life austerity. Wilson is similarly presented as a humane man with a common touch rather than the aloof, withdrawn, temperamental person that he often was in reality.[24]

In Zanuck's movie, the "private" Wilson is a family man with two loving wives, three adoring daughters, and a love of music, family dancing, and the Vaudeville theater. An early scene shows him enjoying a music hall visit with his family to see a popular performer of the day, Eddie Foy (played by Eddie Foy Jr.). His despair over the death of his first wife and possible scandal of his hasty second marriage adds pathos to the representation of Wilson the man. The film neatly avoids any moralizing about the president's remarriage by effectively having his first wife give her deathbed blessing to any future relationship.

The movie further humanizes Wilson by highlighting his Southern heritage (he was born in Virginia and grew up in Georgia and South Carolina) and affinity with Teddy Roosevelt's advocacy of "outdoor life," represented in scenes showing him playing golf, going to baseball games, and watching college football. Paralleling the real Wilson's brief spell as Princeton football team coach, an early scene shows him extolling students of that college about the virtues of taking part in the game rather than winning. In other words, the private Wilson is an all-round "good egg," a characterization that is supposed to have the audience in his corner when the movie reaches its climactic third act.

The "Public" Wilson: The Domestic Reformer

In its insistent depiction of a heroic Wilson, the movie overlooks the mixture of light and shade in the twenty-eighth president's political makeup. Initially it presents Wilson as a passive political figure on whom greatness is thrust, rather than the ambitious politician who was instrumental in creating the modern presidency through his appreciation of its potential for programmatic, partisan, and political leadership.[25] The cinematic Wilson is invariably a wise leader, but the real Wilson's tendency to see the world in starkly simplistic terms as a struggle between good and evil made it difficult for him to compromise with those who did not share his views. Most significantly the movie ducks any reference to the twenty-sixth president's racism. At one of his first Cabinet meetings, the real Wilson assented to a proposal for racial segregation in all federal departments. The storm of protest from African American, Progressive, and church leaders induced him to retreat from this policy, but he continued to insist that segregation was beneficial to blacks.[26]

In a reflection of reality, Wilson is more focused in the Zanuck biopic on the political and regulatory goals of Progressivism than its social justice agenda. In the scene showing the first major speech of his gubernatorial election campaign, he speaks out against bosses, trusts, and machine politics. True to his beliefs, he promptly distances himself from the New Jersey machine and later refuses to cut a deal with New York's Tammany organization in order to win the 1912 Democratic nomination. As a demonstration of his "man-of-the-people" status, the film attributes his eventual nomination to the support of the so-called Great Commoner, William Jennings Bryan, leader of the party's Populist wing. Paradoxically, it unintentionally undercuts the effect of this by presenting the 1912 election as a three-cornered Ivy League contest. The fictitious Henry Holmes character gleefully comments of the respective Progressive, Republican, and Democratic presidential candidates: "Teddy Roosevelt's a Harvard man. Bill Taft is from Yale. And I'd give five dollars any day to let a Princeton boy have a crack at them in the same game." Missing from this roster is Socialist Party leader Eugene Debs, who won a respectable 6 percent of the vote (compared to Wilson's 41.9 percent, Roosevelt's 27.4 percent, and Taft's 23.2 percent). The fact that he was written out of the movie is unsurprising since he was handed a ten-year prison sentence in 1918 for denouncing U.S. participation in what he deemed an imperialist war.[27]

Once elected, Wilson is presented as instrumental in the passage of a series of progressive laws, such as the Federal Reserve Act and the Clayton Anti-Trust Act, to an accompanying salvo of trumpets! Of course, the limitations of his reform agenda are not discussed, notably his refusal to support federal child-labor legislation and rural credits for farmers. To reassure business, Wilson also appointed conservatives to leading positions in the regulatory agencies created during his presidency, the Federal Reserve and the Federal Trade Commission, prompting novelist John Dos Passos, among others, to denounce him as the tool of the corporations. Few historians would support this bald assessment, but most would characterize the twenty-eighth president as a cautious reformer at best.[28] The Zanuck movie is unconcerned with such nuances because its fundamental focus is on Wilson the Internationalist rather than Wilson the Progressive.

Throughout the first-term section of the film, the incipient concerns about world peace and the Wilsonian position of moral international leadership come increasingly to the fore. In the 1912 campaign, a key Wilson speech introduces his vision for the United States as a world power and protector of human rights. Introduced halfway through the movie, Lodge is shown being unintentionally snubbed by Wilson in his hurry to meet his political aide, Colonel House, who has returned from unspecified business from Europe. This suggests a personal grievance motivated the senator's later truculence over the League of Nations. In reality, if personality issues did foment their political quarrel, both men were equally guilty. While Lodge certainly loathed Wilson, the president felt the same about him. The movie also seeks to rationalize Wilson's conversion from initial belief in neutrality to eventual support for American entry into the war. To this end, he is shown basing his decision to remain neutral after the sinking of the *Lusitania* as necessary to preserve America's ability to define a lasting peace after the hostilities have finished in Europe. The slogan on which Wilson campaigned to win narrow reelection in 1916—"He kept us out of War"—is only referenced once. More significantly, Wilson is shown as increasingly ambivalent about the policy of nonintervention.

The "Public" Wilson: The International Statesman

The film's principal concern comes to the fore with the scene of the German ambassador informing Wilson of his government's decision to renew U-Boat attacks on the U.S. merchant marine. In berating the Kaiser's messenger, Wilson delivers a speech about freedom, justice, and democracy that implicitly links the aggression of Imperial Germany with that of Nazi Germany. Wilson also announces that America's entry into the war shall have a purpose greater than its own security owing to its disinterested ambition of shaping a lasting peace settlement founded on a League of Nations.[29]

The film endorses the real Wilson's belief that visionary and humane internationalism rather than narrow self-interest should shape U.S. foreign policy. This is presented as the core of his disagreement with Lodge. By the final section of the movie, Wilson's determination to secure approval of a treaty without reservations about America's participation in the League of Nations has become his obsession. It develops the image of a leader sacrificing his health for the greater good of seeking to mobilize popular support for his vision of international peace. This sets up a respectful ending that glossed over the reality that presidential refusal to compromise over Article X ultimately condemned the

Versailles Treaty to rejection by the Senate in November 1919. Instead, the celebration of Wilson's hopes for lasting peace in the movie's finale sent domestic audiences a clear message about the value and relevance of his legacy to America and its allies in World War II.

In focusing on Wilson's efforts to get the United States to accept its responsibilities as a great power, the movie suggests that the internationalist cause did not end with his defeat in the battle for the League of Nations. In its narrative of this struggle, the emphasis on international peace, collective security, and the U.S. duty to act as world policeman is intended to underline the contemporary significance of the twenty-eighth president's story. As Trotti wrote to Ray Stannard Baker, the film sought to awaken audiences "to the dangers of indifference, isolation, and reaction, so that the tragedy of the present war which the Wilson dream might have prevented, may never again be permitted to occur."[30]

Critical and Box-office Reception

Zanuck expected *Wilson* to be his finest achievement as a dignified homage to a great man, a paean to world peace, and a box-office success. With top stars and famous politicos in attendance, the premiere took place on August 1, 1944, at the 6,000-seat Roxy Theatre (known as "the cathedral of motion pictures") in New York, an event also broadcast on radio. Zanuck spent a reported $250,000 on the opening, buying up 4,000 radio spot announcements and 35,000 lines of newspaper coverage. He paid $18,000 for a 50 x 75 foot Broadway mural depicting the main scenes of the movie. Some three hundred exhibitors were also invited to attend the premiere that was the opening gambit in a national promotion campaign with a budget of $1.8 billion. Underlining his personal identification with the movie, Zanuck made a triumphant hometown visit to Wahoo, Nebraska, to show it to local dignitaries at a cinema in nearby Omaha.

The contemporary critical response was overwhelmingly stacked in favor of *Wilson*. Almost the only note of criticism centered on its partisanship, with many Republicans accusing it of pro-Democrat bias. More typically, the film drew widespread praise for the quality of the acting, script, direction, and production values. Its message of international cooperation was also well received. *New York Times* reviewer Bosley Crowther declared it the film to stop World War III through its "uncommon dignity...good taste...humour and understanding." *Variety* was particularly effusive in its praise for the production values (including "splendiferous" Technicolor), the impressive crowd scenes, the attention to detail, and a "flawless cast" that included a "newborn star" in Alexander Knox. "The keynote of *Wilson*," it declared, "is authority, warmth, idealism, a search for a better world."[31]

Reflecting its strong critical reception, *Wilson* made it onto several "top ten" films-of-the-year lists. Zanuck had high hopes that it would do well in the 1944 Academy Awards after it received a clutch of nominations, including best picture, best director, and best actor. Knox's award of a Golden Globe from the Hollywood Foreign Press Association seemed a good omen. Even more encouragingly, the Academy's high regard for *Wilson* earned Zanuck its special Irving Thalberg Memorial Award for a second time. However, Twentieth Century Fox's message movie lost out to Paramount's sentimental comedy about two Catholic priests, *Going My Way* (1944), which won Oscars for best picture, best director (Leo McCarey), and best actor (Bing Crosby). *Wilson* did win five Oscars, including best screenplay for Trotti and best color cinematography for Leon Shamroy, but Zanuck was disgusted at its failure to win any of the big three awards for production, direction, and acting. On eventually receiving a best picture Oscar for *Gentleman's Agreement* (1947), the still bitter mogul declared in his acceptance speech, "Many thanks but I should have won it for *Wilson*."[32]

The disappointing outcome of the Academy Awards ceremony in March 1945 denied *Wilson* a much needed box-office fillip. In contrast to its critical reception, the movie was not popular with the American cinema-going public. Poor word-of-mouth regarding its entertainment value, together with regional scepticism about its internationalist message, hurt its cause in the Midwest in particular. Despite the huge promotion budget and large openings on the East and West coasts, where it played to full houses in New York, Los Angeles, and San Francisco, *Wilson* did not resonate with audiences in the American heartland. In only the second night of its run in Omaha, a mere seventy-five members of the paying public bothered to see the film. Zanuck's old family doctor from neighboring Wahoo told him, "Why should you expect people to pay 75¢ to see a movie about Wilson when they wouldn't give 10¢ to see him alive?"[33]

Just before his movie's release, Zanuck had told one reporter that he had made it "for the regular mugs and bobby-sockers, and we don't want them getting the idea that it's highbrow." Despite his best efforts, however, audiences regarded *Wilson* as a message movie rather than entertainment, which limited its box-office appeal. Even

though its release came at a time when Allied military success indicated that the war was close to being won and actually coincided with
the holding in Washington, D.C. of the Dumbarton Oaks conference
that laid the foundations of the United Nations, *Wilson* gained little
from the growing public interest in the shape of the postwar world.
Audience research clearly demonstrated that wartime cinemagoers
wanted movies to entertain rather than enlighten them.[34] Significantly
the biggest grossing film of 1944 was MGM's lavish musical *Meet
Me in St Louis*. Zanuck's movie was further disadvantaged by a War
Department ban on it being shown to U.S. troops on grounds that it
violated the Soldier Voting Act as a work of political propaganda.[35]
Though lasting only a month, this prohibition strengthened popular
perception that *Wilson* was a message movie.

   The biopic did respectable but not spectacular business abroad
where audiences were more receptive to serious films. It made its best
showing in the United Kingdom. While critical of its inaccuracies,
especially pertaining to the 1919 peace treaty negotiations, British
reviewers found much to applaud in the movie. According to the film
critic of the *Times*, *Wilson* "tells at least half the truth, and tells it
honourably, and the League of Nations Union could ask for no more
powerful or persuasive advocate."[36] However, it would have required
truly exceptional foreign box-office returns to make the movie profitable. Ultimately grossing $4,053,000 from a total audience of ten
million, *Wilson* was Fox's second highest earner among 1944 productions behind *Home in Indiana*, a slice of Americana about horse
farms and harness racing. However, this fell well short of paying for
its mammoth costs. *Wilson* ended up a massive $2.2 million in the red
on the Twentieth Century Fox ledger, making it the studio's biggest
loss-maker prior to *Cleopatra* (1963).[37]

A Forgotten Film

Looking back on his career, Zanuck later commented of *Wilson* that
it was the "nearest to my heart…an artistic and sociological success
but a financial failure."[38] Such was his personal distress as the scale
of its commercial flop became evident that he banned any mention of
the film at future Fox meetings and in memos. While the Woodrow
Wilson Foundation produced a special booklet about *Wilson*'s critical reception in the hope that the movie would gain further cinematic
runs, it was shelved in 1945. Even a July 1945 opinion poll ranking

the twenty-eighth president the fifth greatest man in American history could not breathe new life into the market for the film.[39] Except for occasional showings on television, it became a largely forgotten movie, seen only by film historians and other movie enthusiasts in years to come.

In the case of *Wilson*, Zanuck had failed badly in the primary duty of a Hollywood producer—that of "foretelling public taste."[40] Many reasons were advanced as to why the movie was a box-office flop. Zanuck himself later reflected that he should have told Wilson's story through the eyes of his second wife to ensure greater human interest. Others blamed the absence of big stars from the cast or the one-word title that did not truly convey what the film was about (contemporary audience research suggested that 25 percent of moviegoers bought tickets on the appeal of a film's title[41]). Another line of criticism blamed the premature timing of the movie's release that could have awaited the inauguration of the United Nations to enhance its popularity.

More fundamentally, *Wilson* failed to promote a sense of feel-good inspiration in its concern to be portentous. In many ways its commercial failure stemmed from Zanuck's reverential approach to Wilson, his ambitions to make the film a message for world peace, and his hubristic conviction that it would be counted as one of his greatest achievements. The movie often has the feel of a civics lesson with an emphasis on showing great moments from the twenty-eighth president's political history rather than that on human drama and entertainment. Despite Zanuck's attempts to humanize Wilson, his characterization in the movie was stiff, humorless, and bordering on pomposity. Notwithstanding the quality of his Oscar-nominated performance in the lead role, Alexander Knox's brief career as a star never recovered from the debacle.[42]

Before *Wilson*'s release, Zanuck quipped that if it failed he would never make another movie without making blonde, wartime pin-up Betty Grable its star. If he did not actually go this far, the mogul never placed worthiness ahead of profitability in his later films. One casualty of his new realism was his half-formed plan to make a semi-sequel to *Wilson* based on Willkie's *One World*. As had been the case for the real Wilson, the idealist in Zanuck had been beaten down. As two film scholars observed, "On seeing *The Birth of a Nation*, [Woodrow] Wilson had supposedly remarked, 'It is like writing history with lightning.' In *Wilson*, the lightning flirted with history, but struck Hollywood and Darryl F. Zanuck."[43]

Conclusion

Scholarly assessment has been broadly respectful of *Wilson* for its artistic merits and worthy political values. For some analysts the movie had considerable personal resonance because of the positive audience reaction when they first viewed the movie years after its making. Nevertheless, there is also broad agreement that Zanuck's film fails to make Wilson an accessible and appealing figure to contemporary audiences. If the real Wilson was the first president other than Theodore Roosevelt to understand the importance of rhetoric as a tool of presidential leadership, the screen Wilson fails to convey the power of his words to a movie audience—even though (or, perhaps, because) some actual speeches are repeated verbatim. As Michael Coyne commented: "[W]hen it comes to public speechifying, Knox's Wilson...is too cold, stiff and *preachy* to be appealing. The film shares the same problems. Wilson fails to make the grade as a rousing movie hero."[44]

Along with its dramatic credentials, it is instructive to consider how *Wilson* reflected Hollywood's rendition of American exceptionalism and the film industry's role in perpetuating American values internationally. Throughout the various phases of its development, Hollywood has received U.S. government support not only because its dominance in the international marketplace benefits the American economy but also because its films have effectively disseminated American values across the world.[45] With few exceptions, mainstream Hollywood films have presented an idealistic representation of American cultural artifacts to an international audience. Therefore, a film such as *Wilson* reinforces claims of the uniqueness of America's democratic experiment and its consequent idealism in regard to world politics.

While the primary message of the Wilson biopic focuses on its subject's vision for world peace, the subliminal theme depicts this as a reflection of America's democratic exceptionalism and manifest destiny to promote its values. Despite its commercial failure, the Zanuck movie in many ways established a template for Hollywood political films that generally portray America as an exceptional nation and its leaders as men of greatness and vision. This paean to the twenty-eighth president embodies a national mythology that also infuses the populist movies of Frank Capra, the political movies of Oliver Stone, war movies such as Steven Spielberg's *Saving Private Ryan* (1998), and post-9/11 national security movies such as *Syriana* (2005), *Lions for Lambs* (2007), and *Rendition* (2007). Despite their different hues, such films reassert the essential decency of the American character when faced with difficult moral dilemmas. Therefore, *Wilson* has a pivotal role in Hollywood's promotion of an idealistic democratic vision as America's guiding force at home and abroad. It is a movie that early twenty-first-century audiences could benefit from viewing in light of the contemporary debate about the interrelationship between power and idealism in America's wars in Iraq and Afghanistan.

Notes

1. Leonard J. Leff and Jerold Simmons, "*Wilson:* Hollywood Propaganda for World Peace," *Historical Journal of Film, Radio and Television*, 3 (1983): 4. For a synopsis of the movie, see Harry Keyishan, *Screening Politics: The Politician in American Movies, 1931–2001* (Lanham, MD: Scarecrow Press, 2003), 180–3.
2. Wendell Willkie, *One World* (New York: Simon & Schuster, 1943).
3. Thomas J. Knock, "History with Lightning: The Forgotten Film *Wilson* (1944)," *American Quarterly* 28 (1976), reprinted in Peter C. Rollins, ed., *Hollywood as Historian: American Film in a Cultural Context*, rev. ed. (Lexington: University Press of Kentucky, 1998).
4. For biographical detail, see Mel Gussow, *Don't Say Yes Until I Finish Talking: A Biography of Darryl F. Zanuck* (New York: Pocket Books, 1972); Leonard Mosely, *Zanuck: The Rise and Fall of a Hollywood Tycoon* (New York: McGraw-Hill, 1985); and Thomas Thackerey Jr, "Darryl F. Zanuck, Last of the Movie Moguls, Dies at 77," *Los Angeles Times*, December 23, 1979, 1.
5. Joel Finler, "Darryl F. Zanuck: Don't Say Yes Until I Finish Talking," in Ann Lloyd, ed., *Movies of the Sixties*, (London: Book Club Associates, 1984), 41.
6. Norman Zierold, *The Hollywood Tycoons* (London: Hamish Hamilton, 1969), 256–60.
7. Leff and Simmons, "*Wilson:* Hollywood Propaganda for World Peace," 5.
8. Knock, "History with Lightning," 90.
9. For the Zanuck-Willkie relationship, see John B. Wiseman, "Darryl F. Zanuck and the Failure of 'One World,' 1943–1945," *Historical Journal of Radio, Film and Television* 7 (1987): 279–87.
10. Donald E. Staples, "Wilson in Technicolor: An Appreciation," in Peter C. Rollins and John E. O'Connor, eds., *Hollywood's White House: The American Presidency in Film and History* (Lexington: University Press of Kentucky, 2003), 118.
11. Rudy Behlmer, ed., *Memo from Darryl F. Zanuck: The Golden Years at Twentieth Century Fox* (New York: Grove Press, 1993).
12. Leff and Simmons, "*Wilson:* Hollywood Propaganda for World Peace," 4; Chris Fujiwara, *The World and its Double: The Life and Work of Otto Preminger* (London: Faber and Faber, 2008), 26.

13. Gussow, *Don't Say Yes Until I Finish Talking*, 109–10; Behlmer, *Memo from Darryl F. Zanuck*, 77.

14. Leff and Simmons, "*Wilson:* Hollywood Propaganda for World Peace," 5–6.

15. Knock, "History with Lightning," 96; Alexander Knox, "On Playing Wilson," *Hollywood Quarterly*, 1 (1945), 110–11.

16. Knock, "History with Lightning," 101–102.

17. Leff and Simmons, "*Wilson:* Hollywood Propaganda for World Peace," 5–6.

18. Knock, "History with Lightning," 95.

19. Behlmer, *Memo from Darryl F. Zanuck*, 76.

20. Leff and Simmons, "*Wilson:* Hollywood Propaganda for World Peace," 9.

21. For the text of this address, see "Address to a Joint Session of Congress Requesting a Declaration of War against Germany," April 2, 1917, in John T. Woolley and Gerhard Peters, *American Presidency Project* (Santa Barbara: University of California), available at www.presidency. uscb.edu.

22. For historical discussion, see Robert Ferrell, *Woodrow Wilson and World War I, 1917–1921* (New York: Harper & Row, 1980); Lloyd Ambrosius, *Woodrow Wilson and the American Diplomatic Tradition: The Treaty Fight in Perspective* (New York: Cambridge University Press, 1990); and Thomas J. Knock, *To End All Wars: Woodrow Wilson and the Quest for a New World Order* (Princeton, NJ: Princeton University Press, 1992).

23. For an explanation of Lodge's position, see William Widenor, *Henry Cabot Lodge and the Search for an American Foreign Policy* (Berkeley: University of California Press, 1980).

24. Leff and Simmons, "*Wilson:* Hollywood Propaganda for World Peace," 5; Ian Scott, *American Politics in Hollywood Film* (Edinburgh: Edinburgh University Press, 2000), 142.

25. John Milton Cooper, *The Warrior and the Priest: Woodrow Wilson and Theodore Roosevelt* (Cambridge, MA: Belknap Press, 1983); See too Stephen Graubard, *Command of Office: How War, Security, and Deception Transformed the Presidency from Theodore Roosevelt to George W. Bush* (New York: Basic Books, 2004), chapter 6; Peri Arnold, *Remaking the Presidency: Roosevelt, Taft and Wilson, 1901–1916* (Lawrence: University Press of Kansas, 2009).

26. The president's racial attitudes are thoroughly discussed in John Milton Cooper, *Woodrow Wilson: A Biography* (New York: Knopf, 2009). For African American reaction, see W.E.B. Dubois, "Another Open Letter to Woodrow Wilson," *The Crisis* (September 1913), http://teachingamericanhistory.org.

27. James Chace, *1912: Wilson, Taft, Roosevelt and Debs: The Election that Changed the Country* (New York: Simon & Schuster, 2004). Wilson denounced Debs as a traitor for his antiwar speeches that were deemed to

have obstructed military recruiting under the terms of the Espionage Act of 1917. When the conflict was over, an unforgiving president rejected his attorney general's recommendation that the ailing sixty-five-year-old Debs be released. Wilson's successor Warren Harding finally set him free on Christmas day, 1921. See Howard Zinn, "Eugene V. Debs and the Idea of Socialism," *The Progressive* (January 1999), http://www.third-worldtraveler.com.

28. John Dos Passos, *USA*: Vol. 2: *1919* (Boston: Mariner Books, 1919). For Wilson the reformer, see Richard Hofstader, *The American Political Tradition and the Men Who Made It* (New York: Knopf, 1948); and John M. Blum, *The Progressive Presidents: Theodore Roosevelt, Woodrow Wilson, Franklin D. Roosevelt, Lyndon B. Johnson* (New York: Norton, 1980).

29. Interestingly, there is no mention of the so-called Zimmerman telegram that the German government sent to Mexico on February 25, 1917. This promised Mexico significant territorial gains in New Mexico and Arizona if it joined the war on the side of Germany. It was undoubtedly a factor in Wilson's decision to go to war. The omission may have reflected Zanuck's intent to present Wilson as an international idealist standing above narrow concerns of defensive security. It may also have been influenced by commercial calculation—Mexico and Latin America had become more significant markets for American movies because the war had closed off a significant portion of the European market.

30. Knock, "History with Lightning," 99.

31. Bosley Crowther, "'Wilson': An Impressive Screen Biography, in Which Alex. Knox is the Star, has Its World's Premiere at the Roxy," *New York Times*, August 2, 1944, http://www.movies.nytimes.com/review; *Variety* Staff, "Wilson," *Variety*, August 10, 1944, http://www.variety.com/review.

32. Knock, "History with Lightning," 89.

33. Gussow, *Don't Say Yes Until I Finish Talking*, 119–20.

34. Leo A. Handel, *Hollywood Looks At its Audience: A Report on Film Audience Research* (Urbana: University of Illinois Press, 1950), 170.

35. "Army Bans Wilson as a Film for Troops," *New York Times*, August 1, 1944, 1.

36. "*Wilson*," *Times* (London), January 4, 1945, 6.

37. Leff and Simmons, "*Wilson*: Hollywood Propaganda for World Peace," 11.

38. Behlmer, *Memo from Darryl F. Zanuck*, 78.

39. Geoffrey Perrett, *Days of Sadness, Years of Triumph: The American People, 1939–1945* (New York: Putnam, 1973), 236.

40. Finler, "Darryl F. Zanuck," 41.

41. Handel, *Hollywood Looks at its Audience*, 36.

42. Subsequently, Knox returned to Hollywood character roles but was later blacklisted as a result of the House Committee of Un-American Activities

investigation into communist influence in the film industry. He returned
to the United Kingdom to become a supporting actor in British films and
television programs. Knox again played a U.S. president, on this occasion a fictional one, in the James Bond film *You Only Live Twice* (1967).
Zanuck also hired him once more to play the small role of General Bedell
Smith in his D-Day epic, *The Longest Day* (1962). For his obituary, see
"Alexander Knox, 88, Actor Who Played Woodrow Wilson," *New York
Times*, April 29, 1995.
43. Wiseman, "Darryl F. Zanuck and the Failure of 'One World,' 1943–45,"
    281–287; Leff and Simmons, "*Wilson:* Hollywood Propaganda for
    World Peace," 15.
44. Michael Coyne, *Hollywood Goes to Washington: American Politics on
    Screen* (London: Reaktion Books, 2008), 61; emphasis in the original.
45. Mark Wheeler, *Hollywood: Politics and Society* (London: British Film
    Institute, 2006), 163.

Chapter 5

The "Confidence" President:
Franklin D. Roosevelt in Film

Harry Keyishian

A newspaper cartoon from the first hundred days of the Roosevelt administration, which is on prominent display at the Franklin D. Roosevelt Presidential Library and Museum in Hyde Park, New York, portrays FDR as the engineer of a train called "US Recovery 'New Deal' Special." Strong-jawed and determined, the new president looks boldly down the tracks before him. His left hand, encased in thick railroad gloves, is on the lever, while his right is clenched for action. With Uncle Sam cheering him on from trackside, a confident FDR looks ready to drive that train right out of the Great Depression.

Confidence, as this sketch indicated, was from the start the defining theme of Franklin D. Roosevelt's presidency. If, as he famously asserted in his first inaugural address, "the only thing we have to fear is fear itself," then all the challenges facing the United States could be overcome by tackling them boldly. Other presidents stressed the same theme, of course. Theodore Roosevelt used it to promote national and personal self-reliance; John F. Kennedy claimed to embody a new generation of leadership born in the twentieth century and ready to "pay any price" in the name of liberty; Ronald Reagan's "morning in America" slogan associated his presidency with national renewal; Bill Clinton touted himself as "the man from Hope"; and Barack Obama carried the day with the slogan "Yes, we can." However, confidence was the most characteristic and fundamental leitmotif in the leadership success of the thirty-second president, whom scholars conventionally rank among the three greatest holders of the office in American history.[1]

The confidence mantra worked in different ways at different times for Roosevelt. This essay explores its various manifestations in cinematic depictions of him both during his lifetime and since his death in 1945. Films that are about FDR, or reflect his personality, are—like all presidential movies—also about their own times, using his iconic figure to shed light on contemporary events and problems. In this regard it is no accident that motion pictures featuring Abraham Lincoln were especially popular during the Great Depression, perhaps more so than at any other time. This embodied the enduring appeal of his belief in the nation's capacity for renewal to Americans facing the economic and social crisis of the 1930s. Roosevelt's presence in cinema has proven just as durable in finding applications during later times when America faced very different challenges from those of his era.

The first stage in the evolution of FDR's cinematic image was not about him at all. It was an imagined person created in the last months of Herbert Hoover's administration, based not on any real individual but on yearning for vigorous leadership in Washington amid the palpable failure of business and government to deal with the severest economic crisis in the nation's history. Several popular films made in 1931–34 pictured presidential "strong men" willing to suspend the Constitution and act unilaterally to solve America's problems in a bold and decisive manner.

In its second phase, the movie Roosevelt elaborated on the personality and policies of the real FDR to portray him as a vital, confident, and highly active president, one with big ideas for the country's future and expressing special concern for the poor and disadvantaged—in his own phrase, "the forgotten man." With his cocky smile, raised chin, and a cigarette holder held in his teeth at a jaunty angle, Roosevelt provided the face of optimism that America could overcome the economic problems of the Depression. With the onset of World War II, movies adapted this image to represent or reference him as an inspirational commander-in-chief, frank about the need for sacrifice but firm in his belief in ultimate victory.

With America enjoying prosperity and preeminence in the years after FDR's death, the historical significance of his transformative leadership in the crucible of depression and war became manifest. At the same time, there was growing awareness of his polio-related disability, which the media had colluded in shrouding during his presidency. Melding these two strands of his story, the most significant movie representation of Roosevelt in the postwar era, *Sunrise at Campobello* (1960), focused on his struggle to deal with the personal crisis of his illness in the early 1920s in order to fulfill his destiny to lead America at a time of great national crisis in the 1930s and 1940s.

Backlash against Lyndon Johnson's Great Society and the incapacity of Keynesian economics to deal with stagflation undermined the New Deal legacy in the 1970s and beyond. Growing skepticism about big government also coincided with cynicism about presidential trustworthiness in the wake of Vietnam and Watergate. Nevertheless, Hollywood continued to depict FDR in inspirational mode during this age of uncertainty. In *The Way We Were* (released October 1973), the devotion to the Roosevelt ethos that marks the radicalism of its fictional heroine stands in marked contrast to popular disillusion with Richard Nixon as his presidency tottered toward destruction. In more direct fashion, the musical *Annie!* (1982) revived the image of FDR as a visionary and compassionate national leader at a time when American government was floundering in the face of the new economic crisis of stagflation.

Finally, in a series of films about World War II—usually large-scale, epic affairs—FDR makes cameo appearances as a strong national leader, shrewd, sagacious, and determined, whose conquest of his physical disability was a strength—and an important element of his heroism—rather than a weakness. His greatness is understood to have dwelt in his will, his heart, and his unshakeable determination in the face of challenge.

A Savior Sought

In the last months of Herbert Hoover's administration (1929–33), many Americans called for drastic and extraordinary action to deal with the worsening economic depression. The key problems were the interrelated calamities of a collapsed stock market, rising unemployment, and a banking crisis. Constrained by outdated orthodoxies, government had only made matters worse in its response to these developments. The Federal Reserve helped to precipitate and then perpetuate the downturn through its overly restrictive monetary policy; Congress enacted highly protectionist trade measures to boost domestic industry but this only undermined the entire international economy; and—driven by concern about the rising budget deficit—Hoover's shift in 1932 from hesitant economic activism to fiscal restraint flattened already weak consumer demand. Of course, Roosevelt himself lacked effective solutions to set the economy right. Even after eight years of the New Deal, the nation's economic output had still not regained its 1929 level by 1940. Nevertheless, FDR's willingness to experiment in pursuit of recovery and his mastery of political communication sustained the nation's confidence that prosperity would eventually return.[2]

The new president's immediate challenge was to restore confidence in the banking system that had tottered to the verge of collapse in the interregnum between his election victory on November 8, 1932, and his inauguration on March 4, 1933. Especially harmful were the runs on banks by panicky depositors, fearful that the failure of these establishments would obliterate their savings. Roosevelt directly and dramatically confronted the crisis by declaring a temporary bank holiday on March 5, the day after taking his oath of office. New legislation was then rushed through Congress to lay down regulations that restored confidence in the banking system. These decisive initiatives reassured the public that America's leaders were getting to grips with the crisis. As influential political commentator Walter Lippmann noted, "In one week, the nation, which had lost confidence in everything and everybody, has regained confidence in the government and itself."[3]

Frank Capra's film *American Madness* (released August 1932) offers a melodramatic perspective on the developing bank crisis—it is a bank robbery that causes the panic, not economic conditions in general—but it brilliantly dramatizes the hysteria of depositors rioting to get their money out. The day is saved by heroic bank president Thomas Dickson (Walter Huston) who rescues his bank by investing his own money in it (somewhat like the real J.P. Morgan in the Banker's Panic of 1907). Anticipating the fictional George Bailey in the same director's *It's A Wonderful Life* (1947), the protagonist explains to depositors that the money a bank possesses does not reside in the building, but in its investments—in particular, its investments in the good character of those to whom it lends money. As he puts is, "Character is the only thing you can bank on." Faith therefore solves the problem and a strong leader who can inspire confidence saves the day.

As Roosevelt's biographer Kenneth S. Davis observes, the national mood in the weeks prior to his inauguration "had running through it a broad streak of messianic authoritarianism…a longing for the Leader, the Messiah in whom a passionate communal faith could be invested and who would take responsibility for everything."[4] A host of influential voices urged the new president to take whatever actions were needed without heed to constitutional restraint. Comparing the government's task with that of wartime emergency, FDR's predecessor both as New York governor and Democratic presidential nominee, Alfred E. Smith, urged that the nation's supreme law be "laid…on the shelf and left…there" for the duration of the crisis. However, Roosevelt lacked the inclination to exploit such expectations for the sake of power. Retaining faith in the ideals of Thomas Jefferson, he strove instead to achieve what one contemporary scholar called "a working balance between liberty and equality, the basic concepts of democracy."[5]

In contrast to Roosevelt, a number of Hollywood movies depicted a strong president drastically expanding his executive power to deal unilaterally—with, without, or against the consent of Congress—to alleviate the Depression and other social ills. *Gabriel Over the White House*, which premiered four weeks after FDR's inauguration, featured a president—Judd Hammond (also played by Walter Huston)—possessed by the spirit of the Angel Gabriel. Prior to this metamorphosis, he is no more than a genial political hack, awaiting the orders of his (unnamed) party before initiating any action or declaring any policy. The heavenly possession is dramatized in a scene in which Hammond, lying near death after a car accident—he has driven recklessly, his vehicle as out of control as the nation's economy—rests in his hospital bed. The curtains of his room rustle and a mysterious breeze floats toward him to signal divine intervention. Immediately the puppet president is transformed into a wise, thoughtful, and bold leader, one capable of setting the nation on course to salvation.

Hammond initiates a series of actions to deal with two national problems. One is organized crime, centralized in the figure of a gangster named Diamond (seemingly a reference to recently convicted racketeer, Jack "Legs" Diamond). The other is unemployment, symbolized by a march on Washington by World War I veterans (reminiscent of the "bonus" army of 1932 that sought financial redress, only to be forcibly dispersed, on Hoover's orders, by military troops under the command of General Douglas MacArthur). Hammond suspends the Constitution, fires the Cabinet, and overrides a resistant Congress to declare a "Jeffersonian dictatorship." Armed with new powers, he destroys organized crime, repudiates national treaties, compels foreign nations to pay their war debts, and establishes world peace. Though some at the time objected to the film's message—*The Nation* said that it was an attempt "to convert American movie audiences to a policy of fascist dictatorship"—it was a great success at the box office and satisfied many as a fable of national redemption.[6] FDR saw the film several times and judged it "intensely interesting" in a letter to newspaper magnate William Randolph Hearst, who had helped develop the project and actually wrote some of the speeches delivered by Hammond. The real president further declared that the reel one's message "should do much to help."[7]

In *The President Vanishes* (released November 1934), an American president defeats the plans of a fascist war lobby by vanishing mysteriously, thereby galvanizing public opinion in his favor and permitting him to take extraordinary executive action to prevent military conflict being fomented by the arms industry. In *The Cat's Paw* (released

August 1934), the son of missionaries (played by Harold Lloyd) applies the wisdom of an Oriental sage to the political problems of a corrupt American city. Overriding the courts, he stages a series of faked beheadings that terrorize local politicians into confessing their crimes and returning their ill-gotten gains. "I'll confess to anything," cries one panicked victim.

Roosevelt's Jeffersonian ideals prevented him taking up in real life the role created for him by these allegorical films. Nevertheless, there was significant juxtaposition between presidential politics and presidential motion pictures in the early New Deal era in spite of their divergence over leadership methods. As film historian Michael Coyne notes, each fulfilled "the mythic ethos and expectation cardinal to both Hollywood movies and American presidential campaigns—that one man, the right man, truly *can* make all the difference and ensure the triumph of virtue."[8]

Of course, the broad acceptance of FDR's strong leadership in the Washington of 1933 ultimately gave way in his second term to conservative suspicion that he was intent on unconstitutional usurpation of power. In particular, the Supreme Court packing plan of 1937 to circumvent judicial opposition to the New Deal raised fears among conservatives that Roosevelt was threatening the separation of powers. In contrast, Hollywood never bought into this more negative view of FDR. Despite abandoning its initial flirtation with quasi-dictatorial strong men, particularly as concern grew about real-life foreign dictators Adolph Hitler and Benito Mussolini, the movie industry continued to portray Roosevelt as hero, savior, and fount of national confidence throughout the remainder of the Depression decade.

FDR, Movie Star, and the Great Depression

In the words of one analyst, Roosevelt's dour, dispirited predecessor, Herbert Hoover, "invariably...appeared solemn and sad, an unhappy man, a man without hope." In contrast, FDR was immediately a media star thanks to his "vibrant cinematic personality." Quick to exploit his charisma, he flooded screens with his exuberant, virile image that was perfectly suited to the development of his "Newsreel Presidency." Until Roosevelt, *Variety* remarked, "no chief executive in the recollection of newsreel men has possessed all the screen qualifications."[9] Primarily remembered as the first "radio president" because of his Fireside Chats, FDR was also fully aware of the significance of newsreels and looked to control his image in this medium as much as he did in still photographs of him. To this end White House press officer Stephen Early laid down guidelines to Hollywood studios preventing the use of newsreel shots of FDR in fiction films.[10]

Much of Hollywood was quick to support the new president in his image-management. Studio boss Jack Warner, in particular, displayed an "abiding faith in the words and works of [FDR, who] became an invaluable plot device, a way to rescue [topical films] from their own bleak implications, an unseen sheriff cleaning up the town."[11] In the Warner Bros. film *Heroes for Sale* (released in June 1933), Great War veteran Tom Holmes, having endured a series of personal and social disasters, joins a workers' movement to find redemption and a new life. He concludes, "Did you read President Roosevelt's inaugural address? I cut it out of the newspaper yesterday, and the more I think about it, the more I realize that...it takes more than one sock in the jaw to lay out 120 million people" These lines of dialogue were a change from the original script. Studio vice president Darryl F. Zanuck, who was responsible for their insertion, thought that the film would benefit dramatically from linking itself to Roosevelt. As he reasoned, it was better for Tom to be referencing FDR's words because "we can believe that the President could be a prophet but it is hard for us to believe that a down and out bum could be a prophet."[12] In like vein, MGM's *Looking Forward* (released in April 1933), in which the main character (played by Lionel Barrymore) fights to keep open a family department store in the Depression, took its name from a compilation of Roosevelt articles and campaign speeches, published the previous month and now riding high in the *New York Times* best-seller list. Having gone through several working titles beforehand, the movie establishes its links to FDR's words and spirit by quoting from his book in its opening credits: "We need enthusiasm, imagination and ability to face facts—we need the courage of the young."[13]

The Disney cartoon *Confidence* (released July 1933) also used the Roosevelt image to develop an upbeat message for economic hard times. Directed by Walter Lantz and Bill Nolan and running under eight minutes, it featured Oswald the Rabbit, an early cartoon favorite. The film depicts a happy, productive farm, populated mainly by dancing chickens that regularly lay eggs, are content in their work, and take pride in their productivity. One night, however, the farm, and the world in general, is invaded by the ghastly specter, "Depression." Next morning, the cock cannot crow, the chickens are listless, and all production ceases. In a parallel action, panicked depositors are withdrawing their money from banks and sticking it under their mattresses. Seeking medical help for his sickly charges, Oswald is told by his physician, who points to a poster of FDR, "He's your doctor." At this, the cartoon hero flies to Washington to visit the president in the White House. Asked what is to be done about the nation's ills, FDR strides out from behind his Oval Office desk and bursts into cheery song. The opening line is "Confidence—can lick this whole depression," and the word "confidence" becomes a constant refrain in the ditty. In the corner of the president's office stands an entire barrel of "Confidence" medicine, from which Oswald extracts a full syringe (figure 5.1). On his return home, Oswald sprinkles the now padlocked local bank with the elixir of FDR's "Confidence," with the effect that depositors come rushing back with their cash, in bags and wheelbarrows. Back on the farm, he injects all his animals with this potion, instantly restoring them to vitality and productivity.[14]

Perhaps the most spectacular "Roosevelt scene" in movies of the early 1930s—certainly the one most celebrated today—occurs in the Warner Bros. backstage musical *Footlight Parade* (released in October 1933). In the final "Shanghai Lil" dance sequence, staged by Busby Berkeley, James Cagney (directing as well as performing in the show in his role as Chester Kent) is reunited with his love, Ruby Keeler,

Figure 5.1   Confidence: FDR explains what America needs to get out of the depression in "Confidence."

while a troupe of sailors holds up flash cards that, on one side, form an American flag and then, flipped over, form the face of FDR. The group then reassembles in the form of the Blue Eagle symbol of the National Recovery Administration, the mainstay of the early New Deal's anti-Depression program, as the sailors fire their rifles. The brilliantly staged and shot sequence perfectly captures a cumulative mood of national success and victory as the finale of a movie about showbiz triumph over adversity. Significantly, preproduction notes show that this was shot and added after the film was finished to capitalize on FDR's immense popularity. Later film historians have also seen the movie as deliberately portraying the James Cagney/Chester Kent character "as a surrogate for FDR, a strong director leading the 'little people' in the chorus into the order and success of the completed show."[15]

Later in the 1930s, the Roosevelt image was implicitly if not literally conveyed through the character of a "government man" who intervenes to help people in distress.[16] Frank Capra's films in particular are cited as offering a "metaphorical God" who stands in for FDR. As one analyst put it, "Roosevelt is the presiding spirit…, admonishing injustice and encouraging righteous belief, never more so than in the Vice President's (Harry Carey) kindly and encouraging attitude toward Senator [Jefferson] Smith through the climactic filibuster scene (of *Mr. Smith Goes to Washington*, 1939)."[17] The image of government as benign—the last, best friend of the downtrodden—was another element of FDR's broad cinematic motif. This was notably conveyed in *The Grapes of Wrath* (released in March 1940), which was based on the novel by John Steinbeck. It tells the story of the Joads, whose failure to maintain mortgage payments leads to bank repossession of their Oklahoma farm. Embarking on an optimistic but hazardous journey to a new life in California, the family finds its only refuge at a government-run camp for work-seeking migrants.

Some have suggested that Roosevelt stands behind the Great Oz in *The Wizard of Oz* (released in August 1939). Morris Dickstein sees in the film the "collective energy" of Depression America, reflected in the fact that the heroine, Dorothy, can get home to Kansas "only by working with others who also need help"—the Lion, the Tin Man, and the Scarecrow—but who simultaneously manifest the qualities FDR was trying to instill: "courage to face up to the social crisis, empathy for the sufferings of others, a break with past thinking about how we ought to live." The Wizard is in one sense a fake—a good man, but a very bad wizard, he admits—but in another, as a stand-in for FDR, he manages to convince Dorothy and her friends that "they already have [the powers they need] within themselves. By working together, they discovered their own strength and found their own home."[18] As in films that are more overtly "Roosevelt movies," therefore, faith and confidence win the day.

The Commander-in-Chief

When war came, a different note was required. The "day that will live in infamy" speech that FDR made to Congress on December 8, 1941, after the Japanese bombing of Pearl Harbor, set the United States on a course of determined retaliation and national mobilization against foreign foes. But the note of confidence remained an essential focus in facing up to this new crisis. In his Fireside Chat of February 23, 1942, FDR struck a fiery note in response to the perception that Americans were too spoiled and rich to fight a war:

> From Berlin, Rome, and Tokyo we have been described as a nation of weaklings—"playboys"—who would hire British soldiers, or Russian soldiers, or Chinese soldiers to do our fighting for us. Let them repeat that now! Let them tell that to General MacArthur and his men. Let them tell that to the sailors who today are hitting hard in the far waters of the Pacific. Let them tell that to the boys in the Flying Fortresses. Let them tell that to the Marines![19]

In the patriotic epic *Yankee Doodle Dandy* (released in June 1942), FDR invites entertainer and impresario George M. Cohan, memorably played by James Cagney, to the White House amid the run of the political satire *I'd Rather Be Right* (book by Lorenz Hart and George S. Kaufman, music by Richard Rodgers). The real Cohan, a fierce critic of the New Deal, played a dancing, singing FDR who takes time from balancing the budget to deal with the problems of a young couple unable to get married because of economic conditions. The stage FDR frets, "I'm really quite a hero. I only have to say, 'My friends...,' and stocks go down to zero," and confesses, "The trouble with the country is that I don't know what the trouble with the country is."

Worried that the president has taken offense, Cohan is surprised instead to be presented with the Congressional Medal of Honor for his musical contributions to the American spirit in World War I through his songs such as *Over There* and *Grand Old Flag*. Cohan protests, "This medal is for people who have given their lives for the country or done something big. I'm just a song-and-dance man." Roosevelt replies that a man may serve his country in many ways, not least by penning songs that inspire patriotism. He continues: "Today we're all soldiers. We're all on the front. We need more songs to express America." The president is seen from behind his desk, his features never clearly glimpsed but his resonant voice is reproduced by actor Art Gilmore. In this representation, he speaks to a nation at war about its identity and values, and the expression of national spirit in a confident song like *Over There* about America's ability to take on and finish a hard job—"we won't come back till it's over over there"— both for itself and for the world at large.

Roosevelt also made cameo appearances in his commander-in-chief role in films made during World War II. He was played by Canadian actor Jack Young in such movies as *Action in the North Atlantic* (released June 1943), *This is the Army* (released August 1943), and *Up in Arms* (released February 1944). Whether he appears as an actual character or merely in a photographic image in these films, his confidence-inducing demeanor continues to manifest itself. As a sailor in *Action in the North Atlantic* avows, "I got faith in God, President Roosevelt, and the Brooklyn Dodgers, in the order of their importance."

Personal Heroism: Conquering Polio

When Franklin Roosevelt died on April 12, 1945, with the Allies on the brink of victory in Europe, the nation lost the man who had led it for twelve years through economic depression and world war. Having no real historical memory of any other president, many Americans could not imagine what life would be like without him at the helm. Testifying to this sense of his everlastingness, a character in Preston Sturges's *Palm Beach Story* (1941) had quipped, "Nothing is permanent in this world except Roosevelt, dear." As the nation moved on under the leadership of Harry Truman, it faced new challenges. Eleanor Roosevelt, always an important element of FDR's presidency when traveling on his behalf and her own for the worthiest causes and acting as his eyes and ears on the world, now became the focal point of remembrance of her husband. After the war, she served as the nation's first ambassador to the United Nations, the organization that Roosevelt had played the essential role in creating, and spoke out on issues of world peace and nuclear disarmament. To ardent New Dealers such as playwright and film producer Dore Schary, Eleanor Roosevelt represented FDR's legacy in a prosperous post-1945 America that bore onerous responsibility for ensuring the emergence of a better world from global conflict.

Partly to support Eleanor Roosevelt in this role, Schary wrote the play *Sunrise at Campobello* in 1958. In this, FDR's polio—downplayed during his presidency—became the focal point of his heroism and dedication to serve his nation. After the play's successful Broadway run, Schary produced a film (released in September 1960) that expanded the action to present a pre-polio Roosevelt (Ralph Bellamy) playing actively with his children at the family vacation residence on Campobello Island in Maine. At this juncture, FDR can look forward to a glittering political career on the basis of his noteworthy campaign for vice president in what otherwise had been for Democrats the woeful election of 1920. When his illness manifests itself, and its full extent and irreversibility become clear, the narrative settles into a struggle between the future president's mother, Sara Roosevelt (Anne Shoemaker), who wishes her wheelchair-bound son to abandon public life, and his wife, Eleanor (Greer Garson), and advisor, Louis Howe (Hume Cronyn), who encourage and empower him to resume his political career. For them, FDR's illness is a test rather than an obstacle. Eleanor says, "God takes man into deep waters not to drown him but to cleanse him." FDR, admitting "deep, sick despair" in the early days of his disease, comes to conclude that it must have a deeper purpose: "I feel I must go through this trial for some reason."

Roosevelt admits that a lesson in humility was perhaps essential. "I was snobbish, haughty," he says of his early days, "a mean cuss." ("Never mean," answers Eleanor; "perhaps inexperienced.") Now—morbidly afraid of being trapped by fire at home and unable to escape when on his own—he declares, "I've been learning by crawling." Indeed, much depends on Roosevelt's efforts to strengthen his upper body, required both to crawl at home and—essential to his image—to stand in public, projecting the appearance of mobility. Despite his mother's efforts to infantilize him, FDR gives himself over to the task of becoming a spiritually and physically stronger person.

To forward her husband's career, Eleanor overcomes her personal shyness and public awkwardness to deliver political speeches to Democratic women's groups. Meanwhile Howe keeps FDR's name alive within the political establishment, positioning him to advance to the governorship of New York and then the American presidency. In one of the film's key scenes, this trusted adviser mocks William Ernest Henley's banal poem *Invictus*, but then drops into serious register to deliver its stirring closing lines—"I am the master of my fate: I am the captain of my soul"—as a message to Roosevelt and to forward their mutual enterprise.

The heart of the film—as it was of the stage version—is a scene in which FDR, after a bruising argument with his mother about his future, shuts the doors of his room to all, even Louis Howe and Eleanor, in order to test and build his strength. He deliberately drops from his wheelchair onto the floor and then repeatedly struggles his way back into it, using only the strength of his arms and upper body. We are to understand that this determined exertion was his silent and private struggle to make himself strong enough in spirit and physique to endure the challenges that lay ahead.

Roosevelt's values are introduced by references to causes that continued to echo in the late 1950s and early 1960s. His internationalism is certified by a letter from Woodrow Wilson—champion of the League of Nations—thanking him for his concern about world peace and order. His lack of religious prejudice is illuminated in his dismissal of those viewing Al Smith's Catholicism as a bar to national office, a scene that had contemporary relevance in relation to John F. Kennedy's upcoming run for the presidency. The influence of Eleanor is manifest, as she urges her husband to "pursue principle without calculating consequences."

At the same time, FDR is a canny shaper of his own image and political career. In one episode, when he must leave Campobello Island for medical treatment on the mainland, he contrives to get secretly to a waiting train by bypassing inquiring reporters. In real life, by contrast, reporters and photographers knew of, but deliberately suppressed information on, his physical status. FDR and Howe maneuver an invitation from New York governor Al Smith to deliver his nominating speech in his unsuccessful bid to become the Democratic Party's presidential candidate in 1924. The film ends with Roosevelt's mastering of the braces and crutches he needed in making the walk to the national convention podium (with his son at his side) to deliver the "Happy Warrior" address that would burnish his own ambitions of high office. This climax may puzzle those seeing the movie in the twenty-first century. However, it was not necessary to dramatize what followed 1924 for audiences of the early 1960s—including Roosevelt's election as governor of New York in 1928 and as U.S. president in 1932. This was history to which most Americans still felt close.[20]

Late Nostalgia for the New Deal

In the 1960s Lyndon Johnson's Great Society program completed the outstanding agenda of the New Deal and took liberalism in new directions through its concern to promote racial equality and eradicate poverty.[21] In the following decade, however, reaction against the new socioeconomic reforms and disillusion that government could not cure an ailing economy engendered a vigorous conservative movement that looked to roll back Roosevelt's legacy. The assault on the New Deal had started in the disastrous but portentous 1964 presidential campaign of Republican candidate Barry Goldwater, who attacked it as a counterproductive government intrusion against free enterprise and personal liberty. The economic woes of the 1970s brought new legitimacy to conservative claims that the state was a hindrance not a help to the development of prosperity. This viewpoint found its most famous expression in Ronald Reagan's 1981 inaugural address declaration that fundamentally challenged the New Deal ethos: "Government is not the solution to our problems. Government is the problem."[22]

Nevertheless, some self-consciously nostalgic films sought to show what Roosevelt meant and represented in his time. In *The Way We Were*, directed by Sydney Pollack, FDR is the inspiration for the idealism of radical activist Katie Morosky (Barbara Streisand). Though never seen, he is a perpetual presence in the movie. Devoted to his legacy, Katie is in constant conflict with the conservative circle of her husband, Hubbell Gardner (Robert Redford). Many of its members are Roosevelt haters, who bandy about "Eleanor jokes" and sneering references to FDR as "The Yaltese Falcon" because of concessions he made to the Soviet Union at the 1945 Yalta conference with Winston Churchill and Joseph Stalin. Katie's stout defense of both Roosevelts marks her off absolutely from her husband's WASP world. Seemingly lacking any ideals of his own, even conservative ones, Gardner complains that she cares too much about the causes in which she believes: "When you love someone, from Roosevelt to me, you go deaf, dumb, and blind." This was a movie made early in the 1970s "me decade," a self-centered spirit that the Redford character embodies.[23] At one level, therefore, it presents FDR as a symbol of an antique, if admirable, idealism that has lost relevance for all but a few true believers like Katie. On the other hand, the film's obvious sympathies for the Streisand character convey a message that the loss of the Rooseveltian ethos has diminished America and undermined its moral purpose.

Nostalgia also permeates the Great Depression-set *Annie!* (released in June 1982). The heroine of Harold Gray's *Little Orphan Annie* cartoon strip—also a long-running radio program—was a plucky red-haired waif, accompanied by her dog Sandy, who held her own in orphanages and on the streets and had adventures with pirates and criminals. She also benefits at times from the support and guardianship of the fabulously wealthy Oliver Warbucks. Cartoonist Gray was a fierce opponent of New Deal, so it is ironic that the 1977 Broadway musical *Annie* (book by Thomas Meehan, lyrics by Martin Chamin, music by Charles Strouse) presented Warbucks as a friend of Roosevelt and ultimately a supporter of his programs. In the film version, *Annie!* (note the enthusiastic exclamation point), directed by John Huston, the heroine is plucked from her orphanage as a holiday gesture by the Warbucks household in an attempt to spruce up its patriarch's negative image as a hard-hearted plutocrat. Annie soon endears herself to and becomes indispensable to her new benefactors and then to Warbucks himself, who is charmed by her feisty independence.

The stage musical was developed at a time when America was facing its worst economic problems since the Great Depression. The old industrial heartland underwent a process of partial deindustrialization as traditional manufacturing jobs began to be shipped overseas. The nation's increased dependence on foreign oil also exposed it to energy shortages and the end of cheap gasoline. Meanwhile government seemed incapable of addressing the new problem of "stagflation," an unprecedented combination of severe inflation and low economic growth. Federal Reserve determination to choke off price instability through monetary tightening also produced three recessions in 1974–75, 1980, and 1981–82. *Annie!* was released when the last and most severe of these downturns was at full tilt.[24] It is no wonder, therefore, that cinema audiences were ready to see and identify with a musical about economic conditions in 1933!

Having first-hand experience of economic hardship through her own days in the orphanage, Annie prevails upon Warbucks to introduce her to the president and first lady. When FDR (played by Edward Hermann) asks her advice about how to handle the Great Depression, Annie replies that the nation's morale must be sustained by giving it faith in the future. To this end, she sings for Roosevelt the song that cheered her up in her orphanage days and now speaks to his efforts to uplift national confidence. Its opening line—"The sun will come out tomorrow"—perfectly epitomizes the universal hope for a better future.

Looking to make a New Dealer out of the self-described devotee of "money and power and capitalism," FDR tries to enlist Annie's guardian to work for the government. An appalled Warbucks responds in the voice of the contemporary New Right that the state is harmful to free enterprise, the essential source of prosperity: "The New Deal is badly organized. You don't think your programs through...you don't think what they're going to do to the economy in the long run." In an obvious reference to economist John Maynard Keynes's famous dictum against future-oriented caution amid present-day crisis ("In the long run, we're all dead"), FDR responds, "People can't think 'in the long run.'" Eleanor chimes in, "They have to feed their children. The lucky ones end up in orphanages; the older ones are abandoned in the field to starve." FDR touts the Works Progress Administration that marked his administration's efforts to provide relief jobs for unemployed workers while contributing to national infrastructure: "I want to feed them and house them and pay them—not much but enough...so that they hold their heads up again and be proud to be Americans."

While Annie thinks FDR's plan is "swell," Warbucks still calls it "mistaken foolishness," "big-hearted" but "empty headed." "Who's going to run it?" he asks. Roosevelt responds, "I was hoping you would." Soon enough, with Annie's enthusiastic support, Warbucks has been enlisted to organize the effort. FDR then turns to Annie to handle morale: "You can help me recruit the young people...Many of them have given up hope, Annie. They think that government doesn't care whether they live or die." Annie will inspire the young to make the extra effort to raise themselves from poverty and to dream of better days—the cue, of course, for a reprise of "The Sun Will Come Out Tomorrow." As ever in the Roosevelt saga, it is attitude that comes to the rescue, the conviction that individuals already have within them the capacity to survive.

The War President Once More

Roosevelt makes cameo appearances in many later films, both American and foreign.[25] Arguably his most significant appearance was in *Pearl Harbor* (2000). He was played to generally very good reviews by Jon Voight, an actor who had personally journeyed from radicalism in the Vietnam era of his youth to conservative Republicanism in his later years.[26] A commercially very successful blockbuster, the movie showed little concern with historical accuracy in portraying the events prior and subsequent to the Japanese attack that brought America into World War II. Within a short time of its release in May 2001, however, the 9/11 attacks on New York and Washington signaled a new day of infamy with historical parallels to Pearl Harbor.

In this context, FDR's principal scene in the 2001 movie could be seen anew as a defiant statement of America's determination to hit back at its attackers (figure 5.2). In the wake of the Japanese air strike, Roosevelt is portrayed as demanding immediate retaliation in kind against the aggressor's homeland, but is told by his generals that America is unprepared to mount an offensive of any kind after such a

Figure 5.2 The resolute war leader: FDR (Jon Voight) in *Pearl Harbor.*

catastrophic blow to its Pacific fleet. A defiant president sees no other option but to send the enemy an immediate signal of his country's determination to emerge victorious from the conflict:

> Gentlemen, most of you did not know me when I had the use of my legs. I was strong and proud and arrogant. Now I wonder every hour of my life why God put me into this chair. But when I see the defeat in the eyes of my countrymen—in your eyes right now—I start to think that maybe he brought me down for times like these when we all need to be reminded who we truly are, that we will not give up or give in.

When a general objects, "Mr. President, with all due respect, what you're asking can't be done," FDR seizes the table, snaps his braces into place, and, with immense strength, rises painfully out of his wheelchair to stand unaided, declaring, "Do not tell me it can't be done." The Roosevelt message is all there in that scene: courage in the face of adversity, absolute determination, and ferocious personal power. Of course, this episode was a complete fabrication masquerading as reality, but Roosevelt was playing the perennial role as the embodiment of national confidence—admittedly without the usual jaunty smile—that Hollywood had assigned him some seventy years previously and still had relevance into the twenty-first century.

Conclusion

The adaptability of Roosevelt's screen image to fit changing times testifies to its elasticity. In a sense there were two FDRs on offer in the cinema of the 1930s and beyond—one was the symbol of benign government that was capable of helping America cope with the Great Depression, the other was the leader that restored Americans' confidence to help themselves in the face of unprecedented economic crisis and later global war. As demonstrated in *The Way We Were* and *Annie!*, the former continued to have some resonance even as the nation turned away from the New Deal in the 1970s and 1980s. Moreover, the confidence element in the FDR image had appeal far beyond the liberal spectrum. Roosevelt's most conservative twentieth-century successor, Ronald Reagan, could claim to be his heir in that regard. While praising Calvin Coolidge as the embodiment of small government, the fortieth president could also lionize FDR as the fount of inspirational leadership at a time when his predecessor, Jimmy Carter, had seemingly proclaimed the existence of a national malaise.[27]

No matter which of his images was on display, the movie FDR did not operate in a substantive political environment. None of the films in which he appears or is referenced, whether in the 1930s or later, in reality offer commentary on the New Deal. Policy discussions about how to deal with the Great Depression and the Roosevelt administration's failure to bring it to an end have not made it to the silver screen. For all the uplifting imagery about government helping the downtrodden, there is precious little movie reference in regard to the failure of the New Deal—and, by implication, FDR—to significantly improve the economic conditions of groups that were marginalized before the economic crisis of the 1930s, notably African Americans, women workers (particularly those in sweatshops and domestic service), tenant farmers, and sharecroppers.

Similarly, there is virtually no cinematic treatment of how FDR shaped the institutional structure of the modern presidency. In contrast to historians and political scientists, Hollywood has shown little interest in the development under Roosevelt of the legislative presidency, the establishment of White House media operations, and the reorganization that created the executive office of the presidency. Even the vexed question of his role in pushing the presidency beyond the Constitution in World War II and the significance of this for the development of what ultimately became known as the imperial presidency is not an issue that has engaged moviemakers.[28]

The cinematic Roosevelt gives what Americans have looked for but so often failed to find in their real presidents—bold leadership, a feeling of compassion for those in need, and the capacity to instill belief that the nation would always overcome any problems it faced. In a sense, of course, these qualities paralleled the real achievements of the actual Roosevelt. What may look like showmanship and humbug to some cynical twenty-first-century eyes offered important reassurance at a moment of very great crisis in America's history. As such, scholars and the cinema are at one in recognizing the significance of the thirty-second president's leadership.

Significantly, memory of FDR has always focused on FDR himself rather than the cinematic depictions of him by the likes of Ralph Bellamy and Jon Voight. For historian Rick Shenkman, this was because FDR was a better actor than any of the people who played him. Roosevelt himself was not shy in declaiming his skills as a dramatic performer. As he reportedly told Orson Welles, "There are two great actors in America today. You are the other one."[29] Welles played many roles in his career. FDR always played Confidence. Never was the talent of any performer better deployed in the service of America.

Notes

1. For biographies of FDR, see James MacGregor Burns, *Roosevelt: The Lion and the Fox* (New York: Harper & Row, 1956) and *Roosevelt: Soldier of Freedom* (New York: Harcourt Brace Jovanovich, 1970); Conrad Black, *Franklin Delano Roosevelt, Champion of Freedom* (London: 2003); H. W. Brands, *Traitor to His Class: The Privileged Life and Radical Presidency of Franklin Delano Roosevelt* (New York: Anchor, 2009). Probably the most vivid in term of narrative detail is Kenneth S. Davis's massive biographical series: *FDR* Vol. 1—*The Beckoning of Destiny, 1882–1928*; Vol. 2—*The New York Years, 1928–1933*; Vol. 3—*The New Deal Years, 1933–1937*; Vol. 4—*Into the Storm, 1937–1940*; Vol. 5—*The War President, 1940–1943* (New York: Putnam/Random House, 1972–2000). For short but still very insightful studies, see Roy Jenkins, *Franklin Delano Roosevelt* (New York: Times Books, 2003); and Richard Polenberg, *The Era of Franklin D. Roosevelt, 1933–1945: A Brief History with Documents* (New York: Bedford Books, 2000). Essential for understanding Roosevelt's impact on his successors is William E. Leuchtenburg, *In the Shadow of Roosevelt: Harry Truman to George W. Bush* (Ithaca, NY: Cornell University Press, 2001).
2. William E. Leuchtenburg, *Franklin D. Roosevelt and the New Deal, 1932–1940* (New York: Harper & Row, 1963); Herbert Stein, *The Fiscal Revolution in America: Policy in Pursuit of Reality*, 2nd rev. ed. (Washington, DC: AEI Press, 1996), chapters 2–8.
3. Quoted in Arthur Schlesinger, *The Age of Roosevelt: The Coming of the New Deal* (Boston: Houghton Mifflin, 1958), 13
4. Kenneth S. Davis, *FDR: The New Deal Years, 1933–1937* (New York: Random House, 1986), 38.

5. Ibid.; Charles M. Wiltse, *The Jeffersonian Tradition in American Democracy* (1935; reprint, New York: Hill and Wang, 1960), 266.
6. Andrew Bergman, *We're in the Money: Depression America and its Films* (New York: Harper & Row, 1971), 118.
7. Michael G. Krokones, "Motion Picture Presidents of the 1930s: Factual and Fictional Leaders for a Time of Crisis," in Peter C. Rollins and John E. O'Connor, eds., *Hollywood's White House: The American Presidency in Film and History* (Lexington: University Press of Kentucky, 2003), 153, 174.
8. Michael Coyne, *Hollywood Goes to Washington: American Politics on Screen* (London: Reaktion Books, 2008), 22; emphasis in the original.
9. Thomas Doherty, *Pre-Code Hollywood: Sex, Immorality, and Insurrection in American Cinema 1930–1934* (New York: Columbia University Press, 1999), 77–8.
10. Giuiliana Muscio, *Hollywood's New Deal* (Philadelphia: Temple University Press, 1996), 16–35, 77–81.
11. Bergman, *We're in the Money*, 92–3. Warner organized a Hollywood Bowl rally for Roosevelt during the 1932 election campaign. In gratitude for his support, FDR appointed him chair of the Los Angeles National Recovery Administration in 1933. Not all moguls were Roosevelt admirers, however. Louis B. Mayer, an ardent supporter of Herbert Hoover, prevented some MGM stars from attending the 1932 rally. See Mark Wheeler, *Hollywood: Politics and Society* (London: British Film Institute, 2006), 79.
12. Bergman, *We're in the Money*, 100; Muscio, *Hollywood's New Deal*, 98–9.
13. Franklin D. Roosevelt, *Looking Forward* (New York: John Day, 1933). For a review of the movie, see Mordaunt Hall, "Looking Forward," May 1, 1933, *New York Times*.
14. The animated film *Confidence* can be viewed at http://lantz.goldenage-cartoons.com and at www.youtube.com.
15. Muscio, *Hollywood's New Deal*, 98.
16. Ibid., 99–102.
17. Ian Scott, "Populism, Pragmatism, and Political Reinvention," in Rollins and O'Connor, *Hollywood's White House*, 186.
18. Morris Dickstein, *Dancing in the Dark: A Cultural History of the Great Depression* (New York: Norton, 2009), 524.
19. "Fireside Chat. February 23, 1942," in John T. Woolley and Gerhard Peters, *American Presidency Project* (Santa Barbara: University of California), https://www.americanpresidency.org.
20. The story is essentially retold in the commendable HBO film *Warm Springs* (2005), starring Kenneth Branagh. The scene of recovery is changed to the location in Georgia where FDR actually spent time rebuilding his body, starting in 1924. The action is more narrowly focused on Roosevelt's struggle to rebuild his own confidence and dwells on the lessons in empathy that he gained from his experiences, suggesting

that his disability made him a stronger and better person. Like *Sunrise at Campobello*, the film ends with his career-saving nominating speech.

21. See, e.g., Bruce J. Schulman, *Lyndon B. Johnson and American Liberalism* (New York: Bedford Books, 1995); and William H. Chafe, ed., *The Achievement of American Liberalism: The New Deal and its Legacies* (New York: Columbia University Press, 2003).

22. For discussion, see Allen J. Matusow, *The Unraveling of America: A History of Liberalism in the 1960s* (New York: Harper & Row, 1984); Rick Perlstein, *Barry Goldwater and the Unmaking of the American Consensus* (New York: Hill & Wang, 2001); and Donald Critchlow, *The Conservative Ascendancy: How the GOP Right Made Political History* (Cambridge, MA: Harvard University Press, 2007).

23. Tom Wolfe, "The 'Me' Decade and the Third Great Awakening," *New York* 9 (1976): 26–40; Edward D. Berkowitz, *Something Happened: A Political and Cultural Overview of the Seventies* (New York: Columbia University Press, 2006), chapter 8.

24. Barry Bluestone and Bennett Harrison, *The Deindustrialization of America: Plant Closings, Community Abandonment and the Dismantling of Basic Industry* (New York: Basic Books, 1982); Wallace Peterson, *Silent Depression: The Fate of the American Dream* (New York: Norton, 1994).

25. A full list can be found at www.imdb.com (Internet Movie Data Base), under the category "character."

26. Voight became a vocal critic of Barack Obama, arguably a Roosevelt legatee, accusing him of being a "socialist" and "false prophet" who would bring America to ruin. Some conservative bloggers, whether seriously or not, have expressed the life-imitating-art hope that he would run for president in 2012 as opposed to just playing one on film. See "Cody Gault: Obama vs. Jon Voight in 2012?" June 22, 2009, www.network.nationalpost.com.

27. Ronald Reagan, *An American Life: The Autobiography* (New York: Simon & Schuster, 1990), 66–7, 244.

28. Arthur M. Schlesinger, *The Imperial Presidency* (Boston: Houghton Mifflin, 1973), chapter 5.

29. Rick Shenkman, "How Hollywood Imagines American Presidents," *History News Network*, October 21, 2003, http://hnn.articles/1749.html. Shenkman was also one of the dissentients from the favorable critical reception for Jon Voight's performance as FDR in *Pearl Harbor*. He adjudged the actor's reprise of Roosevelt's congressional address of December 8, 1941, calling for a declaration of war on Japan, "One of the profoundly disappointing moments among many in the movie." See Rick Shenkman, "Foreword," in Rollins and O'Connor, *Hollywood's White House*, xiii.

Chapter 6

The Cinematic Kennedy: Thirteen Days *and the Burnishing of an Image*

Mark White

John F. Kennedy's presidential tenure lasted barely more than one thousand days but the substantial body of historical scholarship on his life and times makes him one of the most written about of all America's presidents. Of central importance in the study of Kennedy has been to evaluate whether his policies as president were well conceived and effectively implemented. In the international arena, no example of his decision making was more important than his management of the Cuban missile crisis in October 1962, the most dangerous episode in the history of the Cold War. The price of failure would have been superpower conflict, perhaps even nuclear war that would have cost many millions of lives and unimaginable devastation.

Beyond the issue of policy, Kennedy's character has—apart from his assassination —stimulated the greatest interest. As allegations of JFK's philandering, drug-taking (both for medicinal purposes and recreationally), and dealings with mafioso leaders became commonplace in the 1970s, scholars began to consider what these revelations signified about his sense of morality. Many Kennedy historians became preoccupied in the ensuing decades with debating his character shortcomings and their significance for his leadership.

An issue that has received less attention, despite its importance to an understanding of Kennedy's impact not only on Americans but also on people throughout the world, is how he developed such a mesmerizing image. This topic gained new relevance with the election in 2008 of Barack Obama, America's most charismatic and dazzling president since JFK. While biographers routinely acknowledge Kennedy's iconic appeal, Thomas Brown in his 1988 work *JFK: History of an Image*, and John Hellmann in *The Kennedy Obsession: The American Myth of JFK*, published a decade later, rank among the few scholars to engage in in-depth analysis of a subject that merits further attention.[1]

No less than scholars, filmmakers have been fascinated by and contributed to the canon of Kennedy history. The movie *Thirteen Days* is particularly interesting in this regard because of its interconnected examination of JFK's handling of the Cuban missile crisis, his character, and his image (figure 6.1). The release of this film in 2000 symbolically underlined the enduring significance for the new century of the first president born in the twentieth century, one who promised a new generation of leadership at a time of crisis abroad and turmoil at home This essay considers how its treatment of JFK's management of America's greatest crisis between the Japanese attack on Pearl Harbor in 1941 and the 9/11 terrorist attacks on New York and Washington, D.C. in 2001 added to his reputation in American popular culture as a great, wise, and moral leader.

The Kennedy image is a brand developed and refined in a two-stage process. During his lifetime, JFK, his family, and their acolytes constructed a multifaceted and potently alluring image of his personality that made no allowance for its imperfections and contradictions. His authorship of two books, *Why England Slept* (1940), a study of Britain's appeasement of Nazi Germany that was based on his Harvard undergraduate dissertation, and the Pulitzer Prize–winning *Profiles in Courage* (1955), was used to portray him as a man of letters.[2] This glossed over the reality that he was not particularly cultured and had depended on aide Theodore C. Sorensen to do most of the writing for his second book. JFK's naval service during World War II was used to

Figure 6.1 Bruce Greenwood as John F. Kennedy in *Thirteen Days*.

depict him as a military hero, though subsequent writers would disagree over whether his commandership of the motor torpedo boat, *PT-109*, was heroic or negligent. Another component of Kennedy's dazzling image was the widely held view that he was a gifted politician whose star was rising inexorably to future greatness. His stylish conduct encouraged such a perception, notably his gracious performance during the unsuccessful pursuit of the vice presidential nomination at the 1956 Democratic National Convention and his cool, adroit sparring with Richard M. Nixon in their television debates during the 1960 presidential campaign. An additional element in the Kennedy image was his portrayal as both family man and sex symbol. Thanks to constant media coverage, JFK's large and interesting family, often dubbed the Kennedy clan, helped to underwrite his celebrity status. Magazine and newspaper photographs frequently showed him in the company of his wife or children or siblings or parents. However, the family-man image coexisted alongside that of the handsome politico with a film star's sex appeal. More than any U.S. president before or since, Kennedy had an eroticized image that received consistent public affirmation, notably when Marilyn Monroe sang "Happy Birthday Mr. President" to him, Frank Sinatra crooned at the inaugural gala about women swooning over him, and *Esquire* magazine published a made-up picture of him dripping-wet and bare-chested alongside Anita Ekberg from the Trevi Fountain scene in Federico Fellini's film *La Dolce Vita*.[3]

The second stage of Kennedy image-building began after his assassination in Dallas in November 1963. The "Camelot" myth, the notion that the thirty-fifth president and his team had provided the sort of high-minded, inspiring leadership that was at the core of the Arthurian legend, took root. In 1965 Kennedy advisers Ted Sorensen and Arthur M. Schlesinger, Jr. published works that provided a scholarly underpinning to the claim that JFK had been a great leader. This assertion was only one part of the postassassination reworking of the Kennedy image. To Kennedy the war hero, man of letters, precocious politician, sex symbol, family man, and great president was added a new image of a liberal icon in the mold of Woodrow Wilson or Franklin Roosevelt. In essence, he was now portrayed as a moral crusader rather than a pragmatic politician.

This impulse to depict Kennedy as a caring liberal was attributable to the tragedy of his assassination that left many Americans with the desire to remember him well. The image of him as a man of principle rather than a politician of expediency met this need.[4]

Depicting Kennedy as a committed liberal glossed over the contradictions of his career. For much of it, he had been hawkish on

Cold War issues. Moreover, he had positioned and projected himself as a sensible, centrist Democrat before reaching the White House. He was the solitary Democratic senator neither to vote nor "pair" against Joseph R. McCarthy in the Senate censure of this controversial, red-hunting Republican in late 1954. He had also been embroiled in bitter clashes with leading liberals such as Eleanor Roosevelt and Adlai E. Stevenson. It is true that as president Kennedy promoted liberal initiatives, notably in proposing a landmark civil rights bill to end segregation, launching the Alliance for Progress and the Peace Corps, and signing the Nuclear Test Ban Treaty of 1963. Yet he also promoted what was then the largest peacetime increase in U.S. military spending, authorized a sustained covert effort to destroy Cuban leader Fidel Castro, and substantially escalated American involvement in Vietnam. Seeking to reduce Cold War tensions in the wake of the Cuban missile crisis and to advance the civil rights agenda in response to increasing African American protest activism, Kennedy did chart a more progressive course at home and abroad in the final year of his presidency. In all, however, his record was not that of a quintessential liberal. The postassassination adaptation of his image was aimed at suggesting otherwise, so did not highlight the ballooning military budgets, Operation Mongoose, and the Vietnam escalation. Instead emphasis was put on his civil rights bill and other progressive initiatives to cast him as a leader who would have gone on to fulfill an ambitious liberal agenda had he lived.[5]

This posthumous image of Kennedy was developed in a myriad ways. Memorializing architecture, such as the Kennedy Center for the Performing Arts in Washington, the Kennedy Space Center in Florida, and the John F. Kennedy Presidential Library and Museum in Boston, highlighted his supposed cultural leanings, his vision, and his presidential achievements. Streets and schools were named after him. Popular songs referred to him. Presidential campaigns, notably those of Bill Clinton and of Barack Obama, cited JFK as a key source of inspiration.[6]

The enduring potency of Kennedy's image in American popular culture can be understood by comparing scholarly assessments of JFK's presidency with how the public rated him. In terms of the academic discourse, the Camelot paradigm gave way in the 1980s and 1990s to a more skeptical evaluation. Irving Bernstein's *Promises Kept* praised Kennedy's domestic policies and James Giglio offered a commendably balanced assessment of his presidency, but most analysts were far more critical. Garry Wills's *The Kennedy Imprisonment*, Thomas Paterson's edited work *Kennedy's Quest for Victory*, Thomas Reeves's

A Question of Character, and Seymour Hersh's *The Dark Side of Camelot* typified the counter-Camelot consensus that crystallized during this period.[7]

While the academic view of Kennedy shifted decisively, the popular perception of him remained one of admiration. In a 1983 opinion survey, the American public ranked JFK as the nation's greatest president, ahead of even Franklin Roosevelt and Abraham Lincoln. Significantly, a *Chicago Tribune* poll of historians the previous year rated him only fourteenth, behind Harry Truman, Dwight Eisenhower, and Lyndon Johnson. A 2000 ABC poll saw the public rate Kennedy the second finest president ever—behind Abraham Lincoln, but ahead of FDR and George Washington. In a 2007 Gallup poll, JFK was ranked third. Perhaps in reaction against George W. Bush, Kennedy was ranked sixth, his highest scholarly rating, in a C-Span scholarly poll a month after the forty-third president left office. Nevertheless, the chasm between popular and academic views of Kennedy has more typically been vast, something that is attributable in large measure to the powerful attractiveness of his image.[8]

Films and television became a significant agency of Kennedy's iconic appeal even before the assassination. In 1963, Warner Brothers released *PT-109*, a film of his World War II exploits as a motor torpedo boat commander in the Pacific. Kennedy had pushed behind the scenes for the young Warren Beatty to play him, but the rising Hollywood star wisely judged the script to be weak, so the president had to settle for Cliff Robertson. The 1963 release of the first James Bond movie, *Dr. No*, was linked in the public mind to JFK. Kennedy had cited Ian Fleming's *From Russia with Love* in a 1961 *Life* magazine article as one of his all-time top ten favorite books. In line with this the press often commented on his penchant for Bond novels. Indeed Kennedy had met Fleming and discussed Castro with him. This Bond connection increased Kennedy's sex appeal and associated him with a confident, decisive brand of decision making and leadership.[9]

Other films also had a role in shaping public perceptions of the Kennedy presidency. *The Manchurian Candidate* (1962), directed by John Frankenheimer and starring Frank Sinatra, told the story of a macabre Communist plot to assassinate an American presidential candidate. Kennedy played an important behind-the-scenes role in facilitating the making of the movie. The producer was reluctant to go ahead given the film's disturbing plot, and agreed to proceed only after Sinatra had secured approval from the president himself. In a sense, the film was oddly prophetic, given subsequent events in Dallas. Even prior to JFK's assassination, however, *The Manchurian*

Candidate conveyed a sense of the profound dangers that faced the American presidency in the Cold War epoch.[10]

Films and television productions continued to shape JFK's image after his death. *The Missiles of October*, a 1974 television drama starring William Devane and Martin Sheen as John and Robert Kennedy, respectively, provided a Camelot version of the Cuban missile crisis. A 1983 television miniseries, starring Martin Sheen as JFK, portrayed Kennedy flatteringly. Oliver Stone's 1991 film *JFK*, which advanced the controversial theory that a coup d'etat by reactionary forces within American government lay behind the assassination, emphasized the tragic dimension of events in Dallas. "We have all become Hamlets in our country," declares Kevin Costner as New Orleans district attorney Jim Garrison toward the end of the movie, "children of a slain father-leader whose killers still possess the throne." Stone's movie also depicted Kennedy as a liberal hero in suggesting not only that he would have got America out of Vietnam but also that he had a specific plan to do so. In support of this claim, *JFK* places considerable emphasis on National Security Action Memorandum No. 263 that Kennedy signed in October 1963 to withdraw a thousand U.S. military personnel from South Vietnam. It also links this plan to a broader Kennedy ambition, namely to end the Cold War itself. According to Stone's cinematic conspiracy theory, the U.S. military, intelligence agencies, and defense corporations could not accept these objectives. Kennedy was killed, therefore, to prevent the implementation of these progressive ideals. *JFK* was a tendentious film, clearly lacking any sort of analytical balance. For instance, the huge escalation in Vietnam and the increase in U.S. military spending in general, both of which Kennedy had authorized, were not discussed at all. Still, the film did enormous box office, received Oscar nominations and awards, generated a blaze of publicity, and was viewed by many cinemagoers as credible history.[11]

The historical context of Kennedy's image development that prefaced release of the film *Thirteen Days* featured the construction of a seductive, hagiographic portrayal of a great president and liberal hero committed to peace and reduction of Cold War tensions. *Thirteen Days* would serve to strengthen this impression of his leadership and role in history. The movie took advantage of the declassification in the 1990s of key documents on the Cuban missile crisis. In particular, screenwriter David Self made extensive use of the fully transcribed versions of the tapes of the ExComm meetings provided by Ernest May and Philip Zelikow in *The Kennedy Tapes: Inside the White House during the Cuban Missile Crisis*. Though not a flawless source, as Kennedy Library historian Sheldon M. Stern has made clear, *The Kennedy Tapes* furnished the most complete record of the administration's inner workings during the missile crisis. As such, the information therein was grist to the mill for Self as he sought to craft an authoritative, exciting script.[12]

Self's script told the story of the Cuban missile crisis from the CIA's detection of Soviet missile sites in Cuba until the ending of the confrontation by Kennedy and Soviet leader Nikita Khrushchev thirteen days later. The twist given to the story is the major role played by Presidential Special Assistant Kenneth P. O'Donnell. The impression that a JFK/Bobby Kennedy/O'Donnell triumvirate was largely responsible for the administration's management of the missile crisis is conveyed. To historians, this strikes a jarring note. O'Donnell had been Bobby Kennedy's roommate at Harvard, and had a long-standing political relationship with JFK, having worked on his campaign for the House of Representatives in 1946 and for the Senate in 1952. Along with another aide David Powers, O'Donnell enjoyed a close personal relationship with Kennedy during his White House years, one full of banter and candid, unrestrained conversation. Though appreciative that O'Donnell was so fiercely protective of him, JFK did not give him anything but a peripheral role in the Cuban missile crisis deliberations. Self's decision to highlight O'Donnell was likely meant as a narrative device created not in the name of historical accuracy, but as a way of shedding light on the Kennedy brothers by compelling them to reveal their thinking to a third party. This entailed utilizing him, as distinguished film critic Roger Ebert put it, as "a useful fly on the wall." It is also worth noting that O'Donnell's millionaire son Kevin was an investor in *Thirteen Days'* producer Armyan Bernstein's company.[13]

Working under the auspices of the Beacon Pictures production company, Roger Donaldson, whose credits included the 1980s hits *No Way Out* and *Cocktail*, was recruited to direct *Thirteen Days*. The Washington political thriller *No Way Out* had propelled Kevin Costner to stardom in 1987. In directing *Thirteen Days*, another Washington-based political thriller but one grounded this time in reality, Donaldson once again collaborated with Costner, who took the key part of Kenneth O'Donnell. Costner also represented a link to the last film about Kennedy to make a major impact, Oliver Stone's *JFK*, in which he played New Orleans district attorney and conspiracy theorist Jim Garrison on the hunt for the president's killers.[14]

In assembling the rest of the cast, Donaldson did not recruit stars: Canadian actor Bruce Greenwood won the role of JFK, and Steven

Culp got to play Robert Kennedy. Budgetary constraints may have been a factor, but this approach to casting made the characters more credible than they would have been otherwise. Audiences were more likely to focus on the real characters if played by little-known actors but would be distracted by celebrity images if the parts were taken by big stars. Moreover, the ensemble cast produced some excellent cameo performances, such as Michael Fairman's portrayal of Adlai Stevenson, and Len Cariou's formidable Dean Acheson.

The shoot began in late September 1999, and took in diverse locations: Washington, D.C.; Los Angeles; Newport, Rhode Island; and the Philippines. After editing and the incorporation of a score by Trevor Jones of *The Last of the Mohicans* (1992) fame, the film was released in the United States on Christmas day, 2000. It took in almost $35 million at the domestic box office.[15]

Thirteen Days elicited a generally positive response from reviewers. Roger Ebert of the *Chicago Sun-Times* described it as "an intelligent new political thriller," and thought its "taut, flat style...appropriate for a story that is more about facts and speculation than about action." *Village Voice*'s J. Hoberman opined that director Donaldson and screenwriter Self had "risen above their previous work to fashion a tense and engrossing political thriller." Mick LaSalle of the *San Francisco Chronicle* labeled *Thirteen Days* "a good movie about a profound moment in world history." In the *New York Times*, Elvis Mitchell judged the film to be rather melodramatic but generally competent. Most other leading film critics throughout the United States echoed these commendations. The praise was particularly pronounced for the performances of Greenwood and Culp, especially the former. Mick LaSalle, for example, said that his portrayal of JFK was "the best thing in the movie."[16]

Compared to many historical films, *Thirteen Days* pays a commendable degree of attention to the utilization of key sources, the use of authentic pieces of dialogue, and the incorporation of original news footage into the film. That is not to say there are no significant inaccuracies, but in a relative cinematic sense *Thirteen Days* cannot be simply regarded as a shoddy piece of history (in the way that Oliver Stone's *JFK* can).

Thirteen Days does not present JFK as a two-dimensional, comic book hero. To be sure, the film veers toward idolatry in places. At one point O'Donnell tells his wife things will turn out well because of the intelligence of the Kennedy brothers. "You're smart too," she responds. "Not like them," O'Donnell states reverentially. In general, however, the movie presents a very human view of Kennedy.

He takes pills (presumably to relieve the tension or to deal with his various medical problems). His stress is evident; at one point he tells O'Donnell he is not sleeping well. "I slept last night, though," he adds, "and, Jesus, when I woke up somehow I had forgotten that all this [the missile crisis] had happened...and then of course I remembered and just wished for a second somebody else was president." He was clearly finding his responsibilities very onerous. With the tension mounting during the second week of the crisis, JFK is seen hurling a file across a desk. Indeed he is portrayed as frequently irascible during that period. This attempt to reveal Kennedy the man, rather than Kennedy the myth, is not a wholly convincing portrait. He was in reality a very self-contained man, but sometimes comes across in the movie as more emotional than he appeared to be, even during a confrontation as severe as the missile crisis. *Thirteen Days*, then, avoids a simplistic, knight-in-shining-armor interpretation of JFK.

The film does in more subtle ways, however, advance the idea that Kennedy was a wise, courageous, progressive, outstanding leader—in other words, a view that squares with the prevailing, postassassination portrayal of him in American popular culture. An important element in *Thirteen Days*' laudatory interpretation of Kennedy is not just what it says about his leadership, but what it chooses *not* to say. In particular, it does not contextualize Kennedy's overall policy toward Castro in its focus on his generally adroit handling of the missile crisis. Accordingly, the movie makes no attempt to explain why the crisis occurred in the first place. As Todd McCarthy observes in *Variety*, "No background as to the whys or hows of this development [the Soviet missile deployment in Cuba] are offered." Hence virtually no light is shed upon Kennedy's premissile crisis approach toward Castro.[17]

This omission contrasts with the main thrust of scholarly coverage of Kennedy's Cuban policies during the last two decades, which has been to focus as much on the origins of the missile crisis as on its denouement in October 1962. Examination of the roots of the crisis has induced some historians to conclude that Kennedy at the very least played a significant role in bringing it about. Clearly there would have been no missile crisis had Khrushchev not decided in the spring of 1962 to deploy nuclear missiles in Cuba. But a good many scholars now agree that his missile ploy was in part a response to Kennedy's hostility toward Castro, manifested by the Bay of Pigs invasion of April 1961, Operation Mongoose, U.S. military maneuvers in the Caribbean, the ejection of Cuba from the Organization of American States, the establishment of a strict economic embargo on Cuba, and ongoing CIA attempts to assassinate Castro (which Kennedy probably endorsed and about which Khrushchev may have had an inkling). All of this left the Soviet leader with a strong desire to bolster his close and only real ally in the Western hemisphere.[18]

Moreover, the large military build-up authorized by Kennedy at a time when the United States already enjoyed a huge lead in nuclear weapons over the Soviet Union, as well as his public revelation (unlike the more discreet Dwight Eisenhower) of the extent of America's nuclear lead and his talk in the spring of 1962 of the theoretical possibility of a first U.S. nuclear strike on the Soviet Union, persuaded Khrushchev that a bold step was required to deal with the nuclear challenge posed by the United States. In other words, had Kennedy not appeared so hostile to Cuba and hawkish on defense, it is unlikely that the Soviet leader would have felt the need to install the missiles in Cuba that were the trigger for the October 1962 crisis. Kennedy's handling of the Cuban issue, therefore, was something of a curate's egg—in other words, good only in parts. It earned high marks for his management of the missile crisis, low marks for his ill-considered policies prior to October 1962.[19]

None of this is apparent from *Thirteen Days*. The film could have contextualized the crisis through the use of flashback, dwelling on the Bay of Pigs, Mongoose, Kennedy's defense policies, and Khrushchev's decision to put missiles in Cuba. Instead the narrow focus of *Thirteen Days* facilitates a favorable and ultimately unbalanced treatment of JFK. This is reinforced by its Washington-centered approach to the narrative of the missile crisis. While Kennedy and his advisers are at the heart of the action, neither Nikita Khrushchev nor Fidel Castro is ever on screen. As a consequence the audience identifies and sympathizes with the Kennedy team. How Khrushchev felt—given the context of persistent U.S. attempts to overthrow the Cuban government, a huge American lead in nuclear weaponry, and (as the missile crisis would demonstrate) an unpredictable ally in Castro—is never considered. The made-for-television *Missiles of October*, by contrast, had given viewers some understanding of how the Soviet leader, powerfully played by Howard Da Silva, perceived the crisis. *Thirteen Days* would have been a more rounded movie had it done the same.

The themes that *Thirteen Days* makes salient, as well as those it chooses to ignore, have the effect of idealizing Kennedy's leadership. A major issue explored in the film is the conflict between Kennedy and the military during the missile crisis. The picture that is painted is one of a president with backbone resisting pressure from hawkish military officials to bomb Cuba. The first clear sign of JFK's dismay at soldierly truculence comes at a meeting in which Air Force general

Curtis E. LeMay claims that the Soviets would be compelled to accept a U.S. strike on Cuba without retaliating anywhere. In response the president avows: "They're not just missiles we're going to be destroying, General. If we kill Soviet soldiers, they're going to respond. I mean, how would we respond if they killed ours? No, they're going to do something, General. I can promise you that." Kennedy is then shown on October 23 firmly telling the top military men that they must take no action without his prior approval. As originally recounted in Robert Kennedy's posthumous memoir of the missile crisis, JFK is shown musing on Barbara Tuchman's book *The Guns of August* about how the various European militaries had stumbled into World War I. This was something Kennedy was evidently determined to prevent from happening in 1962. In this way JFK is seen as both strong in character (for being able to stand up to the generals) and progressive in outlook (his opposition to the military implies ethical concerns about the use of force). This aspect of *Thirteen Days* meshes with Oliver Stone's *JFK*: a liberal hero pitted against reactionary forces.[20]

Linked to this theme is the depiction of Kennedy as fundamentally a moral man. Shortly after learning about the Soviet missiles in Cuba, he looks out of the White House at his wife and at his children playing. The implication is that concern about his family and the families of others is what will be uppermost in his mind during the missile crisis, not any sort of macho need to triumph at all costs over his Russian adversaries. Toward the end of the first week of the crisis, Kennedy is shown with his family in church, looking thoughtful. Likewise, in the second week of the crisis O'Donnell decides to go into a church he is walking past so that he can pray for peace. In other words, religious scruples, not just Cold War imperatives, are presented as the guiding influence on Kennedy and his advisers at this dangerous juncture. The opening of the film itself, which shows a series of nuclear explosions, dramatizes the stakes in the missile crisis. The intent is to show what could occur if Kennedy (and, by implication, Khrushchev) got it wrong. A proper concern about the apocalyptic nightmare of nuclear holocaust, the film implies, influenced JFK's thinking (figure. 6.2).

There are certainly grains of truth in the *Thirteen Days'* depiction of Kennedy as a profoundly moral man, prepared to stand up to the Soviets but also battle his own military to keep the peace. Believing that the joint chiefs of staff (JCS) and the CIA had misadvised him in their overoptimistic predictions that the Bay of Pigs invasion would succeed, he had thereafter harbored a healthy skepticism toward the military and the intelligence agency. At the same time, he had

Figure 6.2 The responsibility of command: John F. Kennedy (Bruce Greenwood) orders the U.S. naval quarantine of Cuba operational on October 24, 1962, in *Thirteen Days*.

massively increased defense spending and had considerable admiration for General Maxwell D. Taylor, the JCS chair at the time of the missile crisis.[21]

As for Kennedy's character, it included some impressive traits, but some less admirable ones too. For instance, *Thirteen Days* shows the exchange in the ExComm group on October 20 when UN ambassador Adlai Stevenson urged the president to offer Khrushchev diplomatic concessions (in addition to establishing a naval blockade around Cuba) in order to end the crisis. Kennedy rejects Stevenson's advice but is shown professing respect for his views. In truth, JFK was angered by what he regarded as the veteran Democrat's posturing during the crisis. In his view, this was typical of the woolly minded, indecisiveness that Stevenson had displayed throughout his political career, not least during his failed presidential bids in 1952 and 1956. Shortly after the missile crisis, Kennedy was the key anonymous source for an account of White House decision making written by two journalist friends Charles Bartlett and Stewart Alsop, for the *Saturday Evening Post*. The article was a nasty, small-minded attack on Stevenson, accusing him of supporting a policy of appeasement that would have produced another Munich. There was no mention that Stevenson had backed the blockade (as well as the promotion of a diplomatic settlement) and that other officials had also talked about the possibility of some sort of diplomatic trade. Thanks to his robust, televised confrontation with Soviet ambassador Valerian A. Zorin at the United Nations on October 23, Stevenson had emerged from the missile crisis with his reputation bolstered. Kennedy wasted no time in sullying it through a spiteful and clandestine attack. As this episode showed, he could be petty, even vicious, but *Thirteen Days* does not reveal this side of his character.[22]

If the makers of this movie had wanted to show a warts-and-all view of Kennedy the man, it could have made reference to his astonishing sexual life. The issue is never raised, but curiously there is a comment about Warren Harding's promiscuity. In contrast, a large body of scholarship has focused since the 1970s on the seamier side of Camelot. Garry Wills, Thomas Reeves, and Seymour Hersh have pulled no punches in this regard. It is arguable that too much attention has been given to Kennedy's libidinous conduct as president, when policy and leadership should be the focus. Nonetheless, *Thirteen Days* could have touched on this to give a fuller, livelier sense of the man, but its moral image of Kennedy is not stained by reference to his licentious personal life.[23]

Had the makers of *Thirteen Days* chosen to incorporate aspects of Kennedy's private life into their movie, it would have done more than merely serving the purpose of enlivening the film's narrative. In particular, JFK's continued reliance on quack doctor Max Jacobson, initially enlisted during the 1960 presidential campaign, was arguably relevant to his handling of the missile crisis. Jacobson's treatments were unorthodox to say the least, often involving the injection of his patients, including JFK, with large dosages of steroids and amphetamines. Frequently in pain because of his bad back, the president welcomed the temporary respite provided by such ministrations. The detail we have on his treatment is quite precise because Jackie Kennedy biographer C. David Heymann gained access to Jacobson's personal archives from his widow. These confirm that Jacobson treated Kennedy during the early days of the missile crisis, which prompts speculation that his initial belligerence in contemplating an air strike on the Soviet emplacements was due in some measure to the steroids and speed. It is a legitimate question, and the image of the eccentric Jacobson injecting Kennedy during the most dangerous crisis of the Cold War would seem to furnish exciting cinematic possibilities.[24]

The lack of background to the crisis in *Thirteen Days* is further highlighted by the absence of Judith Campbell from its cast of characters. This Californian socialite with whom Kennedy began an affair in 1960 was also on friendly terms with Chicago mobster Sam

Giancana. The linkage has more than prurient interest. Beginning in 1960, the CIA made sustained efforts to kill Fidel Castro, initiatives that included hiring mafia bosses, such as Giancana, to organize an assassination. Hence the agency was in league with Giancana to murder Castro at the same time that Giancana was seeing a woman with whom Kennedy was sleeping. Much of the information on this connection comes from the 1975 Senate investigation into alleged assassination attempts by the CIA on foreign leaders. In addition, Campbell published a memoir and gave a number of revealing interviews.[25]

One key question is whether JFK knew about and endorsed the CIA attempts to kill Castro. The agency's practice of plausible deniability meant that presidential knowledge of such ethically dubious enterprises was not recorded in any documentation. Whether Kennedy endorsed the drive to assassinate Castro or whether the CIA acted without his knowledge is a point of debate. Kennedy's affair with Campbell is relevant to this issue as she represented a nexus between the president and Giancana, a key figure in the CIA/Mob effort to kill Castro. It increases the chances that Kennedy did know about the assassination plots, especially given Campbell's claims that JFK had asked her to arrange meetings with Giancana and that she had passed on written messages between the two men. Khrushchev's decision to deploy missiles in Cuba was in part a response to America's anti-Castro policy. It is also probable that the Kremlin had some inkling of the clandestine assassination efforts that formed part of this, since Soviet diplomats raised the issue in the United Nations. Hence the president's affair with Campbell, because of its possible relevance to Kennedy's understanding of the CIA/Mob assassination plots, could have reasonably been included in *Thirteen Days* if the film had considered the origins of the missile crisis.

Another intersection between Kennedy's private life and public duties over Cuba again relates to his philandering, this one less significant historically but with comic potential cinematically. On October 27, as the world teetered on the nuclear brink, JFK asked an aide for the name and phone number of an attractive new secretary. He said he wanted to know because he just might be able to save the world that evening and so it might come in handy.[26]

A somewhat rose-tinted view of JFK is also conveyed by the way his management of the missile crisis is either presented or concealed. For example, at the start of the crisis declassified documents and other sources make clear that Kennedy was strongly in favor of an air strike on the missile sites in Cuba. In the first and second ExComm meeting on October 16, in a private conversation with Adlai Stevenson on the same day, and in a discussion with CIA director John A. McCone the following morning, Kennedy showed his determination to use force in order to prevail over the Russians. This was one of the least impressive features of JFK's handling of the crisis. If he had felt it necessary to make a snap decision, the evidence indicates he would have opted for a military strike, to which Khrushchev would have presumably retaliated in some way. In a sense, the ultimately effective decision to blockade Cuba was a case of his advisers dissuading Kennedy from the belligerent approach that he initially preferred.[27]

In *Thirteen Days*, however, the sense of JFK's early hawkishness is muted. It does not include the meetings with Stevenson and McCone or show Kennedy's air-strike preference in the first ExComm meeting. Though the president is seen discussing the military options in the second ExComm meeting, he does so with a marked lack of enthusiasm. Moreover he is shown outside of ExComm urging Bobby Kennedy and O'Donnell to consider the nonmilitary alternatives. The evidence suggests that it was not until the third day of the crisis, after the ExComm debate had evolved so as to encompass the idea of blockading Cuba as well as the military alternatives, that JFK showed signs of countenancing a nonmilitary approach. Hence the portrayal in *Thirteen Days* of Kennedy's initial handling of the missile crisis is skewed in his favor.[28]

JFK's handling of the second week of the crisis was generally impressive, as various historians have demonstrated, but *Thirteen Days* still gives it an overly positive spin. On October 25, the distinguished journalist Walter Lippmann published an article promoting the idea that America's Jupiter missiles in Turkey could be removed in exchange for the withdrawal of the Soviet missiles from Cuba. In the end, the Jupiters did form part of the settlement to the crisis. *Thirteen Days* suggests that it was JFK himself who instructed Robert Kennedy to plant the idea with Lippmann, but there is no solid evidence for this. True, the journalist had good contacts in the Kennedy administration and had met Undersecretary of State George W. Ball the day before the article appeared. On that occasion, however, it was a case of Lippmann informing Ball of his plan to publish an article proposing a trade, rather than Ball recommending that Lippmann should do so. It was not until October 27, after Khrushchev had raised the issue of the Jupiters in his correspondence with JFK, that Kennedy took concrete action to integrate these missiles into a proposed settlement to the crisis.[29]

Thirteen Days also presents a dovish image of Kennedy when he responds positively to Khrushchev's idea that he promise not to invade

Cuba in exchange for the removal of the Soviet missiles. "It never was my intention to invade Cuba anyway," he tells advisers, "until they put the missiles in there." This was simply not the case. The cornerstone of Kennedy's approach toward Cuba for almost the entire preceding year was Operation Mongoose, whose principal objective was to trigger an anti-Castro uprising that would require a U.S. invasion of the island to ensure its success.

The excessively favorable view of John Kennedy's leadership during the crisis is mirrored in the movie's portrayal of Attorney General Robert Kennedy, the president's brother and confidant. The latter's 1969 posthumous memoir of the missile crisis, which Ted Sorensen had helped to complete, created the idea that he had rendered the nation outstanding service in October 1962. The film *Thirteen Days* embraced the same idea in its avoidance of any contradictory imagery. On the first day of the crisis Robert Kennedy was in fact enraged— "Oh shit! Shit! Shit! Those sons of bitches Russians" was how he responded to the news of missiles in Cuba—and seriously interested in the most hawkish of military options, namely an invasion of Cuba. The memoir and film furthermore assert that at the height of the crisis it was he who hatched the plan that ended the confrontation and kept the peace. This plan involved accepting the terms proposed in Khrushchev's October 26 letter to JFK for a U.S. no-invasion pledge regarding Cuba in return for the withdrawal of Soviet missiles and ignoring his October 27 message demanding the additional concession that U.S. Jupiters be removed from Turkey (though RFK would inform Soviet ambassador Anatoly F. Dobrynin off-the-record that these would be withdrawn in due course). The declassified ExComm tapes and transcripts make clear that Robert Kennedy was not the architect of this plan. Defense Department official Paul Nitze, Special Assistant for National Security Affairs McGeorge Bundy, Ted Sorensen, and Adlai Stevenson all suggested this approach before the attorney general came around to supporting it. *Thirteen Days* thus leaves the viewer with the same misleading impressions that Robert Kennedy's memoir left its readers: his initial truculence was obscured and his role at the denouement of the crisis was exaggerated. *Thirteen Days* is then a tribute both to JFK and RFK, making it a familial story, as well as a tale of presidential brilliance.[30]

Thirteen Days ends with a voiceover of Kennedy delivering his American University address of June 1963, the most moralistic foreign policy speech of his presidency. In this he affirmed the need for the United States to reconsider its attitude toward the Cold War and the Russian people. He talked of the common humanity that linked all people together, regardless of ideological differences. This is an appropriate ending, encapsulating the central idea of the film that John Kennedy was a moral leader intent on making the world a safer place. Of course, many other Kennedy speeches give a different message, such as his April 1961 address to American newspaper editors after the failed Bay of Pigs invasion. Its affirmation of his determination to stand up to the communists conveys an image of a different president from the one in *Thirteen Days*. In foreign affairs, nothing could make JFK look more progressive, moralistic, and humane than his American University speech. But the sentiments that Kennedy expressed on this occasion were not representative of his entire presidential record on foreign policy.[31]

It is noteworthy that Oliver Stone also made use of Kennedy's American University speech, its words gracing the opening of *JFK* as they do the ending of *Thirteen Days*. This demonstrates the thematic linkage between the two films: both portray Kennedy as a moralistic leader pitted against his own military and determined to reduce Cold War tensions. In this way, *Thirteen Days* is a kind of prequel to *JFK*. One film is about his foreign policy; the other is about his death. But both movies are singing from the same hymn sheet in terms of their basic interpretation of Kennedy's leadership.

Thirteen Days connects with another notable film about the presidency, namely Stanley Kubrick's bravura black comedy *Dr. Strangelove* (1964). As Art Simon points out in *Cineaste*, both films are about "a U.S.-Soviet showdown, the infighting at the highest echelon of national defense, the threat of nuclear Armageddon," and both use nuclear explosions as a bookend device—in the opening scene of *Thirteen Days*, and at the end of *Dr. Strangelove*. Simon is right to observe that the artistic achievement of *Thirteen Days* pales in comparison to that of Kubrick's masterpiece. But thematically there is significant overlap between the two films, though one is historical and the other fictional. Both show a president facing a very real danger of nuclear war, one magnified by the belligerence of his military advisers. In *Dr. Strangelove*, however, the president lacks Kennedy's luck and/or skill, so the result is a nuclear apocalypse.[32]

In its laudatory view of JFK, and in its depiction of him as a moralistic, progressive leader, *Thirteen Days* is emblematic of the general postassassination thrust in American popular culture to remember Kennedy by idealizing him. It is representative of the way in which film and television have sustained the myth of Kennedy's presidential brilliance—a myth in which the nuances and contradictions of his life and political career are obscured.

Notes

1. Thomas Brown, *JFK: History of an Image* (Bloomington: Indiana University Press, 1988); John Hellmann, *The Kennedy Obsession: The American Myth of JFK* (New York: Columbia University Press, 1997).

2. For discussion of these works, see Hugh Brogan, *Kennedy* (London: Longman, 1996), 15–19, 31–6.

3. Among the best works on JFK's prepresidential years are Nigel Hamilton, *JFK: Reckless Youth* (London: Arrow, 1992), and Herbert S. Parmet, *Jack: The Struggles of John F. Kennedy* (New York: Dial, 1980). The JFK/Anita Ekberg front cover was published by *Esquire* in January 1963.

4. Theodore C. Sorensen, *Kennedy* (New York: Harper, 1965); Arthur M. Schlesinger, *A Thousand Days: John F. Kennedy in the White House* (London: Andre Deutsch, 1965).

5. The most insightful biographies on John F. Kennedy include Herbert S. Parmet, *Jack*, and *JFK: The Presidency of John F. Kennedy* (New York: Dial, 1983); and Robert Dallek, *John F. Kennedy: An Unfinished Life* (Boston: Little, Brown, 2003).

6. For an example of how architecture was used to memorialize JFK, see Roger Meersman, "History of the Kennedy Center," on the John F. Kennedy Library website. For an example of how JFK was represented in popular music, see the lyrics to "Abraham, Martin and John" at www.lyricsdownload.com, by Dion and covered by various artists, including Marvin Gaye. One of the most memorable moments of Clinton's 1992 campaign was the Democratic National Convention screening of footage of his youthful meeting (as a Boys Nation delegate) and handshake with JFK in the White House Rose Garden in August 1963. The Kennedy legacy was a significant element in Obama's campaign, particularly after Senator Edward Kennedy endorsed his candidacy.

7. Irving Bernstein, *Promises Kept: John F. Kennedy's New Frontier* (New York: Oxford University Press, 1991); James N. Giglio, *The Presidency of John F. Kennedy* (Lawrence: University Press of Kansas, 1991); Garry Wills, *The Kennedy Imprisonment: A Meditation on Power* (Boston: Little, Brown, 1982); Thomas G. Paterson, ed., *Kennedy's Quest for Victory: American Foreign Policy, 1961–1963* (New York: Oxford University Press, 1989); Thomas C. Reeves, *A Question of Character: A Life of John F. Kennedy* (New York: Free Press, 1991); Seymour M. Hersh, *The Dark Side of Camelot* (Boston: Little, Brown, 1997).

8. Giglio, *The Presidency of John F. Kennedy*, 282; 1982 *Chicago Tribune* poll (www.bessel.org/presfmy.htm); 2000 ABC poll (www.ranker.com); 2007 Gallup poll (www.gallup.com); C-Span scholars' survey released February 16, 2009, and available at www.c-span.org/PresidentialSurvey/.

9. Microjacket for *PT-109*, British Film Institute, London; David Thomson, *Warren Beatty: A Life and a Story* (London: Secker and Warburg, 1987), 193–4; J. Hoberman, "When Dr No met Dr Strangelove," *Sight and Sound* 3 (December 1993): 18; White House/Fleming cartoon, *New*

Yorker, September 21, 1963; Michael R. Beschloss, *The Crisis Years: Kennedy and Khrushchev, 1960–1963* (New York: Edward Burlingame, 1991), 134–5.

10. Microjacket and SIFT material on *The Manchurian Candidate*, British Film Institute; Hoberman, "When Dr No," 18.

11. Oliver Stone and Zachary Sklar, *JFK: The Book of the Film* (New York: Applause Books, 1992), 176.

12. Ernest R. May and Philip D. Zelikow, eds., *The Kennedy Tapes: Inside the White House during the Cuban Missile Crisis* (Cambridge MA: Belknap Press, 1997); Sheldon M. Stern, "What JFK Really Said," *Atlantic Monthly* (May 2000), digital edition.

13. Entry for Kenneth Patrick O'Donnell, *Dictionary of American Biography* (New York: Simon and Schuster Macmillan, 1995), Supplement Ten, 603–605; Roger Ebert, "Thirteen Days," *Chicago Sun-Times*, January 12, 2001.

14. SIFT record on Roger Donaldson, British Film Institute.

15. C.W., "Thirteen Days," *Film Score Monthly* 6 (April/May 2001): 35, 42; EDI report (United States), British Film Institute.

16. Ebert, "Thirteen Days"; J. Hoberman, "Stone Cold Warriors," *Village Voice*, December 12, 2000; Mick LeSalle, "On the Edge of War," *San Francisco Chronicle*, January 12, 2001; Elvis Mitchell, "*13 Days*," *New York Times*, December 25, 2000.

17. Todd McCarthy, "*Thirteen Days*," *Variety*, December 4–10, 2000, 24.

18. For an example of this sort of argument, see Thomas G. Paterson, "Commentary: The Defense-of-Cuba Theme and the Missile Crisis," *Diplomatic History* 14 (Spring 1990): 249–56.

19. Mark J. White, *Missiles in Cuba: Kennedy, Khrushchev, Castro and the 1962 Crisis* (Chicago: Ivan R. Dee, 1997), 35–6. The differentiation between JFK's premissile crisis policies toward Cuba and the missile crisis itself has certainly been central to my own scholarship on the subject. See not only *Missiles in Cuba*, but also *The Cuban Missile Crisis* (Basingstoke and London: Macmillan, 1996).

20. Robert F. Kennedy, *Thirteen Days: A Memoir of the Cuban Missile Crisis* (New York: Norton, 1999 reprint), 49, 97–8; Barbara W. Tuchman, *The Guns of August* (New York: Macmillan, 1962).

21. Richard Reeves, *President Kennedy: Profile of Power* (New York: Simon and Schuster, 1993), 101–103.

22. Stewart Alsop and Charles Bartlett, "In Time of Crisis," *Saturday Evening Post*, December 8, 1962, 17–20; Bartlett to President Kennedy, October 29 and 31, 1962, President's Office Files, John F. Kennedy Library, Boston, MA; entry for November 11, 1962, President's Appointment Book, Kennedy Library; Walter Johnson, ed., *The Papers of Adlai E. Stevenson* (Boston: Little, Brown, 1979), VIII, 351–2.

23. Wills, *The Kennedy Imprisonment*; Reeves, *A Question of Character*; Hersh, *The Dark Side of Camelot*.

24. C. David Heymann, *A Woman Named Jackie* (London: Heinemann, 1989), 296–319, 648.

25. Judith Exner [Campbell], as told to Ovid Demaris, *My Story* (New York: Grove, 1977); Kitty Kelley, "The Dark Side of Camelot," *People*, February 29, 1988; Liz Smith, "The Exner Files," *Vanity Fair*, January 1997, 30–43; U.S. Senate Select Committee to Study Governmental Operations with Respect to Intelligence Activities, interim report, S.Rept. 94-465, 94th Congress, 1st session, *Alleged Assassination Plots Involving Foreign Leaders* (Washington, D.C.: Government Printing Office, 1975).

26. Dino A. Brugioni, *Eyeball to Eyeball: The Inside Story of the Cuban Missile Crisis* (New York: Random House, 1991).

27. White, *Cuban Missile Crisis*, 115–34; McCone's record of meeting with JFK, 9:30 a.m., October 17, 1962, *Foreign Relations of the United States* (Washington, D.C.: US Government Printing Office, 1996), vol. XI, online edition.

28. See, e.g., JFK's recording to himself around midnight on October 18, 1962, in May and Zelikow, *Kennedy Tapes*, 171–2.

29. Lawrence Freedman, *Kennedy's Wars: Berlin, Cuba, Laos, and Vietnam* (New York: Oxford University Press, 2000), 207.

30. White, *Missiles in Cuba*, 79, 81, 137–8.

31. "Commencement Address at American University in Washington," June 10, 1963, and "Address before the American Society of Newspaper Editors," April 20, 1961, in John T. Woolley and Gerhard Peters, *American Presidency Project* (Santa Barbara: University of California), http://www.americanpresidency.org.

32. Art Simon, "Thirteen Days," *Cineaste* 26 (2001): 43.

Chapter 7

The President Impeached: Tennessee Johnson *and* Nixon

Iwan W. Morgan

Andrew Johnson and Richard Nixon held the presidency a century apart but are linked by the common experience of being charged with "high crimes and misdemeanors" in the impeachment process.[1] The only president other than Bill Clinton to have undergone impeachment trial, Johnson escaped conviction when the Senate came up one vote short of the two-thirds majority required for a guilty verdict in May 1868. The only president to resign office, Nixon quit in August 1974 to avoid almost certain pronouncement of guilt had the Senate considered articles of impeachment that had been approved by the House of Representatives.

Another connection between the seventeenth and thirty-seventh presidents is that both are the subject of cinematic biopics. A comparison of *Tennessee Johnson* (1942) and *Nixon* (1995) provides opportunity to examine the relationship between America's movie history and its political history. This essay considers two key elements of this intersection. First, both films offer insights into the changing attitudes of Hollywood in particular and American society more generally about presidential power, politics, and personality in the fifty years that separated their making. *Tennessee Johnson* presents its main character as a true patriot, one unjustly subjected to impeachment charges because of his staunch belief in the need for national reconciliation and unity after the Civil War. *Nixon* uses its protagonist to highlight the moral decline of America's political leadership class in the era of the Vietnam War. Second, both raise fundamental and perennial questions about the utility of Hollywood film as history by engaging in substantial inaccuracies to develop their message regarding Johnson and Nixon.

Tennessee Johnson and *Nixon*: Production and Main-Character Casting

Tennessee Johnson and *Nixon* are very much movies of their times in terms of their making. A product of the Metro-Goldwyn-Mayer (MGM) studio system, the former is a relatively inexpensive, 103-minute-long, black-and-white film, written by studio scriptwriters, and largely cast with stock MGM players. A prestige project to help the war effort, it aimed to boost patriotic pride through the heroic depiction of a largely forgotten president. The studio expected only to cover its production and marketing costs rather than make a large profit from the movie. Taking a personal interest in the venture, Louis B. Mayer hired William Dieterle to direct on the basis of his success with Warner Brothers biopics such as *The Story of Louis Pasteur* (1936), *The Life of Emile Zola* (1937), and *Juarez* (1939).

Johnson was played to universally favorable reviews by Van Heflin fresh from his breakthrough role in gangster movie *Johnny Eager*, for which he won the 1942 Academy Award for best supporting actor.[2] The casting of this still relatively unknown actor meant that the film did not have to overcome audience conceptions of his star persona. The greater problem it faced was popular ignorance of the seventeenth president. To deal with this, the movie trailer sought to entice audiences by setting a visual quiz to highlight Johnson's historical significance, tying him to better-known presidents—specifically Andrew Jackson and Abraham Lincoln—and providing assurance that it would entertain as well as enlighten. To the latter end, it publicized the film as "One of the Most Important Entertainments of the Year."[3]

Nixon, by contrast, is a poststudio system *auteur* film, directed, coproduced, and cowritten by Oliver Stone, then at the height of his critical reputation and commercial success as an iconoclastic moviemaker. This Technicolor widescreen production can be seen as part of Stone's presidential trilogy—along with *JFK* (1991) and *W.* (2008)—or even as the last of his Vietnam quartet, following *Platoon* (1986), *Born on the Fourth of July* (1989), and *Heaven and Earth* (1993).[4] Given his recent record, particularly the massive success of *JFK*, Stone was confident of *Nixon*'s profitability, but even he found it difficult to secure backing for this expensive project. Warner Brothers, for whom *JFK* was made, did not follow through initial interest in his second presidential movie because of doubts about its box-office potential.

However, the Disney Corporation eventually put up the $44 million costs after Nixon's death in April 1994 revived interest in his life and times. Though also considering other political movie projects on murdered gay San Francisco politician Harvey Milk and on civil rights crusader Martin Luther King, Stone seized the moment to get another presidential film into production. With some justification, he commented, "There are few directors this century who have gotten away with two big political movies that were uncompromised."[5]

Stone also encountered problems in casting Nixon. His first choice, Warren Beatty, a leading light of Hollywood's liberal community, wanted to play the thirty-seventh president as evil, rather than tragic as the director envisaged. The Disney studio then lobbied for a big-star alternative such as Tom Hanks and Jack Nicholson. However, Stone picked Anthony Hopkins for the part because he could project the sense of isolation essential for the character. The Welsh actor also shared the director's view that Nixon deserved to be played with an empathetic pathos because of his Shakespearean qualities as a potentially great leader undone by his personal flaws. Hopkins had won the Academy Award for best actor in 1992 for portraying stone-cold killer Hannibal Lecter while onscreen for only 18 minutes in *The Silence of the Lambs* (1991). Though nominated, he did not win the Oscar for his more complex role in *Nixon*, which required him to be onscreen for some two-thirds of the movie's 183-minute duration. This may well have reflected the problems of casting a renowned actor, albeit one of the most talented of his generation, as a recent president. As one reviewer observed, "One never really forgets that this is an actor giving his best impression of a terribly famous man."[6]

Tennessee Johnson: Themes

The first act of *Tennessee Johnson* deals with its subject's rise from being a runaway indentured tailor's apprentice in the late 1820s to become Democratic Senator for Tennessee (1857–62). Adopting the technique that Darryl F. Zanuck later employed in *Wilson*,[7] the movie aims to gain audience sympathy for Johnson's rags-to-riches story in order that filmgoers would identify with his political struggles in the last part of the movie. The opening scene shows him entering Greeneville, Tennessee, still wearing the shackle meant to keep him in semiservitude to his master in North Carolina. After a friendly blacksmith removes this restraint, he seizes the opportunity for personal renewal in what was still virtually a frontier region by starting up his own tailor's business and learning to read and write. In addition, Johnson discovers his capacity for leadership based on idealism and learning, which enables him to arouse Greeneville's disenfranchised lower classes to challenge the political control of the local establishment. With their support, he wins election as sheriff, progressing thereafter to mayor, state legislator, U.S. congressman, Tennessee governor, and U.S. senator. In this phase of the film, he is depicted as a Jacksonian Democrat dedicated to the interests of the common people.

The second part of the movie traces Johnson's evolution into Abraham Lincoln's legatee. The latter is first referenced when Johnson is shown giving a stump speech urging his defeat in the 1860 presidential election but declaring unswerving loyalty to the Union whoever wins. The next scene shows him as the only Southerner not to withdraw from the Senate in support of the Confederacy as the secession crisis reaches boiling point in early 1861. After this, he appears as the Union military governor of Tennessee successfully defending Nashville against Confederate forces in 1862–63. The film then presents his vice presidential nomination as a Union Democrat on the 1864 Republican ticket as evidence of Lincoln's determination to promote sectional reconciliation after the war. Faced with dissent from Radicals, who want an anti-Southern Republican hardliner, the envoy sent to inform them of the president's desire to have Johnson as his running mate declares, "Mr. Lincoln does not approve of vengeance on anyone." In implying Johnson's agreement with this, the movie conveniently ignores his actual advocacy in early 1865 that Confederate leader Jefferson Davies should be hanged.[8]

The film then uses Johnson's notorious inebriation when delivering his vice presidential inaugural address, the result of taking several nerve-steadying whiskies when his physical constitution was already weakened by illness, to reaffirm his ties to Lincoln. Unsurprisingly, the incident caused a furor at the time, encouraged rumors that he was an incorrigible drunk, and prompted some Radical Republicans to demand his resignation. In the movie, Johnson receives a letter from Lincoln assuring his ongoing support with these words: "You ornery old galoot; don't you know better than to drink brandy on an empty stomach, particularly when you are ill?...In hitting at you, they're hitting at me, and I don't mind."

With Johnson's assumption of the presidency on Lincoln's assassination, the movie's final part focuses on his involvement in the controversy over post–Civil War Reconstruction, which centered on how the victorious North should deal with the defeated South. It portrays

Johnson as dedicated to his predecessor's vision of national reconciliation and his political opponents as blindly vindictive in seeking revenge against the former Confederacy at the cost of enduring disunion. This is dramatized through the confrontation between the president and the Radical Republican leader Representative Thaddeus Stevens of Pennsylvania (played by Lionel Barrymore), which culminates in the congressional attempt to impeach him at the latter's behest.

In its depiction of Johnson's struggle with Congress, *Tennessee Johnson* celebrates the president's moral authority as the guardian of the Constitution long before the notion of the Imperial Presidency as a threat to democratic norms came into being. If anything, the film warns of an Imperial Congress through Johnson's rumination that were he to be impeached, the legislature would be ruled by an "irresponsible tyrant" in the person of Stevens. The impeachment trial itself is presented as a trumped-up political stratagem devoid of constitutional justification to remove the champion of national reconciliation. In all, Johnson faced eleven articles of impeachment, nine of which concerned his alleged violation of the Tenure of Office Act of 1867. Radical Republicans had enacted this measure mainly to prevent him purging Cabinet members who were sympathetic to their Reconstruction program. Johnson's dismissal of Lincoln-appointed secretary of war Edwin M. Stanton provided their fig leaf of a justification for impeachment. The movie had already prepared audiences to see through this charade in a written prelude that concluded: "In 1926 the Supreme Court pronounced the law unconstitutional—as Johnson had contended it was." Though a broadly accurate statement, this conveyed the wrongful impression that the judicial verdict was intended to vindicate the seventeenth president.[9]

As further evidence of Johnson's constitutional righteousness, an early scene in the movie had shown him reading the preamble to the Declaration of Independence as part of his youthful quest for literacy. When he queries whether these words and those of the Constitution apply to a poor white "mudsill" like him, his future wife, Eliza McCardle, who is teaching him to read, declares, "Everything in the Bill of Rights means you personally, Andrew Johnson."

More than anything else, however, it is Johnson's loyalty to Lincoln's legacy that highlights the moral compass of his leadership (figure 7.1). The film's hagiographic representation of the sixteenth president, who remains an unseen but constant presence in its middle sequences, conveys the sense that he is set apart from other politicians as the embodiment of goodness. When Johnson doubts his capacity to live up to his predecessor, Eliza offers reassurance: "You were the

Figure 7.1 Lincoln's legatee: Andrew Johnson (Van Heflin) reads out his predecessor's letter at his impeachment trial, with Chief Justice Salmon P. Chase (Montagu Love) presiding, in *Tennessee Johnson*.

man he chose to fill his boots if needed." Finding comfort in this view, Johnson himself fulminates about his impeachment as the work of men bent on destroying Lincoln's vision for a reunited America: "It's a criminal conspiracy. They'd be doing it to him (Lincoln) if he were still alive."

Tennessee Johnson's conscious pleading for national reconciliation and unity quite evidently reflected the wartime circumstances in which it was made. In its key scene, the impeachment trial, Johnson warns the Senate about the folly of internal squabbles at a time when French Emperor Napoleon III was engaged in military intervention to implant European monarchy in Mexico: "If we continue a divided nation," he asserts, "the day will come when still stronger armies and fleets from overseas will conquer and enslave not only our Central and South American brethren, but *ourselves* as well! As our forefathers knew—united we stand, divided we fall."

The movie's final scene underlines the wisdom of sectional reconciliation as supposedly envisioned by Lincoln and promoted by his successor. In contrast to the earlier depiction of Johnson as the solitary Southerner not to join the pro-Confederacy walkout from the Senate in 1861, it has him back in the upper chamber in 1875 as newly elected Tennessee senator. Johnson observes that the presence of his fellow Southerners, now sitting at desks that had been empty for so long during the Civil War and its aftermath, testify to the completion of national reunion. Naming all the former Confederate states that are back in the fold, he affirms that what Lincoln "fought for, lived for, and died for has come to pass—the Union of these states, one and inseparable, now and forever."

Tennessee Johnson: Reception

Tennessee Johnson earned respectful reviews for its performances, story line, and production values, but it failed to resonate with audiences and quickly disappeared into obscurity. Unlike Lincoln, Johnson was not a president who was infinitely adaptable to changing times because he did not embody personal greatness and national destiny. Making the Civil War a struggle for the Union rather than for renewal of founding values was hardly likely to resonate with audiences at a time when the United States was involved in a global struggle with the forces of fascism and militarism. Nevertheless the MGM film did at least engage with a serious subject at a time when Technicolor fantasies such as *Arabian Nights* (1943) were becoming the profitable distractions for wartime audiences.

For a film that few people went to see, however, *Tennessee Johnson* stirred up considerable political controversy. Premiered virtually one year to the day after the United States entered World War II, it struck reviewers as a commentary on present times. America's involvement in the global conflict had not brought about political truce at home. Republicans and conservative Democrats found a new focus for their animosity to the New Deal in the form of the government agencies created to organize the war effort on the domestic front. Charges that these were socialistic and inefficient had featured in the GOP campaign in the midterm elections of 1942 that culminated in Democratic loss of eight seats in the Senate and fifty in the House of Representatives.[10] Some film critics consequently drew parallels between the Johnson movie's depiction of him as the whipping boy for political critics of Lincoln's Reconstruction policy and contemporary denunciations of wartime government as a smokescreen for attacks on Franklin D. Roosevelt and the New Deal.[11]

Such an interpretation might have been expected to draw condemnation of *Tennessee Johnson* from the political right, but paradoxically the attacks on a film that paid homage to Lincoln and implicitly to FDR came from the left. While in production, the MGM movie came under attack from the communist *Daily Worker* and sections of the African American press for historical distortion. The film ignored the reality that Johnson was a racial bigot to lionize him as the homespun champion of the common people. Conversely, it demonized Thaddeus Stevens for pursuing Radical Reconstruction out of dogmatic determination to punish the South for the Civil War. In truth, however, the Pennsylvanian primarily regarded it as a means to ensure racial equality and protection for newly emancipated African Americans, whose human rights were ignored by Johnson's policy of lenient Reconstruction.[12]

The fracas brought about the intervention of the Office of War Information (OWI), an agency created in June 1942 to coordinate government information services, promote patriotism, and develop propaganda. Having reviewed the unedited film, initially called *The Man on America's Conscience*, OWI Bureau of Motion Pictures chief Lowell Mellett advised MGM to change the title and reshoot some of the scenes involving Stevens to present him as sincerely principled if misguided in his battle with Johnson. The changes did not appease the critics but the studio held out against further alterations, a stand that reflected its determination not to establish a precedent for stronger OWI interventions in wartime Hollywood.[13]

Tennessee Johnson and Reconstruction Historiography

In essence, *Tennessee Johnson* is as much a statement against Radical Reconstruction as was D.W. Griffith's silent masterpiece, *The Birth of a Nation* (1915). In many respects it can be seen as a sequel to this movie and the same director's talkie biopic, *Abraham Lincoln* (1930), in its emphasis on the sixteenth president as the great reunionist rather than the Great Emancipator.[14] The Johnson biopic may eschew *The Birth of a Nation*'s negrophobia but only by writing African Americans out of its treatment of a historical era in which race was the central issue.[15]

There is no depiction of slavery in *Tennessee Johnson*'s pre–Civil War sequences, thereby avoiding reference to the fact that Johnson himself was a slave-owner. Indeed, the only time blacks appear in the film is as stretcher-bearers carrying the sick Thaddeus Stevens into the Senate to conduct the impeachment prosecution. This image has a dual symbolic intent. First, Stevens's physical incapacity is a metaphor for his status as an emotional cripple intent on destroying Johnson to wreak vengeance on the South. A later movie audience would see Barrymore in a parallel role as the evil, wheelchair-bound banker, Mr. Potter, bent on crushing into submission American everyman George Bailey (played by James Stewart) to gain control of the small town of Bedford Falls in Frank Capra's *It's a Wonderful Life* (1946). Second, the scene suggests that African Americans will simply exchange one form of subservience for another as the unwitting tools of new Radical masters whose plans constitute as much a threat to America as did those of the Confederate leaders.

The movie's preference for Johnson's vision of Reconstruction rather than that of Stevens was in line with recent historiographical trends. Early scholarship of the period, much of it written by participants in the events being described, had been almost universally critical of Johnson's obstruction of Radical Reconstruction. By the turn of the twentieth century, however, historians such as James Ford Rhodes and William Dunning projected a new orthodoxy that the post–Civil War effort to bring about racial democracy in the South had been unwise, unnatural, and unjust, but there was no accompanying resurrection of the seventeenth president's reputation. Though convinced that Johnson's policy of leniency and early readmission of former Confederate states to the Union was correct, the revisionists accused him of driving moderate Republicans into Radical arms through his stubborn refusal to give Congress a greater say in Reconstruction. In their assessment, the best that could be said of his presidential record was that he did the right things in the wrong way.[16]

Not until the 1920s would opinion of Johnson truly change in line with contemporary desire for normalcy and an end to the hatreds of the Great War era. Studies of Reconstruction in general and Johnson in particular, mostly written by nonprofessional historians, now presented him as the blameless presidential defender of constitutional liberty. The best-known work, *The Tragic Era*, published by journalist-politician Claude Bowers in 1929, depicted Johnson as the bravest of fighters against the propaganda lies of a brutal and corrupt Radical clique. By the end of the decade academic historians had added a variation to this theme. In *The Critical Year: A Study of Andrew Johnson and Reconstruction* (1930), Howard Beale offered a Beardsian interpretation that presented Johnson as a pre-Populist agrarian radical doing battle against the congressional Republican leaders as the representatives of newly influential big business and industrial interests. The favorable view of Johnson would become the dominant Reconstruction paradigm until the pendulum swung back in favor of Stevens and the Radicals a quarter century later in the era of civil rights.[17]

Tennessee Johnson bridges both strands of Johnson revisionism. It manifestly accepts the interpretation of Johnson as constitutional champion that was the staple of popular histories in the twenty years prior to its making. In more muted fashion, it also nods implicitly to the economic class interpretation of Johnson, but in the interests of wartime unity stops short of depicting Radicals as tools of big business. The movie was based on a dramatization of Johnson's story by Wells Root and John Balderston. Possibly due to the influence of the former, a Screen Writers Guild stalwart who encountered studio hostility for his labor activism, the seventeenth president's plebeian origins are strongly emphasized to arouse audience sympathy.[18]

Nixon: Themes

While *Tennessee Johnson* offers the solitary cinematic representation of the seventeenth president, Richard Nixon is the subject of so many motion picture portrayals that it is possible to identify different genres of films about him.[19] Of these, two are particularly important in providing contextualization for Oliver Stone's movie. Some "Nixon films," notably Alan J. Pakula's *All the President's Men* (1976) and Ron Howard's *Frost/Nixon* (2008), reinforce the Watergate orthodoxy that "the system worked." These show Nixon as guilty of abuse of power and obstruction of justice but celebrate his downfall, particularly the role of the press in exposing his wrongdoing, as proof of America's democratic resilience. Other films, by contrast, see Nixon as representative of the shortcomings of the American political system. Some of these, exemplified by Robert Altman's *Secret Honor* (1984) and Andrew Fleming's *Dick* (1999), resort to fictionalized scenarios to put across their message. Stone's *Nixon*, however, adopts a more realistic approach to depict its subject's downfall as allegorizing the corruption of America's political values that the director considered a consequence of its involvement in the Cold War in general and the Vietnam War in particular.

Early scenes in the Stone movie show Nixon's devoutly Quaker mother, Hannah, anointing him as divinely chosen for a special mission. Following the deaths of his two brothers from tubercular diseases, she tells Richard that his survival marks him out as having a special destiny—"God has chosen thee to save." This links him to America's exceptionalism, the idea of its being God's chosen nation to fulfill an extraordinary destiny as the beacon of liberty for all mankind. If the real Nixon was too much a foreign policy realist to believe in such a sacerdotal mission, movie audiences of the 1990s would have been familiar with Ronald Reagan's recent promotion of this very message as justification for the global struggle with Soviet communism.[20] Instead of being the agent of divinely ordained purpose, however, the movie Nixon ends up as the servant of dark forces characterized as "the Beast." To reinforce this, the key scenes as the film progresses into his presidency all begin to take place at night (including the signing of the resignation letter that actually occurred in daytime).[21]

Far from presenting its subject as inherently evil, however, *Nixon* depicts a man who ends up making a Faustian bargain in order to gain the power to do good. While pulling no punches about his abuse of power, the film is really about the constraints placed on the presidency by the broader power structure in America. According to Stone, "Nixon's potential [to do great things] was limitless, but ultimately limited by powers that even he couldn't control. To some degree, *Nixon* is about the illusion of power."[22] In line with this, the movie Nixon is part of what he continually refers to as "the Beast," an entity that he both serves and seeks unsuccessfully to control.

For Stone, "the Beast" is neither Marxist construct nor small cabal but the representation of Darwinian forces in Cold War America. According to *Nixon* cowriter Christopher Wilkinson, "The Beast became a metaphor for the darkest organic forces in American Cold War politics: the anticommunist crusade, secret intelligence, organized crime, big business. People and entities with apparently different agendas. But at certain moments in history their interests converged." In his assessment, the real Nixon fell foul of these elements through his pursuit of centrist policies (the Strategic Arms Limitation Agreement with the Soviets, the China initiative, school desegregation, and the development of environmental regulation) that did not conform to their aims.[23]

The thirty-seventh president's failure to preserve the moral authority of his office because he is in thrall to "the Beast" is allegorized by reference to Lincoln in reverse effect to *Tennessee Johnson*. The first shot of Nixon shows him alone, beleaguered, and half-inebriated, listening to the Oval Office tapes that testify to his wrongdoing. The setting is the White House Lincoln Sitting Room with its portrait of the sixteenth president looking down on his distant successor as a contrasting image of virtue and legitimate purpose. As the movie progresses, Nixon's frequent efforts to compare himself with Lincoln only serve to reinforce the gap between them.

In a key scene, Nixon's meeting at the Lincoln Memorial in Washington with students protesting his decision to invade Cambodia in May 1970, he declares, "That man up there lived in similar times. He had chaos and civil war between the races." Toward the end of the film, his daughter Julie tells him, "You've done what Lincoln did. You've brought this country back from civil war." In another White House scene, Nixon asserts his common understanding with Lincoln that leaders have to accept the necessity for casualties in conflicts of great national purpose, asking his predecessor's portrait, "Where would we be without blood, Abe?" However, Lincoln's war freed the slaves and renewed America's dedication to founding principles. Vietnam could not achieve such catharsis because it was a geopolitical initiative on the Cold War chessboard rather than an existential conflict to define the meaning of America.

In contrast to Stone's other Vietnam movies, *Nixon* presents the war as part of the global struggle with communism and its prolongation as a stratagem to implement the triangular diplomacy of détente with the Soviets and Chinese.[24] In this context, the conflict is less important for its brutalizing effect on the United States, a key theme previously for Stone, than as a bargaining chip to demonstrate America's resolve in great power politics. In key scenes between Nixon and Chinese leader Mao Zedong in Beijing and Soviet leader Leonid Brezhnev in Washington, the film suggests that his real success was not in ending U.S. participation in Vietnam but in ensuring that the communist powers did not see its withdrawal as a mark of weakness.

The Vietnam War, in which Stone served and drew on his personal experience therein to make *Platoon*, has no broader importance for America and the world in *Nixon* than that of a pawn in the game of the superpower kings. Linked to this, the movie effectively endorses the "decent interval theory" that the Nixon administration knew the peace settlement of early 1973 only bought a face-saving passage of time between American withdrawal and South Vietnam's eventual collapse to communist military offensive. Later release of secret U.S. government documents would prove this to have been correct.[25] Stone's representation of the press conference called by a jubilant Nixon to announce North Vietnam's acceptance of terms clearly signifies that this was not the momentous success that the administration claimed. Instead of becoming the center of media celebration, as had happened when he returned from the breakthrough visit to China in 1972, the president is overwhelmed by hostile questions about Watergate.

In contrast to *Tennessee Johnson*, *Nixon* does not question whether its subject was guilty on one or more of the three charges of impeachment drawn up by the House of Representatives with regard to his abuse of power, obstruction of justice, and contempt of Congress. Nor does it deal with the dynamics of presidential-congressional relations and party politics that are central to the plot of the earlier movie. Nixon's congressional accusers do not even have walk-on roles. Stone's emphasis is on how the thirty-seventh president was the architect of his own downfall because of his ruthless ambition and amoral belief that he had license to destroy his enemies before they prevented him from doing great things for America at home and abroad. In this sense he is the victim of "the Beast" within his own self. As the movie's coproducer, Eric Hamburg, observed, "Nixon is a tragic figure of Shakespearean proportions—an immensely intelligent and gifted man, but one who carried within him the seeds of his own destruction."[26] One of the key lines in the film reflects this viewpoint. When Nixon's resignation has become inevitable, Secretary of State Henry Kissinger (played by Paul Sorvino) remarks, "It's a tragedy, because he had greatness in his grasp, but he had the defects of his qualities."

Nixon was a work of personal revisionism for Stone as the third stage in his relationship with the thirty-seventh president. As the fifteen-year-old son of a conservative Wall Street broker, he had worn a Nixon button in symbolic support of his father's Republicanism in the 1960 election. As a disillusioned Vietnam veteran, he considered going to Washington following the 1970 invasion of Cambodia to assassinate Nixon, whom he now told his father was a "very evil man."[27] A quarter century later, Stone had a more balanced view of his subject's strengths and weaknesses. Comparing his two presidential movies in 2000, he declared, "*Nixon* was not about conspiracy and layers of reality, as was *JFK*. It was about a conspiratorial mindset that destroyed the greatness in a man."[28]

Indeed Stone appears at the end of the film to endorse a view of Nixon that the ex-president had tried to achieve in his own campaign for redemption in the last twenty years of his life.[29] As the camera focuses on Nixon's grave at the Richard M. Nixon Library and Birthplace, Yorba Linda, an unseen narrator, declares: "Nixon always maintained that if he had not been driven from office the North Vietnamese would not have overrun the South in 1975...Cambodian society was destroyed and mass genocide resulted. In his absence Russia and the United States returned to a decade of high-budget military expansion and near war."

The theme of reconciliation, a key issue in *Tennessee Johnson*, also has a part in *Nixon*, in its case between the generations torn apart by the political and cultural conflicts of the 1960s. At the closing credits, documentary film of Nixon's funeral on April 27, 1994, shows the honor guard carrying the dead president's casket to the strains of the national anthem, giving way to a final image: a black-and-white still of the actor who played the young Nixon, "eyes all aglow with the hopes of the new century." As the screen fades, the director superimposes the dedication, "FOR LOUIS STONE/1910–1985," to signify personal reconciliation with his father.[30]

Nixon: Reception

Stone's movie earned praise on the review pages for its nuanced presentation of Nixon as more tragic than evil.[31] Like *Tennessee Johnson*, however, its political reception was marked by controversy, but criticism came from across the spectrum in its case. Conservative editorial writers attacked not only the president's portrayal as a heavy drinker, a constant foul-mouth, and vindictively insecure about his social origins, but also the movie's disregard for certain historical details to make its case. This condemnation drew support from some former members of the Nixon administration. Chief of Staff Al Haig and Treasury Secretary William Simon dismissed the film as "a vicious attack" and "a despicable fairy tale," respectively.

Getting wind of the unflattering images of their father before the movie's release, not least his seemingly asexual dependence on their mother, daughters Julie and Tricia decried it as "character assassination." Seemingly ratifying such attacks, Diane Disney Miller wrote to Nixon's daughters that she was ashamed of her father's company being associated with the film, which she disparaged as "a grave disservice to your family, to the presidency, and to American history." Meanwhile liberal critics took Stone to task for his conspiratorial obsession with "the Beast" and being overly sympathetic to Nixon.[32] Paradoxically, the staunchest political defense of *Nixon* came from George McGovern, whom the real Nixon consigned to landslide defeat in the dirty-tricks affected presidential election of 1972. In his view, "the central character is treated fairly, with balanced consideration of his complicated and contradictory nature."[33]

Despite such controversy, *Nixon* did not repeat the success of *JFK* at the box office. In contrast to the earlier movie's speculations about the Kennedy assassination, there were no surprises in the later one about Nixon's downfall to shock the audience and engage its imagination. Stone used dramatic license in *Nixon*, but could not get the balance right between film as entertainment and enlightenment. In trying to be both things, it failed adequately to be either. The movie grossed just under $14 million at the U.S. box office and quickly disappeared from domestic screens after a disappointing performance in its opening weeks. Unlike the real Nixon, Stone's film did not make a comeback. If *Nixon* engaged in too many simplifications for professional historians, it was too complex for popular audiences. It begins as Nixon's downfall is imminent and rewinds through episodes in his life that he recalls in flashback, but the linear narrative that uses *Citizen Kane* (1941) as its model is confusingly nonsequential.[34] It cuts back and forth over time so that one really needs to be knowledgeable about Nixon's life to follow it properly. Indeed the framing device of the film—that of cutting in and out of Nixon alone in the Lincoln Room going over his life in one night—was what gave the impression that he drank heavily as president, something Stone had not intended.

Nixon and Nixon Historiography

If *Tennessee Johnson* reflected historiographic trends about its subject that were nearly two decades old, the Stone movie was an early statement of Nixon revisionism. Through the 1980s, Watergate tended to dominate the scholarly lens on the Nixon presidency, with foreign policy accorded an important but still secondary role. The publication of a three-volume history by historian Stephen Ambrose in 1987–91 offered the first important scholarly reevaluation of Nixon's entire contribution, both positive and negative, to American politics and public policy over the course of his nearly three decades at the forefront of national affairs. Shortly afterward, the first major reconsideration of his presidency by Joan Hoff, which appeared in 1994, controversially—and not wholly convincingly—argued that Nixon's record should be remembered in history primarily for his domestic achievements (notably multigroup civil rights, environmental reform, and Southern school desegregation), then for his foreign policy, and only last for his Watergate misdeeds.[35] If other scholars did not go this far, a number of studies examining specific aspects of Nixon's policies affirmed that his political significance encompassed far more than Watergate.[36]

The Stone movie's appearance on nearly a thousand screens across the country on release gave it the widest audience for any work of revisionism. In a sense its complex view of Nixon not only endorsed reconsideration of him but also pointed the way to a new wave of Nixon historiography. As battle lines were drawn as to whether Nixon deserved reevaluation, some scholars contended that his image and the disputed meanings it engendered have become as important to understand as what he actually did. In the words of Daniel Frick, "[W]hen we fight about Nixon, we are fighting about the meaning of America. And that is a struggle that never ends"[37]

Tennessee Johnson and *Nixon* as History

Whatever the parallels of *Tennessee Johnson* and *Nixon* with revisionist scholarship on their respective subjects, the two films raise important questions about the possibilities and limitations of film as history. Significantly, both start with disclaimers about their historical accuracy. A preamble to the Johnson film states: "The form of our medium compels us to take certain dramatic liberties but the principal facts of Johnson's own life are based on history." The prologue of *Nixon* states, "This film is an attempt to understand the truth of Richard Nixon...It is based on numerous public sources and on an incomplete historical record. In consideration of length, events and characters have been condensed, and some scenes among protagonists have been conjectured." According to Stone, he inserted such a disclaimer for the first time in a movie of his for two reasons: studio policy required it and because there had been "so much wasted energy and misunderstanding" pertaining to historical inaccuracy in *JFK*.[38] This did not save *Nixon* from being savaged by many historians and op-ed writers for its lack of veracity. By comparison, however, *Tennessee Johnson* was far more blatant in its presentation of a highly dubious version of history that refused to see Reconstruction as a possible lost opportunity for the establishment of racial democracy in America.

At one level the inaccuracies of detail in the Johnson movie may appear acceptable as dramatic license to leaven the wordy scenes needed to explain the issues for the audience. It was true that Lincoln was not put out by his vice president's drunkenness at his inauguration, telling a confidante: "I have known Andy Johnson for many years; he made a bad slip the other day, but you need not be scared; Andy ain't a drunkard."[39] However, he did not write the postinaugural letter that the movie uses to validate Johnson as his legatee, even having the seventeenth president read it out at his impeachment trial as proof that he is continuing his predecessor's work.

The impeachment speech is itself a total dramatic fabrication since Johnson never appeared at his trial, relying instead on lawyers to present his case. Having him deliver his own defense raised audience sympathy and drew parallels with another common man unjustly facing Senate condemnation on trumped up charges in a very popular recent movie. Film viewers could identify Johnson's righteous defiance from Van Heflin's mouth with the heroic filibuster in the same chamber by the fictional Senator Jefferson Smith, played by James Stewart in Frank Capra's populist masterpiece, *Mr. Smith Goes to Washington* (1939). Further emphasizing its hero's worthiness, the Johnson movie suggests that his removal through impeachment will mean the succession of a Radical patsy, Jim Waters, president pro-tem of the Senate. In reality, Senator Ben Wade of Ohio would have come to office. Far from being a political hack, he was unpopular with Republican moderates for his radicalism and with business for his prolabor views. The animosity against him actually contributed to Johnson's eventual survival.

Far more serious than these factual distortions, however, is the movie's depiction of Reconstruction as a simple matter of sectional reconciliation with former Confederates rather than a struggle to create a better country based on racial equality. By the time of his death, Lincoln recognized the necessity of limited suffrage for Southern blacks to make them part of the political nation. Far from supporting this, Johnson had a constitutional belief that the federal government could not impose such a policy on the states. He was also an out-and-out racist, exemplified by his statement in his 1867 message to Congress that "in the progress of nations, Negroes have shown less capacity for government than any other race of people." Johnson's policy of lenient terms for the South's readmission to the Union encouraged its intransigence in resisting the implications of emancipation. Among the consequences were the highly discriminatory Black Codes enacted by Mississippi and other states to limit freedmen's rights and the bloody antiblack riots in Memphis and New Orleans in 1866.[40]

These developments are never mentioned in the movie that promotes the fiction of Johnson following Lincoln's intent to the letter. Moreover, the egalitarian significance of the Civil Rights bills and other legislation that he vetoed (only to be overridden) in 1866–67 is written out of the film. A later generation of historians would hold Johnson responsible for Reconstruction's ultimate failure, which they deem a worse crime than the one for which he was tried. While

agreeing that his impeachment on trumped-up charges was unjusti-
fied, scholars of the 1950s and 1960s saw Johnson as an ineffective
president and his own worst enemy because of his stubborn refusal
to compromise with the Radicals. Writing in 1956, David Donald
charged that he merited conviction "before the bar of history...that
through political ineptitude he threw away a magnificent opportunity." Later revisionists would consider the seventeenth president as
Machiavellian rather than an incompetent, however. His main biographer accused him of racism in intentionally undermining hopes that
Reconstruction could safeguard freedmen's rights in the long term.
"Johnson's adamant opposition at a time when radical measures
might have succeeded," wrote Hans Trefousse, "may well have laid
the foundations for this failure. From his own point of view, therefore, he had not been unsuccessful. He had preserved the South as a
'white man's country.' "[41]

Compared with *Tennessee Johnson*'s lily-white view of history, the
numerous distortions in *Nixon* are more factual than interpretive, but
aroused considerable controversy. Stone's reputed self-description as
a "cinematic historian," a phrase he denied ever using, led a goodly
number of professional historians to challenge the credibility of his
movie.[42] As with *JFK*, he vainly sought to preempt such reaction by
co-writing two books replete with footnotes and other historical conventions to describe his research for the film and point out where
it took liberties with reality. Admitting later that he took dramatic
license to simplify complex developments and in some cases made
unintentional errors of detail, the director still insisted, "I don't think
that defeated the overall truth about what was being said." In like
vein, actor James Woods, who plays Chief of Staff H.R. Haldeman,
commented on *Nixon* that "the essential truth is there in dramatic
form." In further defense of the project, this longtime Stone collab-
orator pertinently asked whether the director's critics would prefer
him to be making serious films of this ilk or the increasingly popular
blockbuster sequels of the multiplex era.[43]

Among the instances of dramatic license, Stone gives real characters lines they never spoke in reality (Mao telling Nixon "You're
as evil as I am"), and puts real statements in the mouths of others
(Kissinger gets Nixon's line that Mao's writings have changed the
world). More seriously, he exaggerates his subject's complicity as
vice president in CIA plots to assassinate Fidel Castro in 1960 and
that Kennedy's own assassination was somehow connected with
this. In the movie, what drives Nixon to sanction the disastrous
Watergate cover-up was fear that the personnel involved in the

break-in could link him to this murky past. While accepting that Nixon knew of CIA planning of the Bay of Pigs invasion, most historians doubt that he had deep personal involvement in the agency's machinations or that President Dwight Eisenhower sanctioned the assassination of Castro, something implied in the movie. In rebuttal, Stone falls back on deductive reasoning that Nixon had form as a militant anticommunist and did not shrink from murderous covert intervention when president, as shown by U.S. involvement in the overthrow of Chile's Salvador Allende in 1973.[44] In essence, therefore, his movie uses the allegation of Nixon's involvement in illegal covert activities against Castro not as literal truth but as a representation of America's dirty deeds in the Cold War and the involvement of its leaders in these.

As conceived by Stone, *JFK* and *Nixon* are prologue and epilogue in portraying the perversion of America's founding values in pursuit of Cold War ends. Such intent prompted Stephen Ambrose, in particular, to accuse him of distorting the past to display America as rotten in the interests of promoting his personal agenda of political change. It is difficult not to share Stone's exasperation that this opinion implied this renowned historian's nostalgic animus against change (one out of keeping with Ambrose's public criticisms of Vietnam at the time) and his own lack of objectivity.[45] Nevertheless, the highly unsatisfactory construct of "the Beast" as the embodiment of corrupting power undermines the seriousness of his case regarding the significance of antidemocratic forces in Cold War America. The employment of a one-dimensional power-elite theory to explain U.S. actions during one of the most complex eras in the nation's history would receive short shrift if advanced in any undergraduate paper.

The clash between dramatic license represented by "the Beast" and the intricacy of historical reality is most clearly revealed in the Lincoln Memorial scene. In a fictionalized construct of this actual event, a female protester tells Nixon, "You can't stop the war, can you. Even if you wanted to. Because it's not you. It's the system and the system won't let you stop... What's the point of being president? You're powerless." As his aides and guards escort him away, Nixon tells Haldeman, "A nineteen-year old kid understands something it's taken me twenty-five fucking years in politics to understand... She understands the nature of 'the Beast.'"

Nixon's impromptu nocturnal visit without Secret Service guards to speak to students protesting the Cambodia invasion (figure 7.2) conformed to his habit of confronting his critics up close and personal (as in South America in 1958 and the kitchen debate with Soviet leader

Figure 7.2 The president faces his antiwar critics: Richard Nixon (Anthony Hopkins), with H.R. Haldeman (James Woods) alongside, meets with student protesters at the Lincoln Memorial in *Nixon*.

Nikita Khrushchev in 1960). However, the real episode did not generate any flash of self-doubting revelation. If anything, it confirmed rather than challenged Nixon's truculence toward antiwar critics. Symbolizing this, as he was being driven away, a protester flipped him the finger, to which he responded in kind. Instead of his damascene confession to Haldeman, Nixon chortled to an aide that the youth could tell "his grandchildren that the president of the United States had given him the finger!"[46] Moreover, far from seeing himself as part of a power elite, Nixon would later rage that the Democrats held "the four aces" that mattered in Washington, namely "the Congress, the bureaucracy, the majority of the media, and the formidable group of lawyers and power-brokers who operate behind the scenes in the city."[47]

Acknowledging his reliance on dramatic simplification of the past, Stone justified this on grounds of his need to "collapse time and go for the greater truth, using not the chronological time in which we live out our lives but that interworld of texture, circumstance, and meaning."[48] This statement obscures more than it resolves. It might rationalize the view of Nixon as creature and victim of "the Beast" at the heart of his movie. However, it cannot illuminate what does not fit into that paradigm. Anyone watching Stone's movie could well get the impression that there were only three issues that concerned Nixon in the White House: Vietnam, triangular diplomacy with the communist powers, and Watergate. Doubtless these were the matters of greatest personal importance to him as president but there were others that had huge significance for his presidency.

Stone's biopic does not deal with the decline of presidential-congressional relations amid circumstances of divided party control of government (Nixon was the first president of the twentieth century to face an opposition-led House and Senate for his entire period in office), presidential use of the impoundment power to challenge congressional budgetary authority, and the attempted development of the administrative presidency to enhance presidential control of the executive bureaucracy. Despite momentous racial developments during the Nixon presidency, African Americans are barely more prominent in *Nixon* than in *Tennessee Johnson*. The only significant allusion to them is during a televised campaign appearance in which Nixon responds to criticism from a black audience member. As well as being silent on civil rights, the movie eschews mention of other key domestic issues, notably economic policy and environmentalism. Of course, these are complicated institutional and political issues that lacked the dramatic significance of the three subjects that dominate the film, not least because their development involved a multitude of political actors rather than just the president and his inner advisory circle.

Conclusion

Arguably the best defense for *Nixon* as a presidential movie is to compare it with *Tennessee Johnson*. Regardless of its simplified construct of "the Beast," the Stone movie is a serious exploration of the light and dark sides of Cold War America through its main character. Whether one agrees or not with its themes, it compels engagement with them. The Johnson movie, by contrast, drips with a subliminal racism that rewrites history as a celebration of American union rather than a frank recognition of the racial divisions that represent the greatest indictment of America's self-belief of exceptionalism.

Seeing the two movies together requires the early twenty-first-century viewer to ask who did more damage to America. In the long term, the scales of history are arguably weighed against Andrew Johnson despite Hollywood's lionization of him as representing the best of American values in his role as Lincoln's legatee. The Stone movie's examination of its subject's wrongdoings is a bleaker commentary on the complex relationship between power and democracy in American history. As George W. Bush demonstrated, however, the imperial presidency was not intrinsic to Nixon and did not die away with his downfall.[49] As such the relevance of Stone's movie has not diminished since its making because it tests Alexis de Tocqueville's dictum in *Democracy in America* (1835) that the greatness of the United States "lies not in being more enlightened than any other nation, but rather in her ability to repair her faults."

Notes

1. For biographical and presidential studies of Johnson, see Hans Trefousse, *Andrew Johnson: A Biography* (New York: Norton, 1989); Albert Castel, *The Presidency of Andrew Johnson* (Lawrence: University Press of Kansas, 1979); and Eric McKitrick, ed., *Andrew Johnson: A Profile* (New York: Hill and Wang, 1969). For Nixon, see Stephen Ambrose, *Nixon*, 3 volumes: *The Education of a Politician, 1913–1962*; *The Triumph of a Politician, 1962–1972*; *Ruin and Recovery 1973–1990* (New York: Simon & Schuster, 1987, 1989, and 1991); Melvin Small, *The Presidency of Richard Nixon* (Lawrence: University Press of Kansas, 1999); and Iwan Morgan, *Nixon* (London: Arnold, 2002).

2. John Douglas Eames, *The MGM Story: The Complete History of Fifty-Four Roaring Years* (London: Octopus Books, 1979), 182.

3. The trailer can be viewed at http://www.tcm.com/mediaroom/index. jsp?cid=B1804.

4. For Stone's films, see Chris Salewicz, *Oliver Stone: The Making of His Movies* (London: Orion, 1997); Robert Brent Toplin, ed., *Oliver Stone's USA: Film, History and Controversy* [henceforth *OSUSA*] (Lawrence: University Press of Kansas, 2000).

5. Anita Busch, "Inside Movies: Cinergi Nabs 'Nixon,'" *Variety*, March 6–12, 1995, 10; Salewicz, *Oliver Stone*, 107–108; Daniel Frick, *Reinventing Richard Nixon: A Cultural History of an American Obsession* (Lawrence: University Press of Kansas, 2008), 216–17.

6. Anita Busch, "Inside Movies: Tricky Bit of Casting," *Variety*, January 23–29, 1995; Michael Singer, "Interview with Oliver Stone," in Eric Hamburg, ed., *Nixon: An Oliver Stone Film* (London: Bloomsbury, 1996), xviii; Holly Millea, "On the Set of Oliver Stone's Nixon," *Premiere* (December 1995); Ron Weiskind, "Hopkins Takes Presidential Duties Seriously," *Pittsburgh Post Gazette,* December 25, 1995; Barbara Amiel, "How Hopkins Saved Nixon from Being Stoned to Death," *The Times*, January 18, 1996.

7. For discussion of this, see chapter four in this volume.

8. Trefousse, *Andrew Johnson*, 198.

9. The Supreme Court judgment referred to in the movie was *Myers v. U.S.*, 272 U.S. 52 (1926), but this actually addressed an 1876 law rather than the Tenure of Office Act [TOA]. It ruled that the president had exclusive power to remove executive branch officials without requiring Senate approval. In issuing this opinion, it also expressly found the TOA to be

invalid for the same reason. However, *Humphrey's Executor v. U.S.*, 295 U.S. 602 (1935) did not extend this interpretation of presidential power to removal of members of independent commissions. For historical coverage of the impeachment, see Trefousse, *Andrew Johnson*, 311–34; Eric L. McKitrick, "Afterthought: Why Impeachment?" in McKitrick, *Andrew Johnson*, 164–92; and David O. Stuart, *Impeached: The Trial of President Andrew Johnson and the Fight for Lincoln's Legacy* (New York: Simon & Schuster, 2009).

10. For wartime politics, see Richard Polenberg, *War and Society: The United States, 1941–1945* (Philadelphia: J.P. Lipincott, 1972); and John Morton Blum, *V was for Victory: Politics and American Culture during World War II* (New York: Harcourt Brace Jovanovich, 1976).

11. "The New Pictures," *Time*, January 11, 1943, 39; T.S., "At the Astor," *New York Times*, January 13, 1943.

12. For historical analysis of the Johnson-Stevens confrontation, see Eric McKitrick, *Andrew Johnson and Reconstruction* (Chicago: University of Chicago Press, 1960); Hans Trefousse, *The Radical Republicans: Lincoln's Vanguard for Racial Justice* (New York: Norton, 1969); and Eric Foner, *A Short History of Reconstruction 1863–1877* (New York: Harper & Row, 1990), esp. chapters 5–7.

13. "Blurred Page," *Newsweek*, January 25, 1943, 78–9. For the OWI, see Allan M. Winkler, *The Politics of Propaganda: The Office of War Information, 1942–1945* (New Haven CT: Yale University Press, 1978). According to Winkler, the Bureau of Motion Pictures was critical of Hollywood for churning out escapist movies that were of little value in educating Americans about the meaning of the war, but had insufficient resources and authority to act as more than "a passive observer" of the movie industry (59).

14. For discussion of these movies, see chapter two in this volume.

15. On *Birth*'s racism, see Michael Rogin, " 'The Sword Became a Flashing Vision:' D.W. Griffith's *The Birth of a Nation*," in Robert Lang, ed., *The Birth of a Nation: D.W. Griffith, Director* (Brunswick, NJ: Rutgers University Press, 1994), 250–93; and Melvyn Stokes, *D.W. Griffith's The Birth of a Nation: A History of "The Most Controversial Motion Picture of All Time"* (New York: Oxford University Press, 2007).

16. For a review of the first century of Johnson historiography, see Eric McKitrick, "Introduction," in McKitrick, *Andrew Johnson*, vii–xxii.

17. Claude G. Bowers, *The Tragic Era* (Cambridge, MA: Harvard University Press, 1929); Howard K. Beale, *The Critical Year: Andrew Johnson and Reconstruction* (New York: Harcourt, Brace and World, 1930). Three favorable biographies also appeared around this time, written respectively by a North Carolina judge, a New York trial lawyer, and a Chattanooga newspaper editor: Robert Winston, *Andrew Johnson, Plebeian and Patriot* (New York: Holt, Reinhart and Winston, 1928), Lloyd Paul Stryker, *Andrew Johnson, a Study in Courage* (1929), and

George Milton, *The Age of Hate: Andrew Johnson and the Radicals* (New York: Coward-McCann, 1930).

18. Dick Vosburgh, "Obituary: Wells Root," *The Independent*, April 10, 1993.

19. For fuller discussion of Nixon movies, see Mark Feeney, *Nixon at the Movies: A Book about Belief* (Chicago: University of Chicago Press, 2004); and Frick, *Reinventing Richard Nixon*.

20. Hugh Heclo, "Ronald Reagan and the American Public Philosophy," in Elliot Brownlee and Hugh Davis Graham, eds., *The Reagan Presidency: Pragmatic Conservatism and its Legacies* (Lawrence: Kansas, 2003), 17–39; and Paul Kengor, *God and Ronald Reagan: A Spiritual Life* (New York: Regan Books, 2004).

21. For discussion of this, see Ian Scott, "Oliver Stone's Nixon: Politics on the Edge of Darkness," *Film-Historia*, IX (1999): 35–45.

22. Singer, "Interview with Oliver Stone," xvii.

23. Wilkinson, "The Year of the Beast," 58–9; Donald Whaley, " 'Biological Business-As-Usual:' The Beast in Oliver Stone's *Nixon*," in Peter C. Rollins and John E. O'Connor, eds., *Hollywood's White House: The American Presidency in Film and History* (Lexington: University Press of Kentucky, 2003), 275–87; David Greenberg, *Nixon's Shadow: The History of an Image* (New York: Norton, 2003), 114-16.

24. Randy Roberts and David Welky, "A Sacred Mission: Oliver Stone and Vietnam," in *OSUSA*, 66–90.

25. See Jeffrey Kimball, *The Vietnam War Files: Uncovering the Secret History of Nixon-Era Strategy* (Lawrence: University Press of Kansas, 2004) and "Nixon and Kissinger's Obfuscations about Vietnam: What the Documents Show," History News Network, February 2, 2004. For transcripts of Kissinger's "decent interval" discussions with the Chinese in July 1972, see "Fatal Politics: The Nixon Tapes, Vietnam and the Biggest...Landslide," Episode 5, Decent Interval 2, http://www.youtube.com/watch?v=JQ3L1q3R6-Q.

26. Eric Hamburg, "Introduction," in Hamburg, *Nixon*, xiv.

27. Salewicz, *Oliver Stone*, 108.

28. Oliver Stone, "On *Nixon* and *JFK*," in *OSUSA*, 255.

29. For Nixon's own campaign for redemption, see Morgan, *Nixon*, chapter 1.

30. For *Nixon* and generational forgiveness, see Frick, *Reinventing Richard Nixon*, 219–23.

31. See, e.g., Roger Ebert, " 'Nixon' a Brilliant Study in Tragedy," *Chicago Sun-Times*, December 20, 1995; Jay Carr, "Baring the Heart of Nixon," *Boston Globe*, December 20, 1995; Hal Hinson, " 'Nixon': A Heart of Stone; Superb Bio is the Tale of Two Tortured Men," *Washington Post*, December 20, 1995. Not all reviews were favorable, however. For a particularly critical one, see Christopher Sharrett, "*Nixon*: Review," *Cineaste* 22 (Winter 1996), 4–9.

32. Frick, *Reinventing Richard Nixon*, 217–18; Salewicz, *Oliver Stone*, 112; Bernard Weinraub, "Nixon Family Assails Stone Film as Distortion," *New York Times*, November 1995.

33. McGovern suggested that were they to see the movie, Nixon's daughters would appreciate "a rather sympathetic portrayal of their dad's better qualities and their mother's special strengths." To the amusement of McGovern's own family, the screen Nixon described him as "that pansy, poet, socialist." Recalling that the real one had refused to mention his name in public, let alone debate him, in the 1972 campaign, the former Democratic presidential candidate felt "cheered to hear my name at long last on Nixon's lips—courtesy of Oliver Stone and Anthony Hopkins." See George S. McGovern, "On *Nixon*," in *OSUSA*, 208.

34. Andrew Anthony, "All the Director's Men," *The Observer Preview*, March 17, 1996, 6–9; James Riodan, *Stone: The Controversies, Excesses and Exploits of a Radical Filmmaker* (London: Aurum Press, 1996), 534–6.

35. Joan Hoff, *Nixon Reconsidered* (New York: Basic Books, 1994). Paradoxically, this revisionist historian condemned the Stone movie as "an attempt to implant an even worse image of Nixon in the public mind than existed when he was forced to resign." See Joan Hoff, "Studying the Nixon Presidency," *Presidential Studies Quarterly*, 26 (1996): 8–10.

36. See, e.g., Allen J. Matusow, *Nixon's Economy: Booms, Busts, Dollars & Votes* (Lawrence: University Press of Kansas, 1999); Dean Kotlowski, *Nixon's Civil Rights: Politics, Policy, Principle* (Cambridge, MA: Harvard University Press, 2002); and Robert Mason, *Richard Nixon and the Quest for a New Majority* (Chapel Hill: University of North Carolina Press, 2004). Going against this trend, historian Stanley Kutler, author of the best Watergate study, *The Wars of Watergate: The Last Crisis of Richard Nixon* (New York, 1991), was dogged in battling Nixon's estate for release of still circumscribed Oval Office tapes that added to knowledge of his misdeeds. He eventually published two edited volumes, *Abuse of Power: The New Nixon Tapes* (New York: Simon & Schuster, 1997), and *Watergate: The Fall of Richard Nixon* (Westbury CT: Brandywine Books, 1997).

37. Frick, *Reinventing Richard Nixon*, 17. See too Greenberg, *Nixon's Shadow*.

38. Stephen Ambrose, "*Nixon*: Is It History?" and Oliver Stone, "Stone on Stone's Image: (As Presented by Some Historians)," in *OSUSA*, 207, 48.

39. Trefousse, *Andrew Johnson*, 190–1. Lincoln's historical words are reproduced in the memoir of Treasury Secretary Hugh McCulloch, *Men and Measures of Half a Century* (New York, 1888), 373.

40. LaWanda Cox and John Cox, *Politics, Principle and Prejudice, 1865–1866* (New York: Free Press, 1963), 151–71; Foner, *A Short History of Reconstruction, 1863–1877*, 83–6. For Johnson's address, see "Third Annual Message to Congress," December 3, 1867, in John T. Woolley

and Gerhard Peters, *American Presidency Project* (Santa Barbara: University of California), available at www.presidency.uscb.edu.

41. David Donald, "Why They Impeached Andrew Johnson," *American Heritage* VIII (December 1956): 21–5 (quotation on p. 25); Trefousse, *Andrew Johnson*, 334. For a more sympathetic recent view, see Howard Means, *The Avenger Takes His Place: Andrew Johnson and the 45 Days that Changed a Nation* (New York: Houghton Mifflin Harcourt, 2006).

42. Robert Rosenstone, "Oliver Stone as Historian," in Toplin, *OSUSA*, 26–39. According to Stone, "cinematic historian" was not a self-description but one assigned him in an interview by a journalist. See Stone, "Stone on Stone's Image," in ibid., 40–1; and Stephen Talbot, "Oliver Stone Keeps Telling Personal History," *Mother Jones* (March/April 1991), 46. For a sympathetic view of the movie by a historian, see Ron Briley, "Nixon and Historical Memory in the Classroom," *Perspectives* 34 (March 1996), http://www.historians.org/perspectives/issues/1996/9603.9603fil2.cfm.

43. Oliver Stone and Zachary Sklar, *JFK: The Book of the Screenplay* (New York: Applause, 1992); Oliver Stone, Stephen Rivele, and Christopher Wilkinson, *Nixon: An Oliver Stone Film* (New York: Hyperion, 1995); Salewicz, *Oliver Stone*, 113–14.

44. Ambrose, "*Nixon*: Is it History?" and Oliver Stone, "*Nixon*: Stone on Ambrose," in *OSUSA*, 202–207, 256–7.

45. Ibid., 207, 255. For Ambrose's part in heckling Nixon during his address at Kansas State University on September 16, 1970, see Ambrose, *Nixon: Triumph*, 376.

46. Tom Wicker, *One of Us: Richard Nixon and the American Dream* (New York: Random House, 1991), 634–5.

47. Richard Nixon, *RN: The Memoirs of Richard Nixon* (New York: Grosset and Dunlap, 1978), 770. Top aides were of the same mindset—H.R. Haldeman liked to speak of "four great power blocs in Washington" (he substituted the intelligence community for lawyers). See H.R. Haldeman and Joseph DiMona, *The Ends of Power* (New York: Times Books, 1978), 181.

48. Stone, "Stone on Stone's Image," *OSUSA*, 54.

49. For commentaries on this, see Mark J. Rozell and Gleaves Whitney, *Testing the Limits: George W. Bush and the Imperial Presidency* (Lanham MD: Rowman and Littlefield, 2009); and Iwan Morgan and Philip Davies, *Assessing George W. Bush's Legacy: The Right Man?* (New York: Palgrave, 2010).

Chapter 8

Oliver Stone's Improbable W.

Kingsley Marshall

Moviemaker Oliver Stone has repeatedly drawn upon historical events and real people to inform his cinematic narratives. *Salvador* (1986) dealt with the El Salvador civil war in which the United States supported the right-wing military against peasant revolutionaries; the trilogy of *Platoon* (1986), *Born on the Fourth of July* (1989), and *Heaven and Earth* (1993) explored America's war in Vietnam; *The Doors* (1991) was a biopic of rock star Jim Morrison; and *Comandante* (2003) and *Looking for Fidel* (2004) were documentary portrayals of Cuban leader Fidel Castro. Operating in a fuzzy hinterland between fiction and truth, each of these films interwove drama with documentary realism and history with cinematic memory, but did not draw precise boundaries between these different movie elements.

Stone chiseled at the boundaries between historical reality and dramatic interpretation most controversially in his film trilogy on American presidents. *JFK* (1991) and *Nixon* (1995) both generated a storm of protest over their factual accuracy, while *W.* (2008) provoked dispute more for its timing than substance. In Stone's estimate, the contentious reception of some of his previous work, notably his first two presidential films, had only served to trivialize them.[1] However, his study of George W. Bush was bound to be the center of controversy as the first of his presidential biopics to reach theaters while its subject still occupied the Oval Office, doing so in the final throes of the campaign to elect his successor. The movie's depiction of Bush inevitably encountered difficulties in representing lived experience through film. Not only was its content familiar to the audience as recent history, but also its power to engage with Bush's presidency critically or with any degree of authenticity was hampered by the limited parameters of the conventions of screenwriting practice.

Stone has observed a commonality between the protagonists of his films in that they have all featured individuals who struggled with their identity, integrity, and soul.[2] This is certainly the case in *W.*, where the formation of Bush's identity is that of the underachieving son perpetually in the shadow cast by his overachieving father, George H.W. Bush. Stone explained that the relationship between the two provided a "juicy source of drama. The father's omissions are visited on the son, in a sense they become the son's sins."[3] The film takes a conventional approach to plotting, using selected factual episodes and fictional anecdotes from Bush's complicated past to inform a simplified filmic present. As such, movie scholar Joshua Clover described the film as a "quintessential biopic" because the manner in which it pyschologized Bush reflected the conventional assumption of film biography that "history unfurls because of character formation and for no other reason."[4]

In contrast to *Nixon*, in which the thirty-seventh president is eventually and inevitably undone by his personal demons, the forty-third president fleetingly escapes from the shadow of his father in *W*. Indeed, the later film suggests that Bush Jr. triumphed where Bush Sr. had failed by removing Iraqi dictator Saddam Hussein from power. It is only in the third act of the movie that this success begins to sour. In the closing moments, a dream sequence presents the Iraq War as a failure, as Bush is berated by his father for having created a toxic legacy. Decrying the U.S. occupation as a fiasco, the former president declares that his son's handling of the conflict has "ruined it for us, the Bush name, 200 years of work." He then passes paternal judgment: "You disappoint me, Junior, deeply disappoint me."

This exact line, together with the sentiment that accompanies it, echoes an earlier scene in the film, set in 1971, in which the two men discuss allegations (actually made by pornographic magazine publisher Larry Flynt in 2000) that George W. Bush had arranged an abortion for his then girlfriend. As Susan Mackey-Kallis has observed, both these devices, of father/son conflict and of speculative dreams, are familiar from Stone's earlier work.[5] In *W*., however, they serve to undermine, rather than underpin, the critical potential of historical accuracy. Dismissed as "high-grade, unadulterated hooey" by Jeb Bush, the president's younger brother and Florida governor, the oedipal relationship on which the entire film hinges is unsupported by history. "The evidence, as it is now assembled," suggested journalist Ron Suskind, "doesn't show 'Junior' to be engaged in such a battle with 'Poppy.'"[6]

Stone's third visit to the Oval Office had come into being through unlikely circumstances. United Artists had cancelled *Pinkville*, his projected film of the U.S. Army's investigation into the My Lai massacre of 1968, partly due to a strike by the Writer's Guild of America.

This industrial action, which brought Hollywood production to a virtual standstill between November 2007 and February 2008, impelled Stone and screenwriter Stanley Weiser, with whom he had previously worked on *Wall Street* (1987), to resurrect the script of a Bush biopic that they had completed prior to the strike.[7] Weiser has recounted that he started out with two treatments, the first charting "the path to war in 2003 to the start of the insurgency [...] the other [...] Bush's formative years, his earlier life, his road to political success, and his relationship with his father and God."[8] It was the second storyline that received the go ahead, but residue from the other remained in the final product. The resultant movie consequently fell in the middle ground between a timeless tale of a family dynasty and a more biting critique of Bush's first term in office.

Having previously penned the made-for-television biopic of Rudy Giuliani, when the New York mayor's star was in its post-9/11 pomp (*Rudy: The Rudy Giuliani Story*, 2003), Weiser saw George W. Bush's life story as a contrasting one of ups and downs. It entailed "an improbable rise from total failure to total success and then [decline] again to total failure". Such a biography, Weiser added, lent itself naturally to the movie industry's preferred three-act structure.[9] Stone elaborated that act one would comprise

> the seeds of the man, young, rebellious, a failure at all enterprises—until the age of 40 when he turned it around. The second act comes off his conversion to Evangelicalism, his turnaround in his personal habits, the imposition of a ferocious self-discipline. [...] The third and conclusive act is his presidency [...] when he finally went to war with Iraq.[10]

Elaborating on this concept in an interview with film critic Roger Ebert, the director explained,

> Act One is [Bush's] youth, intermingled with Act Three, his Presidency, and that interconnects with Act Two, his successful middle years. I think overall the most fascinating thing about this incredible President is [...] the second act of his life seems to redeem the first act. The twist on it, to me, is the third act, which becomes a sinister coda to the inauthenticity of his existence.[11]

According to Marnie Hughes-Warrington, the ambiguity and complexity of historical events are habitually simplified to a limited set of characters and a driving, often singular, issue in film. In essence, therefore, mainstream cinema conventionally offers "a closed, completed and simple past."[12] In the case of *W.*, the result is a study of an individual's personality rather than of his presidency. Somewhat ironically this is based in part on Stone and Weiser's shared conviction that tended to personalize complex situations and reduce major issues "to the me."[13] However, their own reduction of the presidency to personality limited the potential scope of their film. Instead of being a timely and forensic examination of a flawed president who tested the limits of U.S. power abroad and the Constitution at home, it becomes a study of individual character. Accordingly, if anyone had "misunderestimated" the story of George Walker Bush, it was Oliver Stone and Stanley Weiser.

The film's production was beset with problems, with the major studios declining to back the project and funding subsequently difficult to find. The $25.1 million production budget was eventually raised entirely independently, thanks mainly to movie financing company QED International underwriting the film before a studio was attached to distribute it.[14] Stone later explained that casting was similarly problematic, with a number of actors turning down roles in the film, some because of the limited fee afforded by the budget and others because of the controversial subject matter. These casting issues became most fraught when Christian Bale withdrew from the lead role, reportedly due to his concerns that his lack of physical resemblance to Bush would not convince an audience of the authenticity of his performance.[15] Approached to take his place, Josh Brolin initially refused to do so until persuaded by Stone to reread the script. In a further sign of financial constraints, both star and director accepted points—money on the back of profits—rather than their usual fee for their work.

Weiser and Stone were initially adamant that the film was not to be a satire but they allowed it sometimes to stray in that direction. Brolin's critically well-received performance met their original intent in its avoidance of the direct impersonation favored by comedians such as Will Ferrell, who appeared regularly as Bush on *Saturday Night Live* and in the election specials of 2000 and 2004. Nevertheless, the script is littered with Bushisms: statements such as "containment don't hold water," slang including "Ayatollah Cockamamies," and the presidential penchant for nicknames—"Turdblossom" for Special Assistant Karl Rove, "Wolfy" for Deputy Secretary of Defense Paul Wolfowitz, "Rummy" for Secretary of Defense Donald Rumsfeld, and "Brother George" for CIA director George Tenet. The accentuation of these turns of phrase, coupled with the manner in which the narrative jumps between widely reported events and fictional scenes, sits uncomfortably in the film as a whole and provides an uneven tone. Weiser admitted, "We struggled [...] with whether to do this as a pseudo-satire or more naturalistically, like *The Queen* or *Dr. Strangelove*. That was the most difficult part of writing this, because there's so much absurdist information and detail."[16]

Once the funds and cast were in place, W. was rushed into production in the spring of 2008 with a theatrical release date set for October the same year, just five months after shooting was scheduled to begin. A provocative teaser campaign was issued at the Cannes International Film Festival in May, while principal photography was still taking place. Posters pronouncing W. as "The Improbable President" were illustrated with a smattering of Bush's spoonerisms and malapropisms that had been widely disseminated in collections such as Jacob Weisberg's *Bushisms* and in illustrations by *Washington Post* cartoonist Richard Thompson. Considering the tone of this first salvo of the marketing campaign, it was surprising that Stone simultaneously played down the satirical qualities of his film. "If *Nixon* was a symphony," the director claimed in an interview with *Variety,* "this is more like a chamber piece, and not as dark in tone." While declaring that his aim was to paint a "fair, true portrait of the man," he admitted that this reflected a commercial assessment of audience resistance to an anti-Bush polemic rather than artistic altruism.[17] Such calculation is reflected in the marketing material that accompanied W.'s DVD release. Despite citing Stone's own comment regarding the "inauthenticity of [Bush's] existence," this promoted the movie for achieving "what few people would have thought possible—moments of genuine sympathy for one of the world's most hated men."[18]

Following its premiere in New York in October 2008, the film went on general theatrical release as the final curtain descended on Bush's tenure of office. The timing brought debate about the forty-third president and his legacy back to the fore in an election campaign where he had otherwise maintained a low profile. *Entertainment Weekly* commented on the bizarre verisimilitude of trailers for the film that ran in the same television advertising breaks as campaign spots for Republican Party presidential nominee John McCain.[19] Seeing this as a source of the film's power, Mick LaSalle commented, "W. makes up in immediacy what it lacks in objectivity."[20] As Richard Corliss had observed on the release of Stone's *JFK*, "Movies are a persuasive medium because theory exists in the present tense, not the conditional."[21] Stone may have intended to avoid criticism with the softer tone of W.'s narrative, which focused on Bush's attempts to escape the long shadow cast by his father's political career, but the timing of the release—very much in Corliss's present tense—ensured controversy.

Although released nearly thirty years after the death of its protagonist, *JFK* had opened a veritable Pandora's box of criticism through its dizzying unification of a number of conflicting theories regarding Kennedy's assassination. In addition to its resynthesis of the past through the prism of cinema, some commentators noted that the film, perhaps more dangerously, had also directly affected the present. This reflected concern that its appearance in 1991 had influenced the outcome of the following year's presidential election. According to Luc Herman, the success of *JFK*, which grossed more than $200 million at the box office, provided the catalyst for Bill Clinton to "ride a new wave of Kennedy popularity in his 1992 presidential campaign." The image of the seventeen-year-old Clinton's handshake with Kennedy when visiting the White House in August 1963 as a delegate of Boys Nation, the American Legion youth program, made their connection more explicit. Footage of this appeared both in a Clinton biographical film screened at the Democratic National Convention and later in campaign commercials.[22]

JFK's box-office success and its broader impact stood in stark contrast to Stone's second presidential biopic. *Nixon*, released in 1995, failed to resonate with U.S. audiences, taking a domestic box-office gross of less than $14 million against a budget of $44 million. The commercial outcome demonstrated the conventional Hollywood wisdom that political biopics were box-office poison. Nixon's death less than a year before the film's premiere had not generated nostalgia for a presidency that had ended in ignominy. More significantly, the mystery that surrounded the assassination of the thirty-fifth president, which had so intrigued audiences four years earlier in *JFK*, was not so apparent in the Watergate conspiracies that had been picked clean by journalists and historians in the twenty years since their exposure. The events that led to the downfall of the thirty-seventh president were far more concrete, fixed in the collective memory, and lent themselves to less creative interpretation by Stone.

According to Marita Sturken, "the relationship of historical truth to narrative truth [...] forms a primary site of debate for Oliver Stone's films."[23] The outflow of historical and journalistic assessments of Nixon upon his death may have limited the scope for Stone to say something fresh in his movie about the thirty-seventh president. The end of presidency assessments of Bush may have similarly hampered *W.* Nevertheless both films engaged with what Susan Mackey-Kallis described as a "debate about truth, [which] adds to the fodder from which historicity is forged," and created a space in which a "clash between modern and postmodern conceptions of history's function" could take place.[24]

As with the earlier films of Stone's presidential trilogy, the narrative of *W.* jumped backward and forward in history, playing out an event in Bush's presidential present, before leaping back in time to establish the formative experiences that, the film suggests, informed his individual decisions. So reliant is the film on the reported events that had been widely documented both before Bush's election to the presidency, during his campaign, and while he was in office, the film's fictional moments can only complicate, rather than clarify, audience perception of his presidential performance.

An early scene in the Oval Office blurs fact and fiction to introduce key characters from the administration. It shows Bush's team gathered together to work on his first State of the Union address, delivered on January 29, 2002, which would become known as the Axis of Evil speech. Each character's motivation, wants, and needs in screenwriting terms are established within this sequence. Aside from Bush, all are cast in stone during this initial discussion, changing little as the narrative leaps between the administration of Bush's father, and his own. Karl Rove notes that positive approval numbers allow an imperial President Bush the freedom for almost any action, but Secretary of State Colin Powell advises caution, National Security Adviser Condoleezza Rice offers analysis that Bush ignores, and Secretary of Defense Donald Rumsfeld, doodling absent-mindedly, avoids expressing an opinion. Meanwhile, Paul Wolfowitz stresses the importance of linking Iran and Iraq to 9/11, while George Tenet points to flaws within the very notion of an Axis of Evil owing to the absence of direct links between Al Qaida, Iran, Iraq, and North Korea. Vice President Dick Cheney skulks in the background, allowing each of these arguments to play themselves out before he reinforces Bush's own worldview. The power dynamic is later reiterated in a scene of the two men lunching together in the White House. In this Bush orders Cheney to keep his ego in check during meetings, reminding him, "I'm the President. I'm the decider." (Bush did indeed use the latter phrase during his presidency but in an entirely different context.[25])

An on-screen caption puts the Oval Office meeting as taking place in 2002. This dating convention is used in many of the historical vignettes, which serve to construct the presidential Bush, but is not reiterated in later scenes of this filmic present. This staging of the present is further complicated by the film's timeline, which begins after the events of 9/11 but ends in 2004, a period during which the Bush administration enjoyed high approval ratings. As such, W. suggests that Bush's presidency is reborn in the months following 9/11; in doing so, it implicitly links all of the decisions that followed to the atrocities of that date. Ending in 2004, the film clearly signals that the president's star is on the wane, but does not go into great detail about the substance of his decline. Its lack of second-term subject matter also excludes coverage of developments that sent Bush's approval ratings into meltdown, notably the horrific images of Abu Ghraib, accusations of torture and rendition, the mishandling of the Hurricane Katrina disaster, and the onset of the subprime crisis and consequence recession.

Throughout the film, the White House serves as a geographical and chronological anchor for a narrative interspersed with historical vignettes. These interchange with critical incidents in Bush's past that are presented as formative influences on his character development and journey to the presidency. Ordered chronologically, the flashbacks begin with his hazing at Yale, his unsuccessful forays into the oil business, and the confrontations with his father that are vital to the film's portrayal of Bush's eventual redemption.

The second of the father-son stand-offs is flagged as occurring in 1972, but refers to an arrest for drink driving that had actually happened in 1976. Although this appears to be a small change, the switch in chronology allows for a clear delineation between Bush's youthful indiscretions and his road to redemption. While not suggesting that it marked a damascene conversion from good time Charley to go-getter, the film emphasizes his failed run for Congress in 1978 as an important episode in fostering his understanding that politics could be his calling. The assistance he later renders his father as a presidential campaign aide in 1988 offers some scope to improve their personal relationship. More significantly, Bush comes to understand in time that his political talents surpass those of his brother Jeb, the family favorite, and even of his father. The coincidence of his gubernatorial victory in Texas and his brother's gubernatorial defeat in Florida in 1994 establishes his right to be the first of the Bush sons to run for president. Moreover, the lesson he has drawn from Bush Sr.'s reelection defeat in 1992, which he attributes to his father's refusal to capitalize on Gulf War victory by overthrowing Saddam Hussein, is that a president must never appear weak.

Another key moment in the movie's formulation of Bush's presidential identity is its depiction of how he came to join the United Methodist Church. While out jogging in a hung-over condition the day after celebrating his fortieth birthday in 1986, he suffers an apparent heart attack. The next scene shows him praying with his pastor in a church meeting six months later. Implied to have undergone a born-again experience in the interim, Bush's salvation—both in life and within the film's narrative—is emphasized as the shot intercuts with a focus pull on his eyes and those of a mural of Jesus. This religious awakening serves as the critical turning point in the narrative. Imbued with new purpose, Bush finally finds his way in business as part of the consortium that buys the Texas Rangers baseball franchise, whose success provides the foundation for the launch of his bid for the governorship.

According to Gilles Deleuze, cinematic images are "sheets of the past" that can serve to create postmodern narratives where, as Marita Sturken notes, "memory and history are entangled, each pulling forms from the other."[26] In effect, what is realized in W. is drawn from a collective cultural memory. Each of the flashback episodes, from Bush's time at Yale through to his presidential campaign, are fragments that had previously been played out in the news media and been caricatured by comedians and satirists. For the viewer, the intertextual references inevitably compromise the film's efforts to present the truth, which consequently are reduced to half-remembered memories denied the power of authenticity.

A second White House scene situated in the post-9/11 present initially promises but ultimately eschews a more serious critique. The key principals charged with making national security policy meet in the Situation Room to discuss the plan to invade Iraq. Outlining the intelligence on Iraq's stock of chemical and biological weapons, Tenet admits that it does not provide conclusive proof of Saddam's possession of nuclear weapons. Again advising caution, Powell is drawn into an argument with Cheney, who continues to make connections between Saddam Hussein and Al Qaida. Describing the Iraqi leader as a "tin pot dictator," Rumsfeld contends that support for the United States after the 9/11 terrorist attacks on its homeland provides an opportunity to reassert its power and "to drain the swamp" of those who threaten its interests. In his estimate, the crisis also presents Bush with the opportunity to remake his presidency, a development that scholars would later conceptualize as the rebirth of the Imperial Presidency.[27]

Meanwhile, in a replay of the earlier Oval Office scene, Rove reiterates that inaction would result in election defeat for Bush in 2004, suggesting a clear parallel with Bush Sr.'s decision not to press for Saddam's overthrow in the first Gulf War. Powell responds that those behind 9/11 remain in the mountains of Pakistan, rather than Iraq, and asserts that implementation of what Cheney repeatedly refers to as "the plan" amounts to a degradation of the rule of international law. Closing down this discussion, the vice president outlines the details of his plan and expounds America's need to control energy reserves and natural resources. In line with this, he states that there is no exit strategy for Iraq—the United States must stay in order to create "a real empire." Getting the last word, Powell warns that the neoconservative line of "pre-emptive war" will result in a "forever war, everywhere."

The fictionalized Situation Room scene begins to offers some critique on the build up to war and its motivation. It suggests that the administration's desire to act was entirely historical, driven by a long-established neoconservative agenda rather than retaliation for the 9/11 attacks. In addition, it indicates that the case for war was built upon thin intelligence and with little regard for the military or diplomatic consequences. However, the president's almost comic response to the discussion undermines the gravity of the film's message on this score. Bush appears buffoonish in supporting the case for war through simplistic imagery and mangled syntax. Before his presidency, he states, "it was us versus them, and it was clear who them was, but today we're not so sure who the they are, but we know they're there."

Bush comes out no better in another sequence at his Crawford ranch. The president and his entourage, including General Tommy Franks—set to command military operations in Iraq—get lost when discussing the forthcoming war during a walkabout. However, the allegorical message is undermined by the scene's descent into comedy as a way of highlighting Bush's leadership flaws. As was the case in the Situation Room scene, however, this may raise doubts about Bush's memory and integrity, but more significantly it undermines the authenticity of the movie's use of material drawn from the public record. The scene of Bush's meeting at Crawford with British prime minister Tony Blair in April 2002 represents a further missed opportunity to implant a serious tone in the movie. Although the real Blair denies such an exchange took place, his reel counterpart is asked by the president whether or not he is committed to the invasion of Iraq, but the film then cuts away before an answer is given. Conversely, another actual event but one of little consequence—Bush choking on a pretzel in 2002—is drawn out in much more detail because of its comedic effect.

The uneven tone that offers a contradictory vision of Bush as hero (escaping from his father's shadow) and fool (flawed war leader) does not entirely undermine the film's power. In the estimate of film studies scholar Marcia Landy, movie biopics serve as an accessible version of history, so they need only to satisfy the audience's desire for "a loose code of realism."[28] Films recounting historical events make only an assertion of truth, but it is that assertion which has the power to become embodied in popular culture. The widely reported events of the film provide the scaffold that supports the less rigorous understanding of Bush's personality as presented in W. The notion of the president as often lost and bewildered, unclear in the facts but somehow certain of his direction, and ultimately driven by his oedipal complex rather than the national interest lie at the heart of the movie.

With *Nixon*, Stone had attempted to preempt the kind of critical scrutiny to which *JFK* had been subjected by stating within a title card that the film made "an attempt to understand the truth [...] based on numerous public sources and on an incomplete historical record." W. offered no such disclaimer as to its assertions of truth and, inevitably, the recounting of actual events and meetings ensured that critics were quick to draw parallels between the filmic account of Bush and his actual presidency. The screenplay's reliance on secondary sources drew particular comment. However, it was unlikely that anyone connected to Bush would have made himself or herself available for interview by the moviemakers. On its release, White House spokesman Scott Stanzel declared, "[W]e don't have time to comment on Mr. Stone's latest endeavor."[29]

The filmic representation of Bush in W. is further complicated by the inauthentic use of contemporaneous news footage. *JFK* had explored the moments of Kennedy's assassination through the use of the [Abraham] Zapruder film, while *Nixon* had used recordings from the infamous White House tapes. In W., by contrast, the cinematic Bush is digitally inserted into real news footage. As such Brolin's Bush serves as a simulacrum, appearing in front of the real Dick Cheney and cutaway shots of the real John McCain at the State of the Union address of 2003. A later sequence places Brolin's Bush within footage shot on the deck of the USS Abraham Lincoln, where the real Bush declared the end of major hostilities in Iraq and sailors draped their own banner bearing the words "mission accomplished" behind him (figure 8.1). While genuine news footage is utilized to illustrate the many marches and protests against the build up to the war, the actual subject of the film—the president himself—is denied this representation. The effect is to further impress Brolin's caricatured performance into the viewer's memory of Bush.

Figure 8.1 The commander-in-chief in his element: George W. Bush (James Brolin) announces the "end of major combat operations in Iraq" aboard USS Abraham Lincoln in *W.*

W. also makes heavier use of allegory than Stone's other presidential movies through three dream sequences that bookend the main plot and mark its midpoint. Each is situated in the baseball stadium of the Texas Rangers, the team that Bush part owned and made him a wealthy man when he sold his shares in the enterprise before running for governor. The opening shot, an extreme close up of Bush's eyes in the very center of the frame, serves as an apt beginning to a film that centralizes his experiences in an attempt to understand his psychology. The eyes are slightly hooded, and he appears confused. As the camera tracks back, it shows Bush positioned in the diamond raising his arms in triumph to the roar of an imaginary crowd. At the midpoint of the film, Bush takes a spectacular catch in the outfield. The film returns to the stadium for the final time in its closing moments, with a shot of Bush again running into the outfield, but on this occasion the ball fails to land. The camera closes on Bush's bewildered eyes as the closing music by the Blackwood Brothers announces, "Down deep in my soul a melody rings, I'm winging my way back home." It is only here, in these three entirely fictional segments, that Stone's film finally offers a coherent judgment on the presidency. The sequence allegorizes Bush's desire to be consequential, his initial success as president, and then his fall from grace over Iraq.

Oliver Stone has claimed not to "believe in the collective version of history," a position he reiterated in controversial comments accompanying the announcement in 2010 of *Oliver Stone's Secret History of America.* Ed Pilkington described this ten-hour series for US TV as "designed as an antidote to the inaccuracies and biases [Stone] believes exist in the conventional historical narrative dished out in American schools and mainstream media."[30] As Norman Mailer noted, cinema is encumbered with a "power to make new history."[31] While Stone's film has inevitably exerted an influence on the legacy of Bush's presidency, this cinematic history has been one that served to reinforce a collective memory some considerable distance from any sense of history. In W., the cinematic representation of Bush is denied power by the parameters of its screenplay and intertextuality. The history it recounts is one that had already been filtered through the news media, written collections of gaffs and spoonerisms, magazine cartoon strips, and the performance of comedians such as Will Ferrell. By locking his "Improbable President" in the aspic of personality, Stone's W. lacked the power of his other presidential movies that commented on the broader nature of American politics and institutions. As such it cast little light on the political forces that shaped early twenty-first-century America and the world beyond.

According to Mark Carnes, "Hollywood history sparkles because it is so historically ambiguous, so devoid of tedious complexity." The effect is to homogenize complex patterns into accessible form. In like vein, Marcia Landy suggested that film and television have become so powerful that cinematic memory has taken the place previously occupied by folklore, identifying this as a "presumed shared experience," one that is constantly in flux, and often in opposition to history.[32] Understood within this framework, the film biopic relies on a number of devices to condense the significance of a particular life into a structure that allows for both authenticity and drama.

The 1930s cinematic biographies of Lincoln adapted his screen persona to suit the contemporary times of economic and international crisis. Even Oliver Stone's own *Nixon*, made when America basked in the glow of Cold War victory, was intended as a reminder that its subject's wrongdoings were as much a product of the decline of American political morals during that conflict (and of darker forces represented by "the Beast") as of his personal shortcomings. The subject of W., however, was too close to the present to be adapted in this fashion. Instead of adopting a quasi-documentary approach, which audience familiarity with recent events may have permitted and the success of Michael Moore's movies indicated may have been profitable, Stone opted to psychologize Bush in order to make him accessible. The result is a film that works neither as history nor as drama (comic or otherwise). Bush occupies a very low ranking in the presidential surveys conducted since he left office, grouped with such failures as Franklin Pierce, James Buchanan, Andrew Johnson, and Warren Harding. Indeed, historian Sean Wilenz has contentiously adjudged him the worst president in American history.[33] Whether this assessment of the real Bush is justified or not, it is difficult to avoid rating Oliver Stone's cinematic treatment of him as one of the worst of all presidential biopics.

Notes

1. Dan Fierman, "Bush Gets Stoned," *GQ*, October 2008, http://www.gq.com/entertainment/movies-and-tv/200809/oliver-stone-w-director.
2. Gary Crowdus, "An Interview with Oliver Stone," *Cineaste* 16 (1988): 18–21.
3. Lorna Mann, *Lionsgate Films: W. Production Notes*, e-mail publicity message (page 8), November 7, 2008.
4. Joshua Clover, "Based on Actual Events," *Film Quarterly* 62 (2009): 9.
5. Susan Mackey-Kallis, *Oliver Stone's America: Dreaming the Myth Outward* (Oxford: Westview Press, 1996).
6. Scott Galupo, "Jeb Bush calls 'W.' movie 'Hooey,'" *Washington Times*, October 17, 2008; Ron Suskind, "Getting Bush Right: Debating *W.*, the Man and the Movie," *Slate*, October 2008, http://www.slate.com/id/2202667/entry/2202668/.
7. Michael Fleming, "Oliver Stone Votes for 'Bush' Project," *Variety*, January 20, 2008.
8. Stanley Weiser, "You Asked…Interview with 'W' Screenwriter Stanley Weiser," *Storylink*, November 13, 2008, http://www.storylink.com/article/273.
9. Ibid.
10. Mann, *Lionsgate Films: W. Production Notes*, 5–6.
11. Roger Ebert, "Oliver Stone: The XYZs of 'W.,'" *Chicago Sun-Times*, October 15, 2008.
12. Marnie Hughes-Warrington, *History Goes to the Movies: Studying History on Film* (London: Routledge, 2007), 21.
13. Silas Lesnick, "Olive Stone and His *W.* Cast," *Comingsoon*, October 14, 2008, http://www.comingsoon.net/news/movienews.php?id=49633.
14. Mann, *Lionsgate Films: W. Production Notes*, 1.
15. Larry Carroll, "What do Batman and George W. Bush Have in Common? Oliver Stone Explains," *MTV*, October 15, 2008, http://moviesblog.mtv.com/2008/10/15/what-do-batman-and-george-w-bush-have-in-common-oliver-stone-explains/.
16. Weiser, "You Asked…"
17. Fleming, "Oliver Stone Votes for 'Bush' Project."
18. Lorna Mann, *Lionsgate Films: W. DVD Press Release*, e-mail publicity message (page 1), November 7, 2008.

19. Benjamin Svetkey, "First Look: W., Oliver Stone's Bush Biopic," *Entertainment Weekly*, May 7, 2008.
20. Mick LaSalle, "Movie Review: *W.*," *San Francisco Chronicle*, October 17, 2008.
21. Richard Corliss, "Who Killed JFK?" *Time*, December 23, 1991, 68.
22. Cited in Peter C. Rollins and John E. O'Connor, eds., *Hollywood's White House: The American Presidency in Film and History* (Lexington: University of Kentucky Press, 2003), 14.
23. Marita Sturken, "Reenactment, Fantasy, and the Paranoia of History: Oliver Stone's Docudramas," *History and Theory* 35 (1997), 64–79.
24. Susan Mackey-Kallis, *Oliver Stone's America*, 25, 28.
25. See "Bush: 'I'm the Decider' on Rumsfeld," *CNN International*, April 19, 2006, http://edition.cnn.con/2006/POLITICS/04/18/rumsfeld.
26. Gilles Deleuze, *Cinema 1: The Movement-Image* (Minneapolis: University of Minnesota Press, 1986), 190; Marita Sturken, *Tangled Memories: The Vietnam War, the AIDS Epidemic, and the Politics of Remembering* (Berkeley: University of California Press, 1997), 65.
27. For discussion, see Charlie Savage, *Takeover: The Return of the Imperial Presidency and the Subversion of American Democracy* (Boston, MA: Little, Brown, 2007); Iwan Morgan and Philip Davies, eds., *Assessing George W. Bush's Legacy: The Right Man?* (New York: Palgrave, 2010) (especially the essays by Nigel Bowles, Clodagh Harrington, and John Owens); and two works by Andrew Rudalevige, *The New Imperial Presidency: The Resurgence of Presidential Power after Watergate* (Ann Arbor: University of Michigan Press, 2005), and "George W. Bush and the Imperial Presidency," in Mark J. Rozell and Gleaves Whitney, eds., *Testing the Limits: George W. Bush and the Imperial Presidency* (Lanham, MD: Rowman and Littlefield, 2009), 243–68.
28. Marcia Landy, *Cinematic Uses of the Past* (Minneapolis: University of Minnesota Press, 1997), 69.
29. Stephen Galloway and Matthew Belloni, "Bush Biographers Mixed on Script for Oliver Stone's '*W.*,'" *Hollywood Reporter*, April 7, 2008; Galupo, "Jeb Bush calls '*W.*' movie 'Hooey.'"
30. Crowdus, "An Interview with Oliver Stone," 21; Ed Pilkington, "Hitler? A Scapegoat. Stalin? I Can Empathise. Oliver Stone Stirs Up History," www.guardian.co.uk, January 10, 2010, http://www.guardian.co.uk/film/2010/jan/10/hitler-stalin-oliver-stone-history.
31. Quoted in William Grimes, "What Debt Does Hollywood Owe to Truth?" *New York Times*, March 5, 1992.
32. Mark C. Carnes, "Past Imperfect: History According to the Movies," *Cineaste* 22 (1997): 33–7 (quotation p. 37); Landy, *Cinematic Uses of the Past*, 232.
33. Sean Wilentz, "The Worst President in History?" *Rolling Stone*, April 21, 2006. For a contrary view, see Andrew Rudalevige, "Rating Bush," in Morgan and Davies, *Assessing George W. Bush's Legacy*, 11–30.

Index

Index